D1615270

MCGRIGOR, Mary

Wellington's spies

WELLINGTON'S
SPIES

Other books by Mary McGrigor

History of South Lochaweside

Dalmally and the Glens

Argyll, Land of Blood and Beauty

'Grass will not grow on my grave' – the story of the
'Appin Murder' in 1752

History of the Family of Edmonstone of Duntreath *(edited)*

The Scalpel and the Sword. Autobiography of Sir James McGrigor,
father of the R.A.M.C *(edited)*

Rob Roy's Country

Defiant and Dismasted at Trafalgar

WELLINGTON'S SPIES

by

MARY McGRIGOR

LEO COOPER

First published in Great Britain in 2005 by
LEO COOPER
an imprint of
Pen & Sword Books Ltd
47 Church Street
Barnsley
South Yorkshire
S70 2AS

ISBN 1 84415 328 2

A CIP catalogue record for this book is
available from the British Library

Typeset in Sabon by
Phoenix Typesetting, Auldgirth, Dumfriesshire

Printed and bound in England by
CPI UK

Pen & Sword   n & Sword
Aviation, Pen &   Wharncliffe
Local History, P   Classics and

For a co   ntact

47 Church Street, Barnsley, South Yorkshire, S70 2AS, England
E-mail: enquiries@pen-and-sword.co.uk
Website: www.pen-and-sword.co.uk

For my husband, Eddy McGrigor,
Direct descendant of both Edward Charles Somers
Cocks and Colquhoun Grant.

CONTENTS

ACKNOWLEDGEMENTS

My deepest thanks must go, firstly, to Julia Page for her great generosity in allowing me to quote from her book *Intelligence Officer in the Peninsula*, a must for students of Wellington's campaign. Also to James Hervey Bathurst of Eastnor Castle for information and photographs from the archives of the family of Somers Cocks. To my neighbours John and Julia Keay and Georgina Nelson. To my editor Tom Hartman, to Neil Hyslop, designer of the maps, and most specially to Brigadier Henry Wilson, Publishing Manager of *Pen & Sword*, and his wonderful team.

Also to the many people who have helped to find the illustrations: the National Portrait Gallery in London; Shona Corner of the Scottish Portrait Gallery in Edinburgh; Jane Cunningham of the Courtauld Institute in London; Senora Teresa Vargas of the Prado in Madrid; Viscountess Esher for contacting the Prado; and Captain P.H. Starling, Curator of the Army Medical Services Museum in Aldershot. Finally, to my husband Eddy, who did the cooking while I wrote the book!

The line drawings all come from Andrew Leith-Hay's own *Narrative of the Peninsular War*, published in 1831.

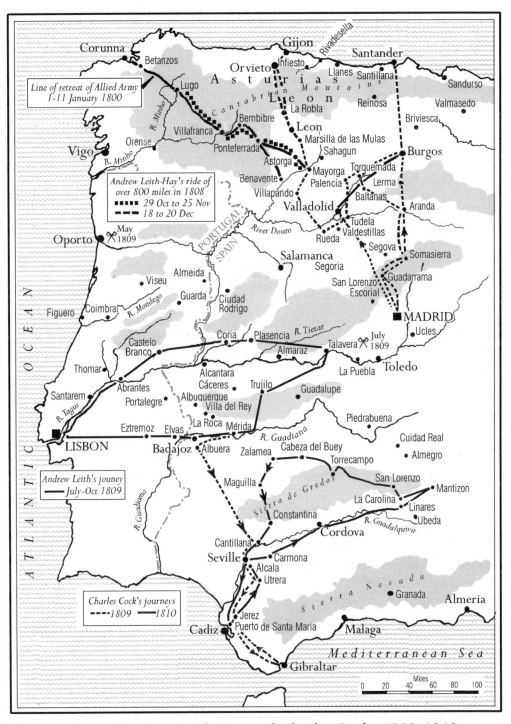

Corunna
Betanzos
Gijon
Rivadesella
Santander
Orvieto
Infiesto
Llanes
Santillana
Sandurso
Lugo
Asturias
Cantabrian Mountains
León
Reinosa
Valmasedo
R. Minho
Bembibre
La Robla
Briviesca
Vigo
Orense
Villafranca
Ponteferrada
Leon
Marsilla de las Mulas
Burgos
R. Minho
Astorga
Sahagun
Torquemada
Mayorga
Palencia
Lerma
Benavente
Villapando
Baltanas
Aranda
Valladolid
Tudela
Salamanca
Valdestillas
Rueda
Segova
Somasierra
Oporto
May 1809
Segoria
San Lorenzo
Escorial
Guadarrama
Almeida
Viseu
Guarda
Ciudad Rodrigo
MADRID
Figuero
Coimbra
R. Mondego
Ucles
Coria
Plasencia
R. Tietar
Talavera
July 1809
Castelo Branco
Almaraz
La Puebla
Toledo
Thomar
Alcantara
Cáceres
Trujilo
Guadalupe
Santarem
Abrantes
Portalegre
Albuquerque
Villa del Rey
Piedrabuena
R. Tagus
Eztremoz
Elvas
La Roca
Mérida
Cuidad Real
LISBON
Badajoz
Albuera
Zalamea
Cabeza del Buey
Torrecampo
Almegro
R. Guadiana
Maguilla
San Lorenzo
Mantizon
R. Guadiana
Sierra de Gredos
La Carolina
Linares
Constantina
Cordova
Ubeda
R. Guadalquivir
Cantillana
Seville
Carmona
Alcala
Utrera
Sierra Nevada
Granada
Almeria
Jerez
Cadiz
Puerto de Santa Maria
Malaga
Gibraltar
Mediterranean Sea
ATLANTIC OCEAN
PORTUGAL
SPAIN
River Douro

Line of retreat of Allied Army
1-11 January 1800

Andrew Leith-Hay's ride of
over 800 miles in 1808
29 Oct to 25 Nov
18 to 20 Dec

Andrew Leith's jouney
July-Oct 1809

Charles Cock's journeys
1809   1810

Miles
0   20   40   60   80   100

The Journeys of Andrew Leith-Hay and Charles Cocks 1808–1810

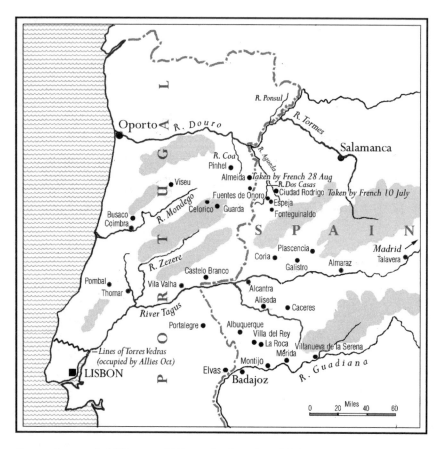

Locations of Allies and French Armies 1810

January   Wellington on Douro – French army centred on Mérida – General Carlos O'Donnell at Villa del Rey and Aliseda.

February   French take Caceres – Town retaken by Don Carlos España – French reoccupy Caceres.

March   Large detachment of Spanish army sent to La Roca – Don Carlos at Montijo – All of Estremadura, north of Guadiana, held by Marques de Romana – Andrew Leith-Hay returns to Lisbon – Marshal Massena, Prince d'Essling, commanding 6th Corps d'Armée, besieges Ciudad Rodrigo and Almeida.

July   2nd Corps d'Armée crosses Tagus at Vila Valha, marches on Castelo Branco, then through mountains towards Guarda – 2 July French cross frontier of Portugal and take fortress of Ciudad Rodrigo.

August   French take Almeida.

September Advance of 2nd Corps d'Armée towards Guarda and Celorico. 8th Corps march on Pinhel – Wellington orders Hill and Leith-Hay to march towards River Mondego – 27 September Battle of Busaco.

October   British army withdraws to lines of Torres Vedras.

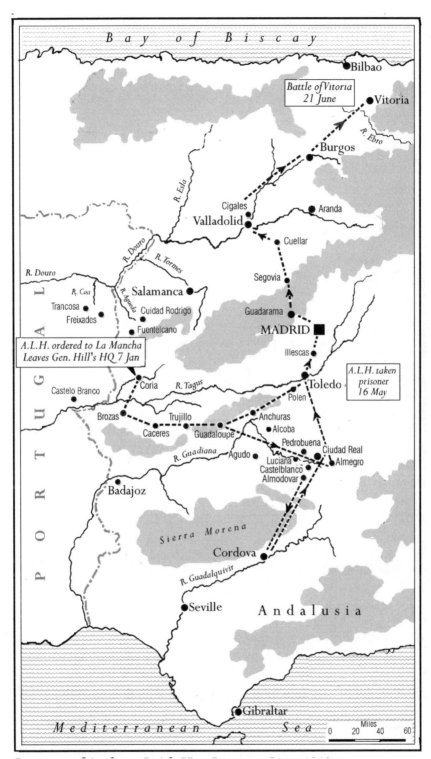

Journey of Andrew Leith-Hay January–June 1813

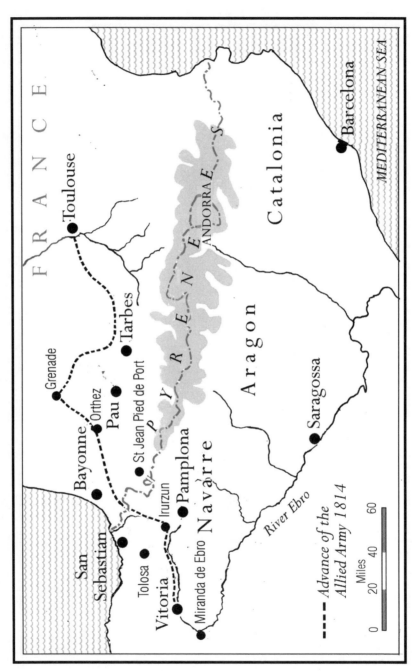

The Final Battles 1813–14

INTRODUCTION

Intelligence officers, more commonly known as spies, have a special place in history if only for the risks that they run. James Bond, 007, the invention of Ian Fleming, is now a household name. Suave, charming and handsome, he survived fictional hazards, in some instances hardly more amazing than those of three of his predecessors during the Peninsular War.

Foremost amongst those who served in Wellington's army, were three men, two of them Scotsmen, the third English. Strikingly different in character, they each left first-hand accounts, as did the doctor, another Scotsman, whose journal supplements the tale.

Andrew Leith-Hay, born in 1785, came from Aberdeenshire. His name is accounted for by the fact that his father, Alexander Leith, had inherited the estate of Rannes, from a relative, Andrew Hay, for which reason he had both added the name of Hay to his own and called his eldest son Andrew.

Commissioned as an ensign in the 72nd Foot in 1806, Andrew went to the Peninsula in 1808 as aide-de-camp to his uncle, General Sir James Leith. In this capacity he spent much time in gaining intelligence. Employed by the army to illustrate locations, when cameras were still unknown, he made sketches of both landscapes and towns which, in 1831, he worked up into two volumes entitled *Narrative of the Peninsular War.** His keen eye for detail is revealed, not only in his sketches, but also in his written descriptions.

Loquacious and sometimes inclined to be pompous, he took himself so seriously that he was a perfect butt for the French who loved to ridicule the British. Nonetheless, thanks to his sense of humour, he saw the funny side of several ludicrous situations which gave his enemies much mirth.

Colquhoun Grant, who like Andrew came from the north-east of Scotland, was quiet and exceedingly reserved. Born at Forres, in Morayshire, in 1770, he was fifteen years older than Andrew and

* Dictionary of National Biography. Vol.X1.Pub, Smith, Elder & co, 1908.

hardened to campaigning before ever reaching the Peninsular. He was known to be extremely clever, having amongst other things, a quick ear for languages which he mastered remarkably well.

Charles Cocks, the scion of a noble family- his father was the second Lord Somers- was born with the proverbial 'silver spoon in his mouth.' Tall and handsome, with all the advantages of wealth, which could have led to a political career, he was nonetheless single minded in his ambition to be a soldier and to reach the heights of his profession. Impetuous and courageous, to the point where he courted danger, he long seemed to bear a charmed life.

From the accounts of these three men, the aspect of each one unique, one can sense the impact of the fighting, the terrible losses both from battle and disease. Yet through the blood and turmoil, the beauty of the country, like sunshine filtering through mist, reaches the reader's mind. Orchards, redolent of orange blossom: the magnificent trees of the forests: water foaming white through dark ravines: boats on the great rivers: the rain, the snow, the wind and the suffocating dust, smothering soldiers and horses below a scorching sun.

In contrast the mountains, cruel as the climate, like shark's teeth guarding the frontier, across which the British soldiers, 'the scum of the earth' as Wellington called them, yet without whom he would never fight a battle, crossed in defiance of all odds.

Most strongly of all comes the realization of the lack of communication at the time of the Peninsular War. Today, when news flashes round the world in seconds, it seems barely credible that generals could still be ignorant of a battle taking place only forty miles away. Thus did Wellington rely on his intelligence officers to bring him, not only the positions of the enemy, but estimations of troop movements, the number of soldiers, both infantry and cavalry, the number and size of his guns, and above all the directions, and the state of the roads, on which they were likely to proceed.

The British general, who vied with the genius of Napoleon as one of the greatest military strategists of all time, was also a sound judge of character. Dependent on the ability of his intelligence officers, 'the eyes and ears of the army', he chose his men with perspicacity and care.

PART 1

1

THE FIRST CAMPAIGN

THE OCCUPATION OF PORTUGAL
NAPOLEON'S BAITED TRAP

August 1808 – January 1809

By the summer of 1808 Napoleon, in a figurative sense, held Europe in the palm of his hand. Prussia and Austria had been overpowered and Russia, through the Treaty of Tilsit, was also under his thrall. England alone stood against him, thanks to her maritime power. The defeat at Trafalgar – largely the fault of Admiral Villeneuve, so Napoleon believed – meant that the survivors of his own fleet, effectually blockaded by the British navy, were no longer a supreme fighting force. His army, on the other hand, was the largest and most superbly trained of any country in the world. Therefore he was confident that the British force, diminutive compared with his own, could be defeated on land.[1]*

Portugal, England's oldest ally, was also one of the countries on which she depended for trade. Napoleon believed that, by installing an army of occupation, he could not only close all the ports to the British but also capture the Portuguese fleet. Only one thing forestalled him, namely that to take an army overland into Portugal he must have the acquiescence of Spain. He was, as usual, triumphant. The Treaty of Fontainebleau, which allowed him to take an army through Spain into Portugal, was signed in October 1807.

The Emperor, acting with his usual energy, had the wheels of war

* See Notes pp. 258–261.

MADRID

in motion while the ink was still barely dry. In less than six weeks Marshal Junot was leading 30,000 men into Lisbon. Almost as they entered the city, the Portuguese royal family, escorted by the British navy, were sailing from the mouth of the Tagus on their way to exile in Brazil.

Napoleon could congratulate himself on achieving a *coup d'état*. However, with increasing arrogance, he then overplayed his hand. The Spanish had promised him freedom of transit through their country. Now, claiming it to be essential to the maintenance of his army in Portugal, he annexed several key fortresses which he garrisoned with French troops. The Spanish people, realizing at that point that, thanks to their leaders, they would soon become a subject state, rose in rebellion on the 'Dos de Mayo', 2 May 1808. Manuel de Godoy, held responsible for the domination of the French, was forced to resign, while the King, Charles IV, also compliant to the liaison, was compelled to abdicate in favour of his son Ferdinand.

Events then escalated. Napoleon occupied Madrid. The Spanish Kings, both Charles and Ferdinand, were forcibly removed to France, whereupon Napoleon, convinced of his omnipotence, installed his brother Joseph Bonaparte as King of Spain. Both Spain and Portugal rose in arms against the usurper. The War of Independence had begun.

Spanish envoys were sent to London where a treaty of alliance between Great Britain and Spain was signed. Thanks to a fortunate but unforeseen circumstance, a force of 9,500 men, originally destined for an expedition against her colonies in South America, was now available to be sent instead to Spain's assistance. Sir Arthur Wellesley, already distinguished for his service in India, was directed to take command of this and of another smaller force, of about 5,000 men, commanded by Major-General Sir Brent Spencer, at that time quartered in Gibraltar.

While the British army was assembling, the Spanish were mauling the French. Besieged garrisons defied them and, more significantly, General Dupont, sent to occupy Andalusia, was defeated by the clever strategy of the Spanish General Castaños, at Baylen, on 19 July. Napoleon raged in exasperation, while his brother Joseph, the newly-made monarch, retreated from Madrid to a safer position north of the River Ebro.

Sir Arthur Wellesley sailed from Cork in the frigate *Crocodile* to land initially at Corunna, on the north-west tip of Spain, on 20 July. The Galician Junta then informed him that no troops were needed. They wanted only arms and gold. Fortunately at that moment an English frigate appeared in the harbour carrying the then enormous sum of two hundred thousand pounds.

Wellesley therefore sailed on to the mouth of the Mondego on the west coast of Portugal where, on 1 August, he landed unopposed. Here, five days later, he was joined by General Spencer, who with his five thousand men, had come from Gibraltar via the Spanish port of Cadiz.

2

SEARCHING FOR INTELLIGENCE

So little was known of Spain that British officers were sent to the northern provinces both to report on the state of the country and to confer with the Spanish commanders as to the means of organizing resistance against the occupying French. Among them was Major-General Sir James Leith, a Scotsman from Aberdeenshire, who was ordered to proceed to Santander to report on the state of the armaments in the Asturias, Guipuzcoa and Las Montañas de Santander. With him, as his aide-de-camp, went his nephew, Andrew Leith-Hay, a young man of twenty–three, whose talent as an artist could now be put to good use. Sailing from Portsmouth aboard the *Peruvian* brig of war, on the evening of 17 August 1808, they sighted the coast of Spain on the morning of the 22nd.

Andrew Leith-Hay was immediately impressed by the magnificence of the country which gradually grew in sight.

> 'As the vessel approached the land the mountains of Asturias appeared in the distance, the wild and varied country, wooded to its summits, exhibiting scenery of striking grandeur and interest.'

Arriving in Santander, they met the bishop, who was regent of the province of Las Montañas. General Leith had been told to question him as to the state of the organization and supply of the armies collecting in the northern provinces to oppose the French. The Condé de Villa Neuva was general-in-chief of the province, being a former officer of the Spanish Guards.

Surprisingly, neither the bishop nor the Condé had any real idea of the situation and movements of the enemy, to the point where they could not say. with any certainty that a Spanish force even existed between the French army and Santander.

The main route from the port of Santander, on the northern coast of Spain, to the interior of the country led through Reinosa and thence by Burgos to Madrid. Because news of what was happening in those areas was of such great importance to the British commanders, Andrew Leith-Hay was sent to reconnoitre.'

His protests that, after only three days in the country, he knew not a word of the language were totally ignored by his uncle. The boy had to go and that was that.

My instructions were to proceed by the pass of Escudo to Reinosa, where it was conjectured I should find General Ballesteros (afterwards so distinguished in the Peninsular War) in command of a body of the Asturians. I was to be accompanied by a Spanish captain of the name of Villardet, twelve soldiers of the regiment of Laredo, to which he belonged, and an old man who was to act as an interpreter.

His description of what happened thereafter was hilarious, as he so aptly describes:

The assembling of this *formidable* cavalcade occasioned a considerable sensation in the town of Santander, and, although late in the evening, a crowd collected to witness our departure. A large and handsome black horse bore the person of the Spanish captain, who was enveloped in his cloak and whose lank and sallow visage was surmounted by a hat of no ordinary dimensions. A mule, caparisoned with all the usual encumbrance of Spanish saddlery, was prepared for me; and as, for the first time, a pair of horse pistols graced my saddle bow, and a cortège appeared to accompany me, I mounted with exultation and derived no ordinary satisfaction from the feeling that I was the hero of this great expedition.

In the midst of these preparations for departure, an incident of ludicrous description rather lessened the importance and detracted from the gravity of the occasion. When the old interpreter proceeded to mount the mule destined to transport

7

him, the solemnity and silence of the scene was suddenly exchanged for the most discordant noise and the most calamitous disturbance. The master of languages, who apparently had neglected the study of equitation, unfortunately for him, had been provided with the only vicious mule in company, which, the moment he ascertained the burden that was intended for him, proceeded with his heels to disperse the crowd, to the terror and annoyance of some, and the amusement of others; nor did he desist from this violent exercise until he had prostrated his rider in the street. [Eventually] the interpreter being mounted upon a more tractable animal, we proceeded on our journey.

After travelling for fifteen miles in increasing darkness they finally arrived at a village where the muleteers insisted they stop for 'refreshment both for themselves and their quadrupeds'. Unfortunately the posada, or inn, like most others in northern Spain, proved to be primitive in the extreme: the main part of the house being used as a stable for both the horses and the mules.

At daybreak they set off again, travelling through very beautiful country. The road ran through narrow valleys, bounded by hills which were covered to the summits by tall and magnificent trees. Only occasionally, where the valleys opened out onto flatter ground, did the land become cultivated.

Shortly they met a party of the Spanish peasants, volunteers in defence of their country, who already were notorious for their brutal treatment of French prisoners.

In the course of the forenoon we perceived smoke ascending from a wood in our front and, upon arriving at it, found an advanced post of three hundred Asturians, all peasants, who had recently enrolled themselves and were but indifferently armed.

From the commandant I learned that General Ballesteros was at Reinosa, and having travelled as expeditiously as the nature of my escort would permit, reached his quarters in the evening.

General Fransisco Ballesteros, to all outward appearances, was a man destined for fame. A native of Asturia aged only thirty-eight, he had gained rapid promotion, from subaltern to major-general, since the

VITORIA

start of the war against France. Andrew described him as superior to any of the other officers whom he had so far come across in Spain.

> Young, active and intelligent, he at once impressed a stranger with the idea that he was an efficient, and likely to become a distinguished, officer.

By the time of their meeting Ballesteros had been for some time at Reinosa in command of a force consisting of about four to five thousand of his native Asturians who, at that point, had not been with either of the two Spanish armies. He gave Andrew a detailed description of all the information which he had acquired of the positions and movements of the enemy's troops. The French head-quarters was in Vitoria and, to the best of his knowledge, nothing so far had indicated that an immediate offensive would take place. ' No force of any description had approached Reinosa and his situation there appeared to be, for the present, secure and undisturbed.'

Andrew, on receiving the assurance that Santander was in no immediate danger, decided he must return immediately to impart this knowledge to his uncle. Thus, having hired post horses, he galloped at midnight through the streets of Reinosa led by a Spanish postillion.

The stillness of a beautiful night was interrupted only by the challenge of the Spanish sentinels as we passed their several posts, and enlivened by the sound of the bells attached to the bridle of my companion's horse; the wild song in which he occasionally indulged, the distant noise, the mirth of travelling muleteers, and the rush of waters falling over their rocky channels in the ravines and closely wooded valleys through which the road is conducted.

The only pace the Spanish horse ever attempts is either a walk or a gallop, and as the postillion invariably precedes the traveller, the transition from the rapid to the slow pace is attended with a species of shock not agreeable to the person unprepared for this mode of proceeding. Notwithstanding this, riding post in Spain is, upon the great routes where the horses are good, a pleasant and tolerably expeditious mode of performing a journey.

In view of Andrew's report General Leith decided that, at least for the time being, disturbance in the province of Las Montañas was unlikely to occur. Therefore, together with Andrew, he re-embarked to sail for Gijon and march down to Oviedo. The Bay of Gijon, one of the most exposed on the north coast of Spain, receives the full force of the swell rolling in from the Bay of Biscay. Fortunately, in late August, it was calm. Andrew and the General were lodged in the château of a nobleman, which, although outwardly magnificent, was, like many such buildings, sadly dilapidated, The huge rooms lacked furniture, weeds grew high in the courtyard and the well was long disused. They stayed there, however, only for one night.

The day after our arrival at Gijon General Miranda and a deputation from the Junta of Asturias came for the purpose of escorting the General to Oviedo, and on the following morning we proceeded to that city. Oviedo, the ancient Ovetum and the capital of Asturias, is situated in a romantic and beautiful valley, surrounded by rich and variegated scenery. The lofty spire of the cathedral forms a conspicuous object, and the background of distant mountain gives importance to the scene.

Their reception was extremely friendly. Amazingly, the Spanish seemed to have forgotten that only three years previously, when still allied to the French, their fleet had been largely destroyed at the Battle of Trafalgar. The members of the provincial Junta, who were assembled to receive General Leith, were headed by General-in-Chief Acevedo, an old man, lethargic and extremely short-sighted. Placed in command of the Asturian contingent. he was just about to set off for the town of Llanes, on the coast, where the new levies were expected to number 10,000 men.

Meanwhile, in Portugal, some fifty miles north of Lisbon, Sir Arthur Wellesley, firstly at Rolica on 17 August 1808 and then at Vimiero on the 21st, had soundly defeated the French army commanded by General Delaborde.

The French, were astounded, deeming it virtually impossible that the troops of their beloved Emperor should be thus overcome. The result was that General Kellerman, on the orders of Marshal Junot, was sent to arrange the armistice which resulted in the Convention of Cintra, signed on the last day of the month.

The terms included the liberation of Portugal, together with the reinforcement of the Spanish army of Estremadura with the four to five thousand Spanish soldiers currently held prisoner on board the vessels in the Tagus. The boundaries were to be be recognized and, most importantly, the French troops, together with their guns and horses, were to be conveyed back to their homeland in British warships, complete with all their possessions including accumulated plunder. The safety of all French residents and their Portuguese adherents was assured and the port of Lisbon declared a haven of neutrality for the Russian fleet.[2]

Sir Arthur Wellesley, much to his fury, was now superseded in command by the Governor of Gibraltar, General Sir Hew Dalrymple, and Sir Harry Burrard, both of them elderly men. Neither was to serve for long, however, for the terms of the Convention of Cintra so enraged the British that a public enquiry ensued. Subsequently, while Wellesley was cleared of all charges, Sir Hew Dalrymple was dismissed and Burrard forced to retire.

On 4 October 1808 the command of the thirty thousand men in Portugal fell upon Sir John Moore. Now aged forty-seven, Moore, the son of a doctor, had been born in Glasgow in 1761, As a young lieutenant, aged only nineteen, he had first won distinction in the American War of Independence. Then, having served in Corsica, the West Indies, Holland and Egypt, and been wounded no less than three times, he had been placed in command of the south-east of England, where, as Napoleon threatened invasion, he had been behind the building of the Martello towers. Also during this period he had trained the Light Division at Shorncliffe in Kent, with so much success that his tactics were copied by Sir Arthur Wellesley (by then Duke of Wellington) in his Peninsular campaign.

Early in October, almost as he took command, Moore received orders from England to move the greater part of his army to northern Spain. There he was to be joined by General Sir David Baird, a fellow Scotsman, acclaimed for his long service in India, where, after capturing the fortress of that name, he had become the 'Hero of Seringapatam'. Baird would shortly sail from England with a force ten thousand strong, to land at Corunna, one of the few good harbours in the north of Spain.

Moore now faced the problem of moving his army for two hundred miles over bad roads made worse by constant rain, To compound his difficulties he was short of money to buy food, for the British, unlike the French, did not impoverish the local people by living, without payment off their land. In addition he had to find transport. Carts had to be bought or hired, together with mules and oxen to pull them over tracks across the mountains in the worst of the winter months,

Already decided on the shortest route through northern Portugal to the frontier fortress of Almeida (in Portugal) and Ciudad Rodrigo across the border, and thence to Salamanca, Moore was told, it tran-spired erroneously, that this was impassible for artillery. Therefore he sent Sir John Hope, with the guns and cavalry, on a longer and divergent way, along the valley of the Tagus to Talavera from where they had to cross the pass over the Guadarrama mountain range before joining him at Salamanca.[3]

Afterwards, much criticized for thus dividing his force, he main-tained that he did so on the assurance of the Spanish authorities that the French were too undermanned to attack from their defensive positions north of the Ebro. Events were to prove, however, that he had been greatly misinformed.

Andrew Leith-Hay, at Ovideo, believed at this time that the Spanish army, despite its obvious inefficiency, could, with the help of the British, overthrow the French. The French army was encamped on the Ebro. General Blake was at Leon from where it

12

was presumed that he would immediately advance. He was to be reinforced not only by the corps of General Acevedo but by that of the Marques of Romana who was daily expected to arrive on the north coast of Spain, now freed from Napoleon's control.

General Blake's army, however, although large in manpower, was very badly equipped: the infantry being both undisciplined and ill-armed. Many of the regiments were composed entirely of recruits, commanded by officers who, being ill-trained themselves, were consequently inefficient. Only a very small body of cavalry, together with the heavy guns, seemed to be in a serviceable state. Andrew, foreseeing what would happen when they faced the French army, renowned as the most invincible in the world, gave it as his opinion that no general, with an army such as Blake now commanded, would want to risk fighting such a force.

But General Blake appeared to have no feeling of this kind. He went headlong to the line of operations, and the result was, as might have been expected, most disastrous.

General Leith, however, apparently convinced that the Junta of Asturias would both arm and equip the troops who were to reinforce General Blake, set off from Oviedo and, together with Captains Lefebure, Jones and Paisley of the Royal Engineers, proceeded to Gijon. From here he travelled along the shores of the Bay of Biscay to Llanes, the headquarters of General Acevedo, and from thence by San Vicente de la Barquera and Santillana to Santander, where he was told of the occupation of Bilbao by a division of the Galician army.

The General, however, thanks to some agreement made with the bishop, could not himself go to Bilbao. Thus he sent Andrew in his place.

He therefore ordered me to proceed to that town, and in an hour after our arrival in Santander I was on my route. Having travelled all night, passed through Santoña, Laredo, Castro Urdiales and Portugalete, I crossed the ferry at the Convent of St Nicolas, a league from Bilbao, which is from thence approached by an excellent road, leading along the banks of the river through a rich and beautiful valley.

Bilbao is a very fine town, the streets spacious, well paved, and the buildings large and handsome. The river [Nerbion] is navigable up to the town, which has long been the most considerable mercantile place upon the north coast of the Peninsula.

The occupation of Bilbao had occasioned a considerable sensation at the French headquarters and an important movement was the result. Marshal Ney with his whole corps d'armée broke up from Logroña, and having rapidly marched the distance, appeared in front of Bilbao upon the 26th [September]

About one o'clock the inhabitants were thrown into the greatest consternation by unfounded rumours that the enemy had entered the town, A more perfect panic could not be well imagined. The street was instantaneously crowded with people, who rushed past uttering the wildest screams. They were accompanied by horses, mules, cars loaded with furniture, and by cattle and sheep; and without pausing to investigate the truth or incorrectness of the report, were flying to gain the road to Portugalete.

General Leith, with the officers of his staff, then appeared to join the Marques de Portago on a hill on the right of the Durango road where two cannons had been mounted. A column of infantry and three more guns were placed on the left side of the road while two battalions of grenadiers defended the approaches to the town. The Spanish artillery tried the range of their guns as the enemy approached, but without effect. The French advance continued and the Spanish, placing their cannon in front of their column, retired to Valmaseda without losing any men.

Then a fresh problem arose.

A considerable quantity of powder having been landed at Portugalete for the use of the Biscayan levies, I was ordered to proceed to that place, endeavour to get it removed, and then cross the country to Valmaseda.'

The weather, which had been fine during the earlier part of the day, had changed. Rain fell in torrents, adding to the misery of the different persons who, escaping from Bilbao, covered the whole extent of the road to Portugalete. On it were to be seen the Spanish merchant and his family toiling through the deep mud – the unattached Spanish officer, who had displayed his uniform during the absence of the enemy (but had now discarded it for safety) – the English amateur, who had visited Bilbao full of curiosity and warlike enthusiasm, but who, unprepared for the reverse of the picture, was now to be seen struggling onwards to a place of safety, drenched with rain, lightly clad, indifferently shod, and perfectly miserable.

At Portugalate Andrew was told that the powder destined for the Biscayan levies was in fact lying in launches at Santoña, a small port on the coast about three miles away. Putting his spurs to his horse, he got there to find to his horror that the launches, containing no less than 400 barrels of gunpowder, were now all lying fast aground.

This presented a real problem, at first sight totally insolvable. To leave the powder in the holds of the boats, in charge of the Spanish guards, was as good as giving it to the French. There seemed to be no means of moving it to a place of safety. What on earth was Andrew to do?

Then, in a flash of inspiration, he suddenly had an idea.

When considering what was most advisable in this emergency, I observed in the crowd a Spaniard of the name of Felix Blanco, an officer who had accompanied the general to Bilbao, and whose manly appearance and fierce sombrero gave hopes that he would have led into contact with the French, but whom, I regret to state, I had passed amongst the fugitives. Whether it was to be attributed to his superior powers of pedestrianism, or to his early departure, I cannot decide. Certain it is that he was very near the head of the column.

Although this hero, who displayed on his hat a very splendid ribbon, on which was inscribed *Vencir o morir por Fernando VII*, [conquer or die for Ferdinand VII] was not exactly the person to be selected for the defence of the post; still, taking into consideration the dislike he appeared to entertain at the sight of anything in the shape of an enemy, and as the launches afforded him the means of escape, as well as a plausible motive for again appearing in his native town, without having carried into effect the martial intentions with which he had left it, I felt convinced that he would strain every nerve to execute this important service.

15

After instructing Don Felix to proceed to sea as soon as the state of the tide made it practicable, I left Santona, and, at three o'clock in the morning, passed to the right of the French corps which had bivouac'd in advance of Bilbao. I entered the village of Valmaseda and again joined the Marquis de Portago's division, the soldiers of which were apparently as unconcerned as if no enemy was near. They were straggling about the streets, which were crowded, and blazing in all directions with the fires which had been kindled. Notwithstanding the inclemency of the weather, groups of military and peasants were to be seen, the former recounting the events, and the latter listening to the adventures of the preceding day.

Andrew returned to Valmaseda to find that General Leith had gone to Frias in search of General Blake. He then set out to follow him up the dangerous, almost perpendicular, road called the Peña de Angulo, to the plateau of Old Castile.

Nothing can exceed the picturesque beauty of the scenery at this point. The country is wooded in the most luxuriant manner, and from the rocky heights, mountain torrents fall in all directions. But having reached the summit of the pass, the aspect of the country is immediately altered, the varied and luxuriant valleys of Biscay are exchanged for the bleak plains of Castile.

Reaching the village of Quincoces, where General Blake had his headquarters, Andrew found that there was no sign of his uncle, General Leith, who had taken a different route to Frias. He then discovered, to his amazement, that General Blake had almost no idea of what had occurred at Bilbao, only forty miles away, and 'exhibited an unpardonable degree of ignorance in a general-in-chief'.

Blake, the descendant of an old Irish family, had, previous to the Revolution, been a colonel of infantry in the Spanish army. Now, aged about fifty, he held the supreme command in the north of Spain. Although reputed to dislike the English, he got on well with General Leith with whom he talked for hours on all subjects connected with the war. Never were they known to disagree. Nonetheless, Andrew strongly suspected that his apparent good will towards his uncle concealed a pressing need to acquire both money and arms.

16

On the morning of 1 October Andrew and General Leith set out for Santander. Having spent the night with a hospitable friar, who actually had glass in his windows and braziers plentifully supplied with charcoal, they arrived at their destination to find it quiet as before.

On the morning of the 8th, however, there was enormous excitement in the town when the *Defiance,* a British ship-of-the-line of seventy-four guns, conveying a fleet of transports, with part of the division from the north, appeared.

Andrew was ordered to go aboard the battleship to communicate with her master, Captain Hotham, but the sea was so rough that the Spanish boatmen turned back, much to his relief. Later, when the wind moderated, the transports entered the harbour. Soon afterwards senior Spanish officers, who included the Conde de San Roman and Brigadier-General Caro, came ashore to confer with General Leith.

Unfortunately the Spanish general the Marques de la Romana had gone to London, leaving his division under the temporary command of Brigadier-General the Condé de San Roman, Colonel of the Regiment of the Princessa. It consisted of four very strong regiments of infantry, a detachment of artillery, two regiments of dragoons and two of hussars.

Previous to the revolution against the French these had been the crack units of the Spanish army, although their arms were out of date. The uniforms of the infantry were white, those of the heavy cavalry a brilliant green. The latter regiments, however, in escaping, had abandoned their horses, thus rendering themselves virtually useless to the Galician army to which they were drafted as reinforcements. General Romana's journey to London could not have been worse timed. Had he only returned to Santander at once to take command of the army from General Blake, the disasters resulting from the latter's mistakes might well have been mitigated if not completely avoided.

Blake now missed a perfect opportunity to strike at the French army before reinforcements arrived. Instead he remained at Bilbao until, on 24 October, he made a feeble and ineffective attack on the French at Zornosa (Amoriebieta). Even as this was happening Napoleon's army from Germany (with which country he had made peace) was crossing the Pyrenees.

If the advance of General Blake, under former circumstances, was rash and dangerous, it now amounted to absolute madness. It was rushing to inevitable destruction, and broken, disheartened, and dispersed as his army soon became, it is a reflection upon the tactic and energy of the enemy that any portion of it was suffered to escape . . . [Blake] continued inactive from the 21st to the 31st – thereby giving Marshal the Duke of Danzig [Marshal Lefèbvre][4] time to assemble a force at Durango of above 20,000 men, with which, on the morning of the latter day, he attacked the Spaniards, overthrew them without the slightest difficulty, and drove them back upon Bilbao.

The Marques de la Romana, whose arrival was so eagerly awaited, had still not arrived at Santander. Therefore, it being thought possible that he might have landed at Corunna and then gone on to Madrid, Andrew was ordered to ride from the north coast of Spain due south to the capital, a distance of almost three hundred miles.

Winter was now approaching and the hours of daylight growing short. Nevertheless, at nine o'clock on the evening of 29 October he set out on the road to Reinosa with a servant or a postillion lighting the road with a lamp. Armed with his sword, a pair of pistols strapped to his saddle bow, he carried the important dispatches for the Marques de la Romana, Mr Frere, the British Minister in Spain, and Lord William Bentinck[5]. The journey was far from easy, as he graphically describes.

The next evening I approached the Somosierra and entered the pass over the celebrated barrier of the Castilles. It was midnight before I ascended the mountain, which was covered with snow. The wind blew loud and the cold was extreme. The village of Somosierra is situated high in the mountain. The houses were covered with snow, almost rendering them imperceptible. Snowed up as was the whole scene, the low and insignificant town, with its flat roofs, appeared from the height above to be but part of the mountainside.

Reaching Madrid, Andrew waxed lyrical about the paintings of the old masters in the Alcazar, or royal palace. The portraits by Velasquez in particular he thought to be superb. 'For all the higher

requisites of art [he] has seldom been equalled and never surpassed.'
Exploring all the great buildings, he reached the Royal Academy of
San Fernando where, among other great masterpieces, he found
Titian's Venus and The Ascension by Raphael, as well as several of
Rubens' greatest works. Eventually, remembering the object of his
visit and having discovered that Mr Frere, the British Minister, had
not yet arrived, 'I went to the house of the Duchess of Osuña and
delivered the dispatches to Lord William Bentinck.'

> His Lordship questioned me very particularly upon the state of
> affairs in the north, and regarding the strength and position of
> the French army. It was quite evident that the Spanish govern-
> ment, either had not the means of obtaining accurate
> information from the immediate scene of action, or, having
> become possessed of it, did not impart what they knew to the
> confidential and intelligent person then acting for the British
> government.

On the evening of the 7 November Mr Frere finally arrived. He told
Andrew to remain in Madrid until he had conferred with the Central
Junta the next day. By this time rumour was running wild in the city,
the generals being made scapegoats for the recent disasters. General
Castaños, a distinguished soldier, later Duke of Bailen, in particular,
was now widely thought to be a traitor.

Soon it became clear that the grand army of Napoleon had indeed
arrived in Spain. The enemy was said to have advanced as far as
Burgos but this was not definitely known. Lord William Bentinck,
however, sent Andrew a message that it was most unlikely that he
would be able to get back to Santander through country held by
enemy troops. Nevertheless, having been given Mr Frere's dispatches
for England and urged by Lord William to attempt the journey, he
set off north from Madrid on the morning of 10 November.

> Having posted all night I arrived at noon the following day at
> Aranda de Duero, where I met with convincing proofs of the
> French army having resumed the offensive. The town was
> crowded with Spanish soldiery, and I soon ascertained that the
> army of Estremadura, the headquarters of which was now in
> Aranda, had been defeated near to Burgos on the preceding
> day.

It soon transpired that Napoleon, from his headquarters at Vitoria, had himself planned the attack of his second corps commanded by Marshal Soult. The Spaniards had been totally overcome. Defeated infantry soldiers. wandering in the streets of Burgos, had been sabred without mercy. People had fled from the town where their houses and shops were being ransacked and plundered by the enemy.

The survivors of the army of Esturia had retreated sixty miles to Aranda which was already crowded with refugees. Andrew entered into a scene of chaos. Soldiers wandered the streets, 'all order or discipline apparently having received a fatal shock from the events of the previous day'.

It was here, in the centre of the mêlée that he found himself forced to witness a scene which, while horrific in itself, brought home to him the intensity of the hatred of the Spanish for the French. In his own description one can still sense his revulsion to the scene, which, all unwittingly, he came across.

> The Condé de Belvedere, a very young man, perfectly unac-customed to command, had been left in charge of the Estremaduran army at this most critical moment. The square, or placa, in which he was quartered, I found occupied by a crowd, evidently in a great state of excitement, This was occasioned by the detection of a Spaniard, said to be employed as a spy, who had been taken in the act of procuring informa-tion. The culprit had been conveyed to the part of the placa fronting the general's quarter, and soon afterwards the Conde himself appeared on the balcony and addressed the populace. The noise and incessant clamour from beneath prevented his being heard at any distance, but I was informed his address was directed with a request to the enraged multitude that they would spare the life of the offender until he might be regularly tried and punished. This temperate appeal appeared not to have the slightest effect. On the contrary, while the Condé and his staff were still on the balcony, I perceived the ponderous swords of some Spanish dragoons hacking at what it could not for a moment be doubted was the person of the un-fortunate spy.

The Condé de Belvedere gave Andrew full details of the recent defeat of the Spanish army, blaming it largely on treachery, [Although] 'how or why that existed he did not explain, and probably to have done so satisfactorily would have been difficult.'

Before leaving Aranda Andrew wrote to Lord William Bentinck telling him that it was now too dangerous to ride directly to Burgos, thanks to the road being held by French troops. Because of this he was going make a detour past the west of the town, through country unoccupied by the enemy, by which means he hoped to reach the north coast.

Riding a post horse, he took the road to Sotillo. On his way he met numerous parties of Spanish soldiers who were heading towards Aranda to rejoin their regiments. All told the same story. The French were rapidly advancing. Passing through Sotillo, he headed for Cevico Nabero, where he could get no definite information, but at Baltanas the Alcalde [Mayor] warned him that the advanced posts of the enemy were only a few leagues ahead. Hearing this unpleasant news, he returned to Cevico Nabero, riding into the village at dead of night.

Some of the fugitive hussars of Valencia had arrived there from Burgos and six of them offered to escort him to Valladolid, still thought to be clear of enemy soldiers. After travelling for nine hours in pouring rain, they arrived at Tudela on the River Duero. Here Andrew was given shelter by the cura [priest], whose house was already full of visitors anxiously asking for news. It soon transpired that Valladolid, only two miles away, had now fallen to the French. 'Never did the people of Tudela pass so anxious or sleepless a night.'

At six o'clock in the morning Andrew's Asturian servant came rushing into the cura's house shouting that the French cavalry were close to the town, which sent Andrew leaping from his bed.

A very few minutes elapsed before I was across the Duero, having passed the bridge amidst a crowd of the inhabitants forming a most singular cavalcade, men, women, children, cattle, sheep, horses and cars, covering the whole road and flying in the utmost confusion.

The Valencian hussars, having purloined his pistols, had now vanished, so, with his servant, he rode on to a place called Valdestillas where new post horses were procured. Having recrossed the Duero by the bridge of Tordesillas, he found to his amazement that the people had no idea that the French were anywhere near their

21

town. Riding on, he met with the same ignorance of any activity in the area. So, deciding to take a chance, he headed across country to a village called Velilla where once again the Spanish clergyman gave him hospitality for the night. The next day could well have been his last.

> At six o'clock in the morning of the 16th, accompanied by two peasants and my servant, I took the road to Villada, on which we had not proceeded above a league, when, through the mist, horsemen appeared upon the road advancing directly towards us. We immediately halted, and soon ascertained they were dragoons. Upon seeing us they retired with precipitation. Supposing them to be a patrol of the enemy's cavalry – for doubtful as was the light, the brazen casque and streaming horse-hair proclaimed without doubt the country to which they belonged – I lost not a moment in following their example in the opposite direction, and galloped back to Velilla.

Now fully aware that the enemy's troops were everywhere to the north, he realized the folly of trying to ride directly to Santander. Deciding then to take the quickest route to Leon, he regained the great road at Mallorga and from thence proceeded to Mansilla de las Mulas. Eventually, at 12 o'clock at night, on what must have been an exhausted horse, he rode into Leon. There he found that while some of the British Commissariat had arrived, none had the faintest idea of the whereabouts of the Marques de la Romana. Neither had any of them heard of the success or otherwise of the Galician army, so vital, not only to his uncle General Leith, but also to his own immediate future.

> In this state of uncertainty, it appeared to me most important to proceed direct to the coast of Asturias and send Mr Frere's dispatches by the earliest conveyance to England.

Andrew left Leon on the evening of 18 November to cross the mountains to Oviedo. The first part of the journey over the cultivated plain surrounding La Robla was easy, but the next stretch of the road to a place called Buiza was atrocious. Streams, flooded by heavy rain, foamed down the hillsides making the fords in some places almost impassable. Worse was still to come. Used as he was by now to the tracks over the mountains, the one from Buiza which climbed up to the Pass of Pajares proved to be the worst he had yet encountered. Extremely rough and full of holes, it would have been bad enough in daylight, but at night, with the darkness made deeper by a violent storm of driving rain, it proved all but impossible to follow. The wretched horse which he rode appears to have stumbled and came down several times while slowly picking its way.

At last, however, after having had more than one roll amongst the rocks, and with the prospect of occasionally accompanying some of the mountain streams into the valleys to which they were rushing with great rapidity, I arrived at the town of Pajares, having been seven hours and a half in travelling sixteen miles. On arriving at Oviedo, the procurador-general of the province and General Ballesteros informed me of the disasters that had befallen the unfortunate army of the left, which had been completely defeated, Generals Acevedo, Requelmé and the Condé San Roman [whom he had met at Santander only a month before] had been killed, while the survivors had dispersed and sought safety in the mountains of Leon. The procurador-general declared, with an expression of solemnity, melancholy and despair, that the whole was to be attributed to the treason of General Blake!

Having failed to learn of the whereabouts of either the Marques de la Romana or General Leith in Oviedo, Andrew rode on to Gijon where he delivered the dispatches to a Mr Hunter to be sent to Canning[6] in London. He then followed the coast towards Santander until told by some Spanish soldiers that his uncle, the general, had gone by a mountain road to a town called Infiesto, from whence he was heading for Oviedo. The town of Infiesto, in the centre of the great chain of the Ariales, proved to be very picturesque, but Andrew was again disappointed in his search for General Leith of whom there was no sign.

Having persuaded the Alcalde to find him horses, he set off after sunset with a guide who very shortly lost his way. They reached a river which the guide said was navigable, so Andrew, at the head of the party, went first into the stream. After several plunges the horse lost its footing and nearly drowned its rider before he managed to force it back to the bank.

La Pola, the nearest village, was four leagues distant, the night excessively cold. I was drenched with water, the guide apparently uncertain where he was and the darkness such that no object could be distinguished at any distance. The guide said there were no habitations in the district, but after a short distance we discovered a light, not far removed from the bank of the river, which proved to come from the window of a cottage. The inmates of this humble dwelling received us with the utmost cordiality and kindness. Our appearance at that late hour must have occasioned considerable surprise, as well as distrust, but the moment the reason for it was explained, all restraint appeared to have vanished, while every effort was made by these poor peasants to render their habitation as comfortable as possible.

Returning to Oviedo, Andrew at last learnt that the Marques de la Romana and General Leith had gone through Potes to Leon, where, to his great relief, he found them both in the palace of the Bishop of Leon. Thus ended his journey of over 900 miles through the length and breadth of northern Spain.

3

'IF THE BUBBLE BURSTS'

The Marques de la Romana, after his prolonged stay in London, had come back to Spain to find his army totally defeated. The first of his soldiers that he came across were flying from the enemy to take refuge in the mountains. There, in the bitter cold, most of them were near starving and without winter clothing and shoes. Many were wounded and all in a state of misery and exhaustion.

Realizing that it was now impossible even to attempt to reorganize the Galician army anywhere near the enemy, the Marques made his headquarters at Leon, which he hoped would become a rallying point for the scattered remains of the army. Andrew admired him, calling him 'the man who, of all others, conducted himself invariably during the struggle with a firmness, an integrity, a prudence, and a courage, worthy of the best of the Spanish monarchy, or the noblest records of patriotism.' Describing his appearance he wrote:

> The Marques de la Romana appeared at this date to be aged about fifty [he was actually forty-seven, just a month older than Moore]. Short in stature, without any great look of ability, his countenance, although it did not indicate the firmness of his mind, had an expression of much amiability of disposition. I was present at his first interview with General Blake, after the disaster of his army. It was conducted by the Marques with the utmost mildness: no expression of irritation or disappointment escaped him, the only restraint appearing on the part of the defeated general.

The Spanish armies of the left and of the centre had both been totally overwhelmed and now even greater danger threatened as Napoleon, who had entered Spain on 8 November at the head of 200,000 men, marched upon Madrid. The Emperor had reached Valladolid on the 13th, just as Andrew had escaped across the Duero to avoid being captured by the French. Sir John Moore, however, had been unaware of the extent of the collapse of the Spanish armies until the third week of November.

On 27 November General Leith left Leon to join the British army. At that time the divisions were widely scattered. Moore's headquarters were at Salamanca, where 12,000 infantry and a battery of six guns were amassed. Sir David Baird was at Astorga and General Hope was still at the southern entrance of the Guadarrama Pass.

Four days previously, on the 23rd, the Spanish Generals Castaños and Palafox had been totally defeated at Tudela. Thus the Spaniards were virtually conquered before the British army had fully assembled in their country.[7]

Napoleon, confident of total victory, was preparing to cross the Somosierra. His guards and the reserve, centred on a new base of operations at Burgos, were poised to move forward either against Madrid or Salamanca. His second corps was on the Deba, threatening Leon and the Asturias, while the fourth, commanded by the Duke of Danzig [Marshal Lefèbvre] was descending via Valladolid on the Guadarrama Pass.

SALAMANCA

Fortunately for the British, the French intelligence was so inefficient that Danzig failed to realize that by marching diagonally across the country to the Guadarrama mountains he could have cut off Hope's division. Had this happened he could have forced him back into Portugal, thus preventing him from rejoining Moore at Salamanca.

On 27 November Sir John Moore had actually written to Mr Frere, the British Minister in Madrid, telling of his planned advance towards Burgos when, on the following night, he heard of the disaster at Tudela. Moore's plans had been founded on the idea of rallying the Spanish armies behind the Tagus. Now, with the strength of Spain broken, this was totally impossible. The French would be across the Tagus before the British. There was no Spanish army to confront them. Accordingly, and with great reluctance, he ordered Sir David Baird to retreat to Corunna or Vigo, from either of which ports he could convey his troops by sea to Lisbon. while he himself fell back upon Portugal.

Napoleon crossed the Somosierra. His fourth corps approached Segovia, threatening Sir John Hope whose leading division had reached Talavera. Don Thomas Morla (the Spanish Secretary of War and one of the delegates who had arranged the treaty between Britain and Spain) urged him to march through Madrid but Hope, having visited the city, realized that the Spanish government was now totally disorganized and, as he rightly guessed, corrupt. Had he agreed to Morla's plan he would have been overwhelmed by the vast French force by then approaching the city.

Somehow he managed to find bullocks to drag his guns over the Guadarrama Pass. Then, once on the plain, he made a series of forced marches to Alba de Tormes, from where a detachment of cavalry escorted his army to Salamanca, where, on 4 December, he joined Moore.

Moore had now come under tremendous pressure both from the Spanish Junta and the British Minister, Mr Frere. The latter informed him that 'the enthusiasm of the Spanish was unbounded, that 20,000 men were assembled in the vicinity of the capital, that reinforcements were arriving daily from the southern provinces, and that the addition of the British army would form a force greatly superior to any the French could bring against that quarter, in sufficient time . . . . It was certain that the latter were very weak . . . while the whole country, from the Pyrenees to the capital, was in arms on their left flank.'[8]

It was largely thanks to this intelligence that, on 6 December, Moore made the momentous decision to countermand his orders for withdrawal and to advance on Burgos. He knew the risks he was running. To Baird he wrote significantly 'If the bubble bursts and Madrid falls, we shall have to make a run for it.'[9]

4

RETREAT TO CORUNNA

Four days earlier, on 2 December, General Leith had set off to join his brigade, consisting of the Royal 26th and 81st regiments at Villafranca. Arriving, with Andrew, he had found the brigade to be continuing its retreat towards the coast.

> On the 7th we arrived at Lugo, (the Lucus Augusti of the Romans), on the River Minho, the principal stream that waters the kingdom of Galicia. The retreat of Sir David Baird's corps terminated here. Upon the morning of the 9th orders were received to march back with the least possible delay to Astorga.

On 11 December Moore began his march to the north and nine days later, on the 20th, joined Sir David Baird at Mayorga. Moore now commanded a combined force of 23,000 infantry and 2,500 cavalry, while Baird led an estimated 10,000 men. Convinced that Marshal Soult was unaware that his force had amalgamated, but, believing that he was still retreating into Portugal, he decided to seize the opportunity to attack him, with the element of surprise.

It was a brave decision to attempt a battle which, but for the military genius of Napoleon, might conceivably have been won.

It is at this point that Andrew Leith-Hay became a witness of the final parts of Moore's campaign. At Lugo his uncle, General Leith, had become too ill to travel, However, Andrew, desperate to see action, had been allowed to head off on his own for the headquarters at Mayorga. He was there when, on the morning of the 21st, a contingent of the French cavalry at Sahagun was totally defeated by Lord Henry Paget with the 15th Light Dragoons. As the French fled, putting spurs to their horses, Baird moved his division into the town.[10]

Moore then ordered a night march on the town of Carrion where Soult's infantry was encamped.

At eight o'clock on the evening of 23 December the troops were actually mustered on the parade ground, on the point of moving off, when Baird received a summons from Moore. The General had just received an astonishing piece of news. Captain Waters, an intelligence officer, had ridden in to Valdesillos to be told that a French officer, rash enough to ride alone, had insulted the post-master, and been murdered by the villagers. Waters, discovering that the man had been carrying dispatches, had bought them for twenty dollars and then galloped to find Sir John Moore.

The messages revealed, not only that Madrid had capitulated, but that Napoleon, with 80,000 men, was marching from there against the British army.[11] Under these circumstances an assault on Soult at Burgos was now out of the question. Sir John was left with no alternative but to order an immediate retreat.

Napoleon had heard, only two days previously, on 21 November, that Moore was advancing against his second *corps d'armée*. Andrew describes what is widely acclaimed as one of the French Emperor's outstanding feats.

His resolution and the carrying it into effect was like lightning – the flash was no sooner visible than the thunder rolled.

The influence of his mighty genius was instantaneously felt. No delay was permitted to take place. The troops were immediately in action, and their great leader rushed to retrieve the errors of his lieutenants. On the 24th he was at Tordesillas, one hundred and twenty miles from Madrid, after having passed his army over a ridge of the Carpentanos, deeply covered with snow, under circumstances that would have effectually obstructed the advance of an ordinary man. The difficulties were such that the artillery, preceding the column of infantry, gave up the point and were returning down the southern ascent of the Guadarrama mountain when met by the Emperor. Napoleon then ordered his troops to follow him and immediately placed himself at the head of the column. Accompanied by the *chasseurs à cheval* of the guard, he passed through the ranks of infantry; then formed the *chasseurs* in close column, occupying the entire width of the road, when, dismounting from his horse and directing the regiment to follow his example, he placed himself in rear of the leading half squadron and the whole moved forward.

The men, by being dismounted, were, with the exception of those immediately in front, more sheltered from the storm, while the dense mass trod down the snow and left a beaten track for the infantry, who, inspired by the presence, as well as the example of Napoleon, pushed forward and the whole descended to Espinar.

Napoleon, with Marshal Ney's troops, reached Valderas on 28 November. The men were all exhausted after their almost unparalleled march in the very worst of the winter weather over country which even in summer was a challenge to both man and beast. Physically they ached for rest but their minds drove their feet forward, urged on by the words of the Emperor who promised them that the certain destruction of the British army would make them heroes one and all.

On 29 November, the day after Napoleon reached Valderas, Lieutenant-General Hope's Division passed through Astorga, just before Sir David Baird arrived to occupy the town on the same day.

The weather had now changed for the worse, the temperature having dropped to the point where it had become unbearably cold. The men, shivering in their greatcoats, glanced in fear at clouds massing on the horizon, knowing they foretold a coming storm. Taking shelter wherever they could, they crowded into houses in the town. The whole of the British infantry was now stationed in Astorga with the exception of some who trudged through the wind and snow on the road to Villafranca.

The Marques de la Romana – now, since the defeat of General Castaños, commander-in-chief of the Spanish army – unable to contend with Marshal Soult, had retired from Leon on his approach. He arrived at Astorga intending to cross the route of Sir John Moore, before taking his shattered and inefficient force to the valley of the Minho.

Nothing, *wrote Andrew*, could be more wretched than the appearance of the Spanish troops that arrived at Astorga. Disease and starvation seemed to struggle for mastery in the

31

annihilation of life. Some of the worn-out wretches, half-naked, stretched on the ground and, in the agonies of death, presented a picture of squalid and extenuated misery not to be described.

The British troops abandoned Astorga on 31 December. The retreat to Corunna had begun.

Hardly had they departed before the French entered the town. They remained well disciplined, but now there was a difference in their confidence and morale. Napoleon, the man who had led them over apparently invincible mountains, for whom most of them would willingly have died, had, in the face of a crisis, been forced to delegate the command of all his armies in Spain.

It was between Benevente and Astorga that a courier, who had ridden flat out from Paris, had managed to reach the Emperor. He had come with bad news. Negotiations with Austria had collapsed. Now, almost certainly, the government would declare war.

Andrew, writing in retrospect, points out that 'This was the most important dispatch that Napoleon ever received.'

> From it may be dated every subsequent disaster that befell him. It saved Spain, divided his power, perilled his invincibility and, by a combination of circumstances, occasioned losses and produced misfortune that laid the foundations for the Russian war, and finally induced the Emperor Alexander to adopt the bold measure of singly taking the field against the man who, after Erfurt, he would willingly have conspired against, but did not openly dare to do so.

It cannot, at this point. have been clear to Napoleon that the hostility of the Austrians was anything more than another challenge which he could overcome. Hitherto, throughout Europe, he had conquered on a monumental scale. An inspiration to his soldiers, he could even overcome the worst forces of nature as his recent success had proved. Nonetheless, it was at this moment, when Spain, in a figurative sense, appeared to be at his feet, that, because of the new threat from Austria, he was forced into fighting on two fronts. To meet this new emergency he had to withdraw divisions from his army now collected at Astorga. While remaining in supreme command, he placed 20,000 infantry, four thousand cavalry and fifty pieces of cannon under the direction of Marshal Soult, to whom he gave emphatic directions to pursue and compel the British either to surrender or embark.

1809

On the morning of the first of January, the commander of the British forces [Sir John Moore] with the reserve, entered Bembibre.

By this time the terrible weather, combined with exhaustion, had resulted in some of the troops falling out of line. This, however, was nothing compared to what happened when the men broke into the wine butts of Bembibre. This marked the beginning of the in-discipline which, thanks to historians, is so much associated with the retreat.

There certainly were good reasons for the soldiers to feel resentment against the authority responsible for the conditions in which they now found themselves placed.

The men loaded with heavy knapsacks, greatcoats, canteens, ammunition and their arms, the route knee-deep in some places, a violent wind bearing alternately snow, sleet or rain, directly in their faces, such was the real situation of the infantry soldier during the greater part of the memorable retreat, added to which he became irregularly and scantily fed.

General Hope's division halted at Lugo on the 5th. The town was completely occupied by troops and Spanish refugees. It was here that Sir John Moore decided to assemble his force to check the advance of Marshal Soult. Therefore on the evening of 6 January Hope's division marched on from Lugo and bivouacked on a position where the whole army was to be concentrated on the following day. Here, in pouring rain, the unfortunate soldiers were forced to sleep without tents, in the damp undergrowth, on high ground exposed to a piercing north-west wind.

Morning dawned, the rain became less violent. The men, suffering from the effects of cold and wet, were without bread, with difficulty preparing some flour and water to appease their

33

craving appetites. Everything was dreary and comfortless, except the presence of the enemy. There was excitement in that, and not a murmur of complaint was heard.

The British army, above the River Minho, faced the French across a ravine. After some skirmishing, five pieces of cannon opened up on General Leith's brigade. At the same moment a column of infantry crossed the ravine, drove in the outposts and headed for the centre of Leith's position.

> The light companies were consequently assembled, met the enemy when near the summit, poured in one discharge and, rushing forward with the bayonet, drove all before them.

With them went Brigade-Major Roberts and Andrew, who continued in the chase until they reached the bottom of the hill on the far side of the ravine.

> The road, or lane, up which the French attacked, was flanked by walls and overhung with trees. Filled with smoke from the incessant and vivid fire of both parties, it was almost im- possible to distinguish friend from foe, but our people cheered and, rushing forward, occasioned great loss to the enemy. When leading the pursuit into the ravine, Major Roberts was wounded and compelled to retire. Sir John Moore was present during the latter part of this affair and expressed himself satis- fied with the manner in which the attack had been repelled.

On the morning of 8 January the troops were formed along the whole extent of the line anxiously awaiting the expected attack. The suspense became worse when no movements became visible in the enemy's lines. It later transpired that the Duke of Dalmatia (Marshal Soult), warned by his spies that the British were prepared, decided not to confront them. Andrew was not the only one who felt that a great chance of victory had been lost. He also paid tribute to the bravery and endurance of the British soldiers, derided by other historians as indisciplined and inefficient.

> I can never look back to the scenes in front of Lugo without a feeling of regret that the battle was not there fought, nor ever

bring to recollection the gallant bearing of the troops, under all their miseries, without admiration of the spirit that appeared to animate them, and must have led to certain victory.

Sir John Moore, realizing late in the morning that the expected onslaught was not going to take place, decided to delude the French into believing that he had abandoned his retreat. To this purpose he ordered the infantry to put up some temporary huts, the materials for which they carried with them on the march. This being done, the enemy saw buildings of various descriptions covering the British lines and the lights of camp fires flickering in the dusk of the winter afternoon.

These were abandoned, however, at ten o'clock in the evening, when, in silence, the whole army filed off to the rear, taking different ways leading towards Lugo.

Although a matter of necessity, this night-march became a most serious evil. It was excessively dark, the wind blew loud, and hail showers superseded the preceding rains. The track by which General Leith's brigade marched was of the roughest and worst description, as may be conjectured from the fact that untired men took five hours in travelling as many miles, the distance from the position to the city of Lugo.

Without halting in that town, the whole moved forward, but even daylight did not materially improve the state of affairs. The storm raged with increased violence; the country, after passing Lugo, becoming more level, the wind, hail and sleet swept resistless across the plains. It was with difficulty, at particular points of the route, that I could persuade my horse to face the tempest.

At last the column of men, by this time weary and confused, staggered into the villages of Guitiriz and Valmeda. They were however, only hamlets, where, there being no room to house them all, there was no alternative other than to march the regiments to some fields on the right of the road. Here, without even a tree to shelter them from the gale, on ground streaming with water and exposed to constant rain and snow, the men, who were already worn down with fatigue, hunger, and want of sleep, were forced to spend the night.

35

When the order arrived to stand to their arms and set forward, they rose wearily, foot-sore, weak and understandably depressed. After a second night's march, conditions had deteriorated to an even more deplorable state. The whole road was now covered with a mass of stragglers, walking like puppets impelled by the instinct to survive. Regiments, brigades and even divisions had become mixed up, men, in the confusion, having lost sight of their officers and their colours.

Then, as Andrew describes it, a near miracle occurred.

On the morning of the 10th we arrived at Betanzos, with the headquarters of the regiments, some of whom had not fifty men to their colours. During the course of the day, however, many joined their ranks, and the alteration produced by a short intermission from fatigue was highly creditable to the soldiers. The battalions that, on the morning of the 10th entered Betanzos reduced to skeletons, marched from thence on the 11th strong and effective. The column, composed of all the in-fantry of the army which ascended the road towards Corunna was orderly in appearance, and perfectly unlike what could have been expected to reform from the debris of an army, which, but the preceding day, had exhibited an alarming state of demoralisation and exhaustion.

On the 11th a favourable change had taken place in the state of the weather, the sun shone upon the troops and, as the columns ascended the winding road from Betanzos, it presented a very different appearance, when contrasted with that of the previous day. It was at Betanzos, and not at Corunna, that the real hardship of the troops terminated.

Lieutenant-General Hope's division, on its arrival, was stationed in the suburb of St Lucia, built along the western shore of the harbour of Corunna. The French were encamped on the opposite side of the River Mero, on high ground which ran from the village of El Burgo to the ocean. The river which divided the two armies was too wide and, being surrounded by swamps, too dangerous to be forded. It therefore provided a safe barrier, the bridge at El Burgo having been destroyed.

General Hill's brigade was posted on the highest part of the ground over which ran the road to El Burgo. On his right was

General Leith, the brigade of Colonel Catlin Craufurd being but a short way behind.

> The following morning everything was quiet. The night had passed without rain, a serene and cloudless sky gave promise of more genial weather. Nothing seemed likely to produce any immediate excitement, when the explosion of four thousand barrels of powder burst upon the astonished ear. It is impossible to describe the effect. The unexpected and tremendous crash seemed for the moment to have deprived every person of reason and recollection. The soldiers flew to their arms, nor was it until a tremendous column of smoke, ascending from the heights in front, marked from whence the astounding shock proceeded that reason resumed its sway. It is impossible ever to forget the sublime appearance of the dark dense cloud of smoke that ascended, shooting up gradually like a gigantic tower into the clear blue sky. It appeared fettered in one enormous mass, nor did a particle of dust or vapour, obscuring its form, seem to escape as it rolled upwards in majestic circles.

The decision to blow up the gunpowder to prevent it falling into enemy hands had been made without proper warning being issued to all in the immediate vicinity. A small quantity which had been first exploded seems, perhaps through carelessness or ignorance of the dangers involved, to have triggered off a succession of larger ones which erupted almost simultaneously. Tragically, because no notification of what was about to happen had been sent to General Leith, a sergeant of the 51st Regiment and two other men belonging to the piquets of his brigade, were killed at a distance of a mile from the magazine.

On the morning of 13 January Sir David Baird's division marched into the position, General Manningham's brigade formed on the right of General Leith's. Lord William Bentinck was on his right, while the Guards were in reserve.

It was not until the next day, the 14th that the French engineers managed to make enough repairs to the bridge of El Burgo to allow the soldiers to cross the river. The moment this happened Marshal Soult ordered a large body of infantry, together with some cavalry, to go across the now mended structure which spanned the wide stream. On the following day, the 15th, he directed a large force to climb the range of hills directly above the northern branch of the Mero, where stood the now ruined magazine. So swiftly was this operation accomplished that, to the watching British, the whole ridge soon appeared to be covered with French troops.

Hardly had this happened, however, before the fleet sent to evacuate the British from of Spain was sighted. The hearts of those soldiers, for whom the dream of returning to England now suddenly seemed a reality, beat fast with excitement at the sight of the line-of-battle ships and transports gliding along the coast towards the harbour of Corunna.

It was now too late to begin an action as darkness overspread the British force. Surprisingly the French made no attempt to launch an attack and hopes rose high as it began to seem possible that the British army might be able to embark in safety before the expected onslaught began.

Andrew, like all those with him, felt the tension of the situation in which they found themselves involved. Common sense made it certain that, under no circumstances, could the French allow them to escape. Compassion, in this instance, would only ensure their return.

> At daybreak on the 16th the enemy's drums beat to arms, but still no firing at the advance posts denoted an immediate attack . . . . It was, however, an anxious period, a battle must in all probability take place. It was not to be expected that an un-interrupted embarkation would be permitted, and, situated as we were, one half- hour was sufficient space of time to bring 40,000 men into close and deadly conflict.

One man, who passed the night in ever-increasing anxiety, was the commander of the army, Sir John Moore, At first light he was in the midst of the troops. Riding to the rocky height in front of General Hill's brigade, he minutely examined the whole range of the enemy's position.

Amazingly, contrary to all expectation, the early part of the day was passed without any offensive movement taking place. Hoping against hope that he might, after all, get his men away in safety, Moore then rode to the town to give his final instructions for the embarkation which was rapidly proceeding in the harbour. All the civilians of the army, the sick, the wounded, the dismounted cavalry and most of the canon were already on board the transports. The infantry and a small force of artillery alone remained on Spanish ground.

Moore became more confident that his army would escape unscathed. At about one o'clock he said, 'Now, if there is no bungling, I hope we shall get away in a few hours.'

Alas, it was not to be. Three-quarters of an hour later, at a quarter to two, the French guns opened fire.[12]

At last the anxiously expected moment arrived. The enemy got under arms along his whole line, his columns were speedily formed and at about two o'clock he descended into the valley, threatening the centre and left, while a serious attack on the right had the twofold object of forcing back the weakest point of the British position. Artillery, placed along the whole ridge on which the enemy had stood, now opened on the British line. He had forced back the advanced posts and Sir David Baird's division received that of General Mermet, which had poured like a torrent down upon the village of Elvina.

Fortunately Sir John Moore had left Corunna and was on horseback when the report of an immediate attack reached him. He galloped on to the field at the critical moment.

The battle began in the lowest part of the ravine which was soon enveloped with smoke. Above, on either side of the valley, the French soldiers stood in their columns, eagerly watching all they could see of the contest taking place below.

Perversely, after all of the terrible weather conditions endured during the march to Corunna, the British troops now found themselves fighting on a beautiful clear winter's day.

The sun shone bright, glittering arms bristled the steep declivity, the rolling fire of artillery and musketry was constant, loud and uninterrupted, the centre became warmly engaged. It appeared that the work of death was extending to the left. The commanding situation of the enemy's cannon was severely felt. Nothing checked their rapid fire. Immovable, they poured from the heights showers of balls. They had no opposed batteries to silence, no position to alter. Unasssailed and in security, their conductors had alone to consider the selection of those points, where, by a judicious direction, the fire might be most effective.

Lord William Bentinck's brigade had from the first borne the brunt of the onslaught of the French troops. They charged with all the impetuosity which the British, through experience, had learned to dread. Nonetheless they remained steady, holding their ground and preventing the flank movement which the French failed to achieve.

The village of Elvina, being directly in the line of advance of the left column of the French army, was eventually taken by the 50th Regiment after a fierce battle. Sir John Moore, directing operations from a hill behind the village, saw the French retreating and believed he was close to a victory. A tall man, conspicuous on his charger, his presence enhanced the confidence of his soldiers as they faced the still-pounding guns.

> In the midst of a fire of musketry of the hottest description, he was also exposed to the effects of the great battery, directly over, and pointed at, this part of the field. A ball struck him from his horse, inflicting a wound of so dreadful a nature that it is a matter of surprise vitality could survive the instantaneous consequence of such a tremendous injury. Thus fell, supporting the honour of his country, this truly excellent and gallant soldier.

When Sir John Moore was fatally wounded General Hope took over his command. As the battle raged on the Guards, commanded by General Paget, who formed the reserve, were brought forward to support Lord William Bentinck. It was they who successfully turned the left flank of the French army.

Meanwhile the left of General Manningham's brigade remained embroiled in a fierce action. General Leith was then ordered to advance one of his battalions to relieve the 81st Regiment, which had not only suffered severely but had nearly exhausted its ammunition. So he marched down the 59th, under a very heavy fire of musketry. However, a successful charge with the bayonet, to the immediate front of the column, silenced the French guns. Andrew, describing this, again takes up the story.

> It was now nearly dark, the firing on the right had ceased, in all directions it seemed to die away, when a warm tiraillade

40

issued from the village of Palavea. Colonel Nichols, with the 14th Regiment, had been sent to drive the enemy from thence. This he accomplished without difficulty, and in so doing terminated the battle.

The British position was unshaken. General Paget, by a judicious movement, had endangered that of the enemy. Darkness alone prevented the complete *déroute* [destruction]of the French army. Cut off from the St Jago road by the advance of the reserve, having that of Betanzos on which alone to retreat, with the difficulty of passing his army, in a state of confusion, across the superficially repaired bridge at Burgo, the Duke of Dalmatia might have been totally routed, could the advantage gained have been followed up immediately after the battle.

The British had won a great victory, which Sir John Moore, the man most responsible, had not lived long enough to see. Moore was only one of the casualties, estimated at eight hundred in all, yet his death was universally lamented as Andrew, so poignantly describes:

At the close of this action there was not the same exhilarating feeling, the same excitement, that usually attends a victory. A stillness prevailed for hours. The repose of the camp was only interrupted by the formation of the troops at midnight, when the whole, with the exception of the piquets, marched towards the harbour.

The men moved with such silence that the French, on the hills behind Corunna, were unaware of what was taking place. Only as day dawned did they look down on the now the deserted position, which, on the previous evening, had been alive with the movements of red-coated men.

Once aware of what had happened, however, the enemy wasted no time in crossing the line of what had been the British ground,

Promptly they set up a battery on the northern point of the range of heights where General Hope's division had been encamped. Fortunately, however, most of the British infantry were embarked before the guns could open fire. Men, now safely aboard the transports, watched the cannon-balls, as they fell, mercifully short of the ships, splashing into the sea.

41

Andrew, describing the evacuation, praises the efficiency of the
the navy.

> Soon after daylight on the 17th General Leith's brigade was
> conveyed to the shipping. The boats of the men-of-war rapidly
> performed this service. The indefatigable officers of the navy
> carried on the embarkation with all the celerity resulting from
> discipline. The consequence was that the service was far
> advanced before the French battery opened. It might otherwise
> have done considerable execution against boats crowded with
> men and covering the whole surface of the water.

Then, as he left the shore of Spain, he was witness to the burial of
the man who had led his soldiers through the hardships, dangers and
final triumph of the first peninsular campaign.

Because it was so necessary to preserve the near complete silence
which successfully deceived the French into the thinking that the
British, while being conveyed in boats in darkness to the transports,
were still on shore, Moore had been carried from the house by the
harbour wherein he died by men who spoke only in whispers.

> Not a drum was heard, not a funeral note,
> As his corpse to the rampart we hurried . . . .
> Slowly and sadly we laid him down,
> From the field of his fame fresh and gory;
> We carved not a line, and we raised not a stone
> But we left him alone with his glory.

So wrote Charles Wolfe in the poem once learned by so many children, which immortalized Moore's name. Andrew Leith-Hay, in the
clear, cold light of the early morning of 17 January 1809, witnessed
the solitary funeral from the boat which carried him out to the
warship, lying in the harbour of Corunna on which he would sail
back to Britain.

> When passing the citadel of Corunna on our way to the
> *Zealous* of seventy-four guns, we perceived in the nearest
> bastion Colonel Graham and one other officer, superintending
> a ceremony which we could not doubt was the internment of
> the brave Commander of the forces. There was something

unusually melancholy in this scene, and in the reflections it occasioned. Nothing around seemed calculated to enliven it. The embarkation going forward had none of the exhilaration attending an operation naturally accompanied with so much of activity, life and spirit. All seemed sombre and depressed. We were flying from the land, which was left in the undisturbed occupation of troops vanquished on the preceding day, but now preparing to fire the last taunting discharges against soldiers whom fortune appeared to have frowned upon, even in victory.

The fleet having been collected off the harbour of Corunna on the morning of the 18th, the admiral made the signal for proceeding, when eleven line-of-battle ships, with the whole of the transports, steered for the shores of England.[13]

PART 2

5

SEARCHING IN SOUTHERN SPAIN

March – May 1809

'Thank God Sir Arthur Wellesley has arrived.'

The retreat of Moore's army from Corunna left the remaining British force in Portugal, of only about 8,000 men, in an extremely dangerous position. Its commander, General Sir John Cradock, was ready to evacuate by sea in an emergency, which fortunately did not materialize.

The Spanish army suffered two more defeats, in January at Ucles and in February at Saragossa, where the gallant garrison, defiant for eight months despite appalling losses, was finally forced to surrender in January 1809.[1]

Marshal Victor, in command of the French corps in the south, was then intent on pursuing General Cuesta with his defeated Spanish army in Andalusia. However, the French suffered a setback when Marshal Soult [the Duke of Dalmatia] failed to force his way through mountainous country in the winter weather and managed to capture Oporto only at the end of March 1809.

In the meanwhile the British position in Portugal was stabilized when the 'regency' acting for the deposed royal family in Brazil agreed to a suggestion that General Sir William Beresford should reorganize and train its army. Thus the combined forces, British and Portuguese, amounted to nearly 17,000 men. In addition to this, the refusal of the Spanish junta to allow British troops to land at Cadiz then meant that the 6,000 men, intended for that purpose, returned to Lisbon.

Subsequently the British government, after much prevarication, decided to send reinforcements. The first detachment, numbering about 5,000, landed in Lisbon in the early spring. It included the 16th Light Dragoons. Among the young officers of this cavalry regiment was a newly promoted captain the Hon Charles Somers Cocks, a man whose journals and letters give a first-hand account of the war in the Peninsula as he saw it for a period of over three years.

In March 1809 Charles Edward Somers Cocks, son and heir of the second Earl Somers, was a young man of twenty-three. Single minded since boyhood and determined to be a soldier, he had, to his father's great annoyance, foregone a parliamentary career. Lord Somers at last relenting, had, with great reluctance, bought him a cornet's commission in the 16th (Queen's) Light Dragoons.

Charles had served first in Ireland, where, during Emmet's Rebellion in the late summer of 1803, his courage and cool-headedness had been noticed. Whilst there he had ridden round the country making sketches and maps, and, in his free time, had concentrated on studying military history from books sent out from home.

The 16th had returned to England in December 1805. Early in the following year Charles's grandfather, the first earl, had died. His father, having succeeded, had entered the House of Lords. Charles had then been put under great pressure by his family to stand as a Whig for the constituency of Reigate, held by his family for two generations. He had eventually agreed, but only on the condition that, in the event of his regiment being sent abroad, he would be free to rejoin. As a member of parliament, with his knowledge of affairs in Ireland, he had voted for the relief of the Irish Catholics.

In September 1808, when Napoleon invaded the Iberian Peninsula, the 16th, encamped at Woodbridge in Suffolk, had been ordered to proceed to Portugal. Charles, once again sending for books, had begun learning Spanish, knowing it would be useful in what he foresaw as a future campaign. Also, in preparation, he had practiced sword-drill and shooting, both on foot and from the back of a horse.

On 1 March he wrote to his mother [styling her as 'Dearest Madam] to say that he had arrived in Lisbon 'after a delightful passage of ten days' and that he had been warmly welcomed by his friends. He also told her that 'The hatred of the French throughout Portugal appears from everything I have heard . . . . I shall probably set off for Spain in a few days to obtain intelligence of the state of organization in Andalusia.'

This casual reference to an expedition to the south of Spain, was, in fact, the only intimation he could impart of the highly secret mission on which he was just about to embark. He did say, however, giving some indication of the importance of the task for which he had volunteered, that he had turned down the offer of Sir Stapleton Cotton [his former commanding officer, now a brigadier], to go on his staff. 'I think this is likely to be an employment of activity and amusement,' he wrote, but then told her to talk about it as little as possible and on no account to mention any political reports which he might send.

Charles reached Seville in March. From there, on the 22nd, he wrote again to his mother. He told her that his Spanish was much improved but that, thanks to an English regiment, the 40th, being quartered in the town, it was too easy to speak in his own language. However, he was setting off for Grenada the next day where he hoped to hear nothing but Spanish. He added, what he knew would amuse her, that he was now known as Señor Capitano Don Eduardo Carlos Cockings!

From Seville he and his companions stopped for the night, first at Arrhal, and then at Assuna. The next day they reached Alameda where they were received by what Charles called a 'deputation'. He vouched for it that even the children were brought up to detest the French and love the English!

Reaching Granada he and his companions then turned in their tracks and headed westward by way of Archidona, Ecija and Constantina to Monasterio. Their route led through the Sierra Morena, one of the wildest parts of southern Spain, which Charles described as 'most romantically beautiful'.

He also reveals that it was a dangerous, being exceedingly remote. Strangers were so unusual that in one place he was stopped and searched as a spy. The local magistrate, 'a most sagacious blockhead', was convinced that a bill, found in his portmanteau, which had been made out in Falmouth for hay for his horses, was in fact a message sent in code. The local people, alarmed, became hostile, but eventually they let him go.

At Constantina, however, it was a different story. Charles was feted as the first Englishman ever to enter the town. The inhabitants seemed 'mad with joy', stuffing him with food and presents of every kind. Leaving there he went on to Monasterio where General Cuesta, a man over seventy, renowned for his bad temper and inflexible views, received him as a welcome guest.

The Spanish army, which Cuesta commanded, at that time consisted of 14,000 men. Charles, when he joined them in an auxiliary capacity, soon discovered, both from the soldiers and the local people, how intensely they loathed the French. It also became clear to him that Spain had been overrun largely because of the incapacity of the officers (who were mostly the local gentry) to organize any proper retaliation. The government he wrote off likewise, calling it irresolute and holding it in scant respect.

The Andalusians as a people, however, did, in his opinion, have a saving grace in that their talent for breeding and training horses was almost unmatched, Charles bought two, one of which may have been the much loved mare of which his friend Tomkinson later wrote.

Hardly had he acquired them before a chance to prove their metal occurred. In the second week of April word came that the French had entered Portugal. He knew it was his duty to return to Lisbon, so back across the wild country he went. We do not know if his horses were shod. General Moore at Corunna could not find nails for horseshoes, but born and bred in rough country the Andalusian horses probably had hard feet. Shod or not, Charles, presumably changing from one to the other, rode almost continuously for over two days. Writing again to his mother on 21 April, he told her that he had hardly been out of the saddle for fifty-three hours. It cannot have done much to relieve her natural anxiety about her son soldiering in Spain.

Charles sent a letter from Lisbon on the eve of his departure to join the British army. He rode north, following the line of the coast, to Leiria and then Coimbra, that town so frequently mentioned in the annals of the Peninsular War. From Coimbra, on 2 May 1809, he wrote to his uncle, the Reverend Philip Yorke, telling him that 'Operations have been for some days at a standstill, in consequence of a change of general. Thank God, Sir Arthur Wellesley arrived this morning.'

[General Cradock, with his increased force, had actually been preparing to march north against Soult when told that Sir Arthur Wellesley was to replace him in command.]

Four days later, in a hasty note to his father when he had just been ordered to march, Charles told him, 'Sir Arthur Wellesley has taken the command of the army and inspired fresh spirit in every breast'.[2]

6

CROSSING THE DOURO

'By God, Waters has done it!'

April – July 1809

Sir Arthur Wellesley, returning to the Peninsula after six month's absence, had landed at Lisbon on 22 April 1809 to find himself threatened by three French armies, hovering like vultures in sight of prey.

Firstly, in Portugal, Marshal Soult, having captured Oporto, had sent advanced posts to Coimbra, some hundred miles farther south. Secondly, in Spain, General Lapisse was near the frontier fort of Ciudad Rodrigo, and thirdly, Marshal Victor was farther south at Talavera. Should the three armies make a pincer movement, the British, outnumbered two to one, would, as Napoleon had declared would happen, be forced to flee in their ships or be driven into the sea.

Wellesley, however, thought otherwise. The French armies were widely separated by mountainous tracts of country. He believed that, from his position on the Tagus, he could defeat them one by one. Not only would he force the French from Portugal but push them out of Spain altogether.

To this purpose he reorganized his army. First he overhauled the commissariat [the administration], making it more adaptable to forces on the move. Then, mainly to ease the problems of communication in wild and often inaccessible country, he formed brigades into divisions which were responsible to their own commanders in the field. A 'light company', largely composed of skirmishers, was added to each infantry brigade. Above all he placed a Portuguese battalion, commanded by British officers, in each of all his brigades. The Portuguese, when trained, became such splendid soldiers that, within the space of four years, they comprised no less than half of the Peninsular army.

Within two weeks of his landing in Portugal Wellesley had completed his plans. Soult was to be his first target, Victor the next. Leaving General MacKenzie with 12,000 troops to guard Lisbon, he headed off, leading his main army on a course running parallel to the Atlantic coast, On 1 May, his fortieth birthday, he entered Coimbra from whence the French pickets had fled.

Coimbra, on the River Mondego, seat of the principal Portuguese university, was noted for the large number of churches, monasteries and convents which it contained. From this ancient city Sir Arthur Wellesley led his army during the first week of May 1809. Having divided his force into three divisions, he commanded the main body himself. With him went the 16th Light Dragoons and Captain Charles Cocks. The young officer, in notes which he later made, was severely critical of some of the confusion which delayed the progress of the march during which, owing to lack of direction, several units got lost. In particular he laid the blame for a skirmish at Grijo, when his friend William Tomkinson was badly wounded, on the muddled orders which had been issued.

Despite what Charles saw as the shortcomings of the high command, the French army retreated northwards before the British from the Mondego, across the Vouga, to Oporto where the Douro runs into the sea. Charles described the capture of Oporto in his journal, beginning on 12 May.

> The column marched off at five and reached Villa Nova about six. This is the suburbs of Oporto, situated on the hill immediately opposite the town and separated only by the Douro.

The soldiers found themselves looking across the river to where a flight of steps led up to the top of a steep escarpment on the other side. The stretch of swift-flowing water appeared to be an impregnable barrier. The French, having destroyed the bridge, had removed every boat, or so they believed.

Now, once again, it was Colonel John Waters, the intelligence officer who had saved Moore's army from annihilation by securing the vital message, carried by the murdered French courier, that

Napoleon was already advancing from Madrid, who rescued Wellesley's force from what appeared to be an impossible situation.

Thanks to his friendship with the local people, Waters had discovered that, on the town side, hidden by a bend of the river, four wine barges lay moored against the bank. Thus, to the astonishment of all those who waited, believing themselves to be stranded by a stretch of impassable water, he appeared, together with a Portuguese barber, a brave patriot, who had rowed across the river in his own boat with this news. Scrambling ashore, Waters also reported that the large building, clearly visible across the river, which was known to be the Bishop's Seminary, appeared to be unoccupied.

'By God ! Waters has done it,' Wellesley exclaimed. The attack was under way.[3]

Waters, with a crew consisting of the barber, a prior and four peasants, brought the barges over the river. Each vessel could only take thirty of the eagerly awaiting men. Charles Cocks, in his journal, describes the crossing.[4]

The Buffs passed over first, huzzaing as the boats shoved off, and reached the top of the steps without opposition, but soon after were attacked. They threw themselves into a house [the Seminary] and maintained their ground. However, it was a critical moment. Sir Arthur appeared very anxious, but fortunately reinforcements arrived and the enemy retreated a little way up the road where they again made a stand. We could see the rising smoke, which pointed out when the heads of the columns were engaged, alternatively advancing and retrograding, while, beyond, large columns of cavalry could be seen in action. From their direction it could not be ascertained whether they were commencing a retreat or coming down on our infantry. Our battery did little execution and occasionally injured our own men, while one gun, which the enemy had brought into action upon a height, appeared to annoy the British column.

Meantime General Hill and General Murray had crossed the river higher up, at separate fords, and the Guards, with two squadrons of the 14th, had crossed opposite Oporto[5]

Only later was it realized how fortuitous it was that, thanks to the Seminary being almost out of sight of the town, the main body of the French garrison had been unaware of what was happening for almost an hour after the Buffs had managed to rush within its walls. Once alive to the danger, they made three separate attacks, the last, led by Marshal Soult himself, being repulsed by the British 1st Division by then marching into the town.

The French were utterly defeated. Sir Arthur Wellesley was told by his spies that Marshal Soult, having destroyed all his guns, had taken the road across the mountains with all that remained of his equipment on the backs of mules. Charles, who had by this time acquired a knowledge of the country, writes that the Duke of Dalmatia had very little choice. There were only three roads leading from Oporto back into Spain. It was reckoned that Soult was heading for Guimares but that he would then cross onto the route leading from Braga to Monte Allegre.

Wellesley, determined to confront him, set off with the larger part of his force on the road to Braga on 14 May. The road was very bad and it poured with rain. The men struggled on, but, as smoke rising from burnt-out villages marked the proximity of the enemy, they increased the pace of their pursuit. Once again Charles, who had such a good eye for detail, described the country.

> The province of Tras os Montes, through which the column was penetrating, is composed wholly of mountains, the foot of one of these is washed by an impetuous stream, rushing along a deep ravine. This stream winds round the projections of the mountains. On the farthest point of these projections is situated the village of Salamonde. In front of it, on each side [of] the road, was the rearguard of the French, 15,000 strong. Observing that the British dragoons were in no force, they took no other precautions than sending out a piquet of cavalry rather more than half the distance towards them, and proceeded in lighting their fires and cooking their dinners.

He then describes how Wellesley, in just over an hour, made his plans. The light companies of the Guards, together with some of the 60th, were sent up round the back of the hill to the summit while the rest of the Guards continued up the road. It was now nearly dark. As the British began firing sparks flew from their guns. The French fled in terror. In the fading light they made for a bridge which crossed over the river behind the village, but it had been damaged by the local Portuguese. The parapet had been broken and men and horses, falling into the river, were killed.

Despite his admiration for Wellesley Charles was again critical of some of the senior staff. Why, for instance, was Colonel Murray, the QMG, so ignorant of the road beyond Salamonde that he could give no directions to the Guards when General Beresford was so well acquainted with the country, and when a few questions to any Portuguese peasant would probably have given sufficient explanation? Also why did General Beresford not send a sufficient force to destroy or defend the passes? . . . I am almost certain he had the time'

Beresford is partly cleared of incompetence when, months later, in a note dated 10 March 1810, Charles writes that 'General Beresford was three days without intelligence of the passage of the Douro through the negligence, or stupidity, of the dragoon who conveyed the dispatch.' His most virulent scorn was poured upon General Stewart of whom he wrote to his cousin Thomas that his only merit in the Battle of Oporto was 'being Lord Castlereagh's brother. Twice when he came in sight of the French he said, "There's your enemy, charge them" and went back'. Charles, having vented his wrath, then finished his letter by saying 'I need not caution you on no account to quote any opinion I may give on speculative points. I am too young a soldier to venture my ideas except to a particular friend.'

Meanwhile, on 17 May, he notes how 'the cavalry and a part of the infantry reached Monte Allegre.' The men were so exhausted that 'they did not advance more than a league. (The enemy) entered Spain, his route was marked by men and horses, dead and dying. A few prisoners were picked up by the army and some were massacred by the Portuguese.'

The Portuguese, renowned for their savagery, killed, in this instance, specifically for revenge. The French had murdered their local guides to stop them helping the English.

Charles records in his diary, on 18 May, that at Monte Allegre the pursuit was given up.

Early in June the 16th Light Dragoons moved from Oporto on the Douro to Thomar on the Zêzere, a tributary of the Tagus. It was here that Charles succumbed to an illness which nearly proved fatal. It was probably typhus, with which the army was infested, or typhoid, as he says the water was very bad. Together with five other sufferers, he was put in a cart which took five days to jolt over the bad roads to the field hospital at Deleytosa, where, on arrival, he was found to be the only one alive. Wellesley, hearing of this, had Charles and another officer from the 16th transferred to the new hospital at Elvas. Lord Somers, when told, swore never again to support the Whigs in deriding the Tory Sir Arthur's conduct of the war in the Peninsula.

Once at Elvas Charles, with his splendid constitution, gradually regained his strength. Bored with recuperation he kept himself occupied by making a detailed report on the hospital, taking in every detail such as its defenses, the water supply and even the type of soil on which it stood.

Recovered, he joined his regiment at Villa Viciosa, south of Elvas, where they were encamped in the Royal Deer Park. Here, in the surrounding countryside, in addition to many deer, he found partridges, hares and even wolves, but, alas, his gun, which he had brought from England had been stolen in the north of Portugal. 'I regret my gun dreadfully' he wrote to his brother James.

In mid-July the army began its long march from Villa Viciosa, in Portugal, into Spain. Once across the border the route lay up the valley of the Guadiana, for some distance, before turning north-east through passes in the mountain range of the Sierra de Guadalupe. Eventually, hungry, foot-sore and weary in the hot weather, the force reached the town of Talavera on the Tagus, a distance of some two hundred miles.[6]

7

TALAVERA

July 1809

Wellesley will probably advance, by the Tagus, against Madrid: in that case, pass the mountains, fall on his flank and rear, and crush him
Translation of Napoleon's instructions to Marshal Soult, 30 June 1809

So bloody an action has seldom been fought. (Captain the Hon. Charles Cocks to his father, Lord Somers, 17 August 1809.)

Captain Charles Cocks was present at the Battle of Talavera but the 16th Light Dragoons did not take a major part. Lieutenant Andrew Leith-Hay, however, as an infantry officer in the 29th Regiment of Foot, was in the thick of it and now, from the moment when he lands in the Peninsula for the second time, he again takes up the tale.

On the evening of the 2nd July, 1809, the *Champion* frigate, Captain Henderson, anchored in the Tagus.

On my way to join the 29th Regiment, I had embarked at Portsmouth with Captain Henderson, and accompanied him to Guernsey, where he took under convoy a fleet of transports, having on board the second battalions of the 34th, 39th and 58th Regiments, which he now saw in safety to their place of destination.

It was late when we entered the river, and darkness prevented us enjoying the beautiful scene. At daybreak, however, the city of Lisbon appeared in all the majesty of its picturesque and grand situation, while the stately river bore on its waters the ships of many nations, Close to where we anchored was the

58

Barfleur, of 98 guns, bearing the flag of Admiral Berkeley, commanding in appearance, as in reality, every vessel that floated on the noble Tagus.

Line of battle ships, frigates and smaller vessels of war, were discernible in every direction; the light, serviceable and elegant rigging of the British navy contrasting with the slack, slovenly, or loaded cordage of all other descriptions of shipping. The Russian men-of-war, detained at the period of the convention of Lisbon [Cintra], dismasted and moored above the town, presented the very beau ideal of hulks, while the large and handsome Portuguese frigates seemed in a state of preparation to carry from their native shores the persons to whom such emigration might become a matter of interest or necessity, in the event of a French army again occupying Lisbon. A large fleet of transports were at anchor; boats passed in all directions; vessels arriving or departing gave life and variety to a scene of the most animated, varied, and interesting description.

At this period, not a French soldier remained in Portugal . . . . Napoleon was at Vienna, his brother Joseph acted as generalissimo in Spain, Marshal Jourdan as his chief of the staff. The other Marshals employed in the Peninsula were without confidence in the military judgement of these persons. They were also jealous of each other – a feeling to which the ablest of them was subjected. Such was the situation of affairs when Sir Arthur Wellesley established his headquarters at Plasencia, on the 8th July, 1809.

Andrew, eager to join his regiment, set off with a fellow officer, Captain Tucker, on the morning of 14 July to row up the Tagus as far as Vila Valha. From there they continued the journey overland. Having spent a night at Santarem they continued to Abrantes, on a height above the Tagus, which Andrew described as 'one of the most beautifully situated towns in Portugal'. Pushing onwards, on increasingly bad roads, they reached the Portuguese frontier fortress town of Castelo Branco.

At last, late at night, they arrived at Plasencia,

a large town, in the centre of fertile plains surrounded by mountains [which] must ever be celebrated from the circumstance of the Emperor Charles V having selected it as the place

59

CASTELO BRANCO

of retirement, to which he dedicated the last years of his eventful and brilliant life.

The British army, however, had already moved on towards Madrid. Only the sick and wounded remained at Plasencia. Therefore, on the morning of the 20th they crossed the mountains in front of the town and descended into the valley of the Tietar. The road, following the river, led through immense forests of oak. In the midst, from a height, at the Casa de las Llomus, they first glimpsed the range of mountains between Estremadura and the province of Salamanca. The towering peaks of the Sierra de Gredos, shone white with perpetual snow.

Andrew was enthralled.

A more splendid scene can scarce be imagined. Nothing could be finer than the bold outline of the mountains, or more magnificent than the broad dark shadow, which, descending from their precipitous and rocky sides, overspread forest scenery on a scale that appeared interminable.

But there was no time to linger. Hurrying on, they reached Oropesa to find it occupied by allied troops. Told of a skirmish having taken place with the rear of the French army, they managed to find horses and arrived at two-o-clock in the morning at the camp of the 29th Regiment at Talavera de la Reina. Here, having slept in a tent, wrapped in their cloaks, for a mere hour and a half, they woke in the dawn as the regiment got under arms.

In the last week of July 1809 Talavera, on the north bank of the Tagus, was the headquarters of Sir Arthur Wellesley and General Cuesta. More then 50,000 British and Spanish troops were lodged in the nearby encampment. In front of them, on the high ground to the south of the River Alberche, was the *Corps d'Armée* of Marshal the Duke of Belluno (Victor).

Similarly, among olive groves in front of the town, on the left of the road to Santa Olalla and Madrid, the 29th Regiment, brigaded with the 45th, and 1st battalions of detachments stationed. These units, commanded by Brigadier-General Richard Stewart, formed part of the Division of Major-General Hill.

Wellesley's main position stretched for about three miles from the town of Talavera to a height, called the Cerro de Medellin, which overlooked the whole area. A stream, the Portina Brook, ran below. On the other side of the valley the French force, inferior in numbers, was assembled on a lower hill called the Cascajal.[7] Wellington wanted to attack immediately, before reinforcements, commanded by King Joseph, arrived, but the Spanish General Cuesta, taciturn and obstinate, refused to comply with his suggestion.

> We were told that old General Cuesta declined fighting on a Sunday. If he did assign that reason, it could only have been in bitterness and derision, but from whatever motive, the combined army permitted Marshal Victor to withdraw his troops uninjured, which he effected during the night. Early on the morning of the 24th the whole army moved to attack his position. It was, of course, found unoccupied. Sir Arthur halted the troops under his orders, but the Spanish general, with characteristic arrogance, singly dashed forward in pursuit. His columns passed the [river] Alberche in rapid succession, as if they were alone to be obstructed by the iron barrier of the Pyrenees.
>
> General Hill's division then re-occupied the same ground on which it had previously been encamped. The state of the campaign, to an uninformed spectator, appeared extra-ordinary.[8]

The army, which had been fighting as one, was now divided. Part of the British force, which had crossed the Alberche, was ten miles in advance of Talavera, while the rest, now very short of rations, remained on the banks of the Tagus. This situation continued for two days until, on the morning of 27 July, they heard that part of General Cuesta's army had passed to the rear.

> From amidst clouds of dust, disorderly chattering assemblages of half-clad, half-armed men, became occasionally visible. Again, regiments marching in perfect order, cavalry, staff officers, bands of musicians, flocks of sheep, and bullocks, artillery, cars and carriages and wagons varied the animated, confused, and singular scene on which we gazed . . .
>
> After the Spanish army had ceased to march past us we returned to the quiet of the olive grove. Cannon and musketry were heard at intervals, but no order to move had yet arrived. Several officers of the 29th were assembled, when the Spanish General O'Donahue rode up from the direction of the Alberche. He appeared in a state of considerable excitement, stating we were probably not aware of the enemy having crossed the river, and that he would be upon us without delay. We merely thanked him, adding, that when it was necessary to get under arms, orders to that effect would of course be communicated. Another hour elapsed – when the firing became so close and constant, that we began to think it extra-ordinary that orders were not received. At last, however, the brigade got under arms, and marched to the left, passing both Spanish and British troops in line, who already occupied the position defended by them on the following day.
>
> As we moved left in front, the 29th, being the senior regi-ment, was in the rear of the column – the 48th leading. In this formation we advanced about half way between the town of Talavera, and the eminence [the Cerro de Medellin] then un-occupied, but which was evidently, from its locality and importance, destined to become the left and also the strongest part of the position

The brigade then halted near to the division of Brigadier-General Alexander Campbell, stationed on the right flank of the British army near to the town of Talavera. It was nearly dark when, at nine o'clock in the evening, Marshal Victor attacked the Cerro de Medellin. General Hill, hearing the firing, went to investigate and suddenly found himself surrounded by French soldiers. One of them seized his horse's bridle, but, spurring on the charger, he just managed to escape.

The 48th Regiment, reaching the foot of the Cerro, was driven back with fierce resistance. This was a critical moment which might well have resulted in defeat. General Hill, however, then led the 29th to the rescue, marching in double quick time.

It was now so dark that the leading company reached the summit before the French could concentrate their guns. Only by the blaze of musketry could the British soldiers pick out human forms. The 29th, almost on the bayonets of the enemy, fired at point blank range

> The glorious cheer of British infantry accompanied the charge, which succeeded. The rest of the regiment arrived in quick succession, forming on the summit a close column, which speedily drove everything before it. The enemy was pushed down the hill, abandoning the level ground at the top, thickly strewn with dead bodies or wounded men. The 29th remained in possession of the ground, lying on their arms in the midst of fallen enemies. The furred shako of a dead French soldier became my pillow for the night.

The heavy fire of musketry, which indicated a fierce fight for the possession of the hill, and the uncertainty of what was happening in the darkness caused much anxiety at headquarters. Typically, Sir Arthur Wellesley himself rode to the scene of action to find out what was taking place. Quickly assessing the situation, he immediately ordered up the guns so that, in the early part of the night, men and horses struggled to pull cannon to the top of the rise.

Wellesley, like Andrew, then slept on the ground wrapped in his cloak. It seemed that there would be little rest for anyone, but, surprisingly, once the guns were in position there followed a strange silence which lasted for some time.

Then suddenly, about midnight, from near Talavera came a thunderous roar.

> A roll of musketry illuminated the whole extent of the Spanish line. It was one discharge, but of such a nature that I never

heard it equalled. It appeared not to be returned, nor was it repeated. All again became silent.

In fact what had happened was that the four battalions of Spanish infantry holding Talavera, at the sight of some French cavalry, had loosed off one huge volley at a range of 1,000 yards. The noise was still reverberating when, shouting 'Treason', the Spanish fled, pausing only to rob the British baggage trains. Wellesley, in his anger, swore he would never trust Spanish troops again.[9]

Meanwhile the British soldiers on the hilltop spent an anxious night, knowing that the rattling of gun carriages meant an early attack. As dawn broke they found themselves looking into the mouths of twenty-two cannons.

> They were posted upon elevated ground, but by no means of equal height to that on which we stood, having, however, the whole face and summit of the hill well within range. To the right of the French cannon were perceived columns of infantry. A renewed battle for the hill became certain.

A single shot marked the start of a tremendous cannonade. The men of the 29th, however, were told to lie down a short distance beyond the brow of the hill so that most of the shot passed harmlessly over their heads.

> An old Scotch sergeant, crouching close to me, permitted his head to attain a very slight elevation, and, with a groan, said, 'Good God, sir, this is dreadfu!' Without discussing the merits of our situation I merely advised him to keep down his head, a hint instantly adopted, and at the close of the affair I was happy to find it was still upon his shoulders.
>
> At this period we had the battle entirely to ourselves, no other part of the army being engaged. When the French columns had mounted the ascent, and were so near as to become endangered from the fire of their own artillery, a scene of great animation was exhibited. The summit, which had appeared deserted, now supported a regular line of infantry. Near the colours of the 29th stood Sir Arthur Wellesley, directing and animating the troops.

General Ruffin had nearly overcome the allied forces opposed to him when a fierce burst of firing checked his advance. His troops wavered. Sir Arthur ordered a charge. With one tremendous shout the right wing of the 29th and the entire battalion of the 48th rushed down the hill like an avalanche, bayoneting and sweeping back the enemy to the brink of the muddy stream [the Portina Brook] which separated the two armies. All order vanished in that headlong chase.

> At this moment, when the whole valley was filled with troops, a column of French infantry appeared close upon our right flank. It became necessary to collect the pursuers, to form a front, and to charge these fresh assailants. So completely were these attacks repelled that the British infantry were quietly collected in the ravine and marched back to the height without being seriously assailed.

The 1st Corps of the French army, commanded by the Duke of Belluno, had been repulsed. Firing continued, but so spasmodically that some of the troops of General Hill's division were able to collect dirty water from the stream. Normally no one would have touched such filthy stuff, but men wearing full uniform, in the burning heat of the day, were desperate for any form of liquid to ease their thirst.

> The lull in the battle lasted only until the early afternoon. when, from the hill, the whole of the French line could be seen standing to their arms. Then, under clouds of dust, the troops advanced against the centre and right of the British army. At the same time the 1st Corps d'Armée, rallying after its earlier defeat, supported by a large body of cavalry, formed to make a renewed attack on the left.
>
> Two French divisions approached from the upper part of the valley and the whole of the flat ground behind it was covered with cavalry in extended lines. Some Spanish soldiers, however, had by now reached the higher hills beyond the plateau and, plunging into the enemy's columns, their fire was incessant and well directed.
>
> In the midst of our troops, these men fought their guns in a manner to excite the admiration of all present, proving that Spaniards only required the confidence given by example to

conduct themselves in the face of the enemy with propriety.

A fire of cannon and musketry, to the whole extent of the British centre and left, was [now] of the most serious description. To those who, elevated as we were, saw every movement, this was the most anxious moment of the whole battle. Heavy columns of French infantry seemed following in succession to press upon the weakest part of the line. Nor did it appear within the reach of probability that the centre could successfully resist this overwhelming force.

General Sherbrooke, in command of the Guards division in the centre of the British position now bore the full brunt of a furious attack. The columns of French infantry appeared to throw themselves upon the bayonets of the British. They reeled back in confusion and, in the heat of pursuit, the Guards lost their formation. At the same time the German Legion, beside them, gave way under heavy fire.

There was no reserve of infantry. One single file of Germans had stood between us and destruction. This had now disappeared. It was an awful moment. Promptitude, and the inertness of the Duke of Belluno, alone saved the army.

Wellesley, watching from the same viewpoint, reacted with his usual decision. He ordered the 1/48th battalion to move forward to support the Guards, while at the same time instructing General Mackenzie to move his brigade to the left to fill the gap,

To the onlookers it seemed impossible that Mackenzie's thin line of 3,000 men could withstand the onslaught of the advancing French force which more than trebled their number. The enemy seemed to engulf them before the British opened fire. Then their deadly volleys thudded into the enemy ranks. The French retaliated at point-blank range. Both General Mackenzie and the French commander Lapisse were killed in the desperate battle which ensued.[10] Then the watchers on the hill cheered themselves hoarse as the French were seen to withdraw.

Sir Arthur Wellesley [then] crossed with rapid step from the right of the 29th to the part of the hill looking directly down upon General Anson's brigade of cavalry, which mounted on the instant. It was immediately known that a charge would take place.

The ground upon which this brigade was in line is perfectly level, nor did any visible obstruction appear between it and the columns opposed. The grass was long, dry, and waving, concealing the fatal chasm that intervened.

For some time the brigade advanced at a rapid pace, without receiving any obstruction from the enemy's fire. The line cheered. It was answered from the hill with the greatest enthusiasm. Never was anything more exhilarating or more beautiful than the commencement of this advance. Several lengths in front, mounted on a grey horse, consequently very conspicuous, rode Colonel Elley. Thus placed, he, of course, first arrived at the brink of a ravine, which, varying in width, extended along the whole front of the line. Going half speed at the time, no alternative was left to him. To have checked his horse and given timely warning became impossible.

The great grey charger drew back on its haunches to clear the chasm in one tremendous leap. Behind it many others fell or unseated their riders as they failed to clear the ravine. Only the German Hussars managed to draw rein in time.

The line of the 23rd was broken. Still the regiment galloped forward. The confusion was increased, but no hesitation took place in the individuals of this gallant corps. The survivors rushed forward with, if possible, accelerated pace, passing between the flank of the square [formed by the French] now one general blaze of fire, and the building on its left.

Colonel Elley and Major Frederick Ponsonby, galloping flat out, led the men who had managed to cross the dry ditch. With swords pulled from the scabbards, they dashed forward against the cavalry drawn up in the rear.

The watchers in the British army could hardly believe what they saw then as the chasseurs, amazed by the impetus of the attack, reined back in confusion, it seemed without reason, before these broken but gallant horsemen.

Some of the survivors of that mad charge managed to regain the valley, but it had taken many lives. Charles Cocks, writing to his father, told him that 'The 23rd Light Dragoons were nearly cut to pieces, of 450 men not 120 were left fit for duty. Of 8 captains, 6 are killed, wounded or prisoners.'

Meanwhile, as the cannonade continued, the tinder-dry grass on the plain caught fire. Andrew, told by Colonel Bathurst, the Military Secretary, to station himself near the cannon on the summit [of the Cerro de Medellin] to report on the enemy's motions, described the dreadful scene.

> The whole face of the country over which the conflagration extended soon formed one black scorched mass, studded with bodies of the dead and wounded.

Horrified by what was happening, his mind was nonetheless diverted by the final drama of this tremendous conflict when Wellesley narrowly escaped being killed.

> After serious attack had ceased on all parts of the line, and even the light troops had become more distant, Sir Arthur Wellesley was seated, with some officers of his staff, upon the south-eastern ridge of the hill, observing the retiring columns of the enemy, when a musket ball struck him on the breast with sufficient force to give a severe and painful blow, without penetration. It would be idle to descant upon the destinies depending on the degree of impetus possessed by this small portion of lead!

At last, as darkness closed upon the armies, the dull sluggish sound of artillery, when heard alone at intervals or at a distance, seemed to knell the close of the Battle of the Spanish town, forever associated with its name. [11]

8

'THIS MORTAL AND UNNECESSARY INFLICTION'

August – September 1809

On the morning of 3 August 1809 Wellesley heard that Marshal Soult, marching south from Salamanca with 50,000 men, was threatening to cut off his army from Portugal.[12] Andrew Leith-Hay, who was with him, describes his own reaction to this news

> His [Wellesley's] situation at Talavera, upon the morning of the 3rd of August, was one of incomparably greater danger than that of Sir John Moore at Sahagun; but, as has previously been stated, the method of extrication must deservedly be given to his own great military talent, his firmness of determination, his clear insight into the real state of affairs, both with regard to his allies, his enemy, the country to which he was committed, or his own numerical means. But all this must have been unavailing had he been opposed by generals of military talent. The Battle of Talavera proved what pretensions Marshal Victor had to that character, the Duke of Dalmatia [Soult] was only great when acting under the immediate orders of Napoleon.
>
> There was no possible safe line of operation now left on the right bank of the Tagus. One passage across that river alone remained open – that by the Puente del Arzobispo, over which, during the 4th, the army passed, encamping in the woods on

the left bank. At daybreak, on the morning of the 5th, we marched in the direction of Mesa de Ibor, halting for the night in a ravine . . . .

On the 6th the army continued its route, passing over a rugged and precipitous road. To drag the artillery up by the usual means became impossible. The infantry were put to the guns, who, with considerable difficulty and exertion, forced them along the mountain road.

Now, as on the retreat to Corunna, Andrew was once again to marvel at the stoical fortitude of the British soldier. The men had endured much hardship and near starvation, but it was only as they struggled in full uniform to pull the guns up steep hills under the blazing sun that he heard murmurs of complaint. 'Nonetheless a few words of encouragement restored their good humour, even on the tenderest point.'

It was largely thanks to Marshal Victor's incompetence that the British army was saved. Had he, prior to the Battle of Talavera, had the foresight to send part of his force across the Tagus to Almaraz, the escape route to the south-west could have been blocked. Victor had missed his chance before General Craufurd's brigade, which had not been involved in the action, advanced to protect the passage of the river at this important place.

Wellesley, with the main part of his army, reached Deleytosa, a small village on the road to Trujillo, where, in comparative safety, he set up his headquarters on 8 August. Next morning, as the Spanish cavalry and infantry appeared, on the tracks of the British army, he heard that the bridge of Arzobispo had been forced. He had crossed the Tagus just in time.

A field hospital was hastily constructed at Deleytosa to receive the British sick and wounded from Talavera. This was where Charles Cocks, delirious with fever, was taken before being sent on to Elvas on Wellington's personal instructions.

On 11 August the British crossed the Rio del Monte to encamp by the road to Trujillo, at the verge of extensive forests of cork, chestnut and oak trees. Andrew writes:

By this time the Spanish army had disappeared to our front, nor did we hear any tidings of the enemy. Nothing could be more dull or monotonous then the camp at Jaraicejo.

70

He was not bored for long. On the 13th, together with a Captain Gell of the 29th, he rode to Trujillo. Their main reason for going there was to buy provisions. Nonetheless, a change of scenery was most welcome and Andrew was also keen to visit the birthplace of Francisco Pizzaro, the Spanish conqueror of Peru.

> Trujillo is a large town, commandingly situated on a height rising from a level of great extent. It appears the monarch of the plain. Upon the approach of the armies, its inhabitants had fled, but returned upon becoming acquainted with the fact that payment would in all cases be obtained from the British. Every thing was of course charged enormously. Wine was sold in profusion. The Spaniards, conceiving that their allies were persons who must have wine and at the same time would not be particular as to the quality, diluted and mixed the originally poor produce of the grape of Estremadura in such a manner, composing so horrible a description of drink, that it is only extraordinary more fatal effects were not immediately produced by its deleterious qualities.
>
> As might naturally be expected, all parts of the camp sent forth its foragers, flocking to the emporium of Trujillo where scenes of a ludicrous kind were constantly occurring . . . . The quartermaster-sergeant, the regimental officer, the soldier's wife, the officer of the Guards, were alike employed in the inelegant and vulgar avocation of purchasing meat, vegetables, chocolate, groceries, or even bread!
>
> In one part of the Plaza was to be observed the scion of aristocracy in the act of dispatching his servants after having completed the degrading service on which he had been from necessity most unwillingly proceeded. In another the more humble messenger of a subaltern's mess had just heaped upon his sinking quadruped the last deposit of his purchased store, the accompanying soldier almost lost in a forest of canteens, containing enough to poison a whole regiment.

It was late when they returned to the camp. Riding through the dusk, as they saw thick smoke rising in front of them, they wondered what the cause of it might be. Then, as they drew near to the encampment, they saw that the forest was on fire. Andrew clearly remembered the terrifying but unforgettable sight.

71

The crackling of the branches and the sheet of fire which enveloped the stems of the ilex or chestnut had in the darkness a brilliant appearance. The trunks of these venerable trees blazed not, but, red with fire that appeared eating to their hearts, resembled innumerable pillars of light . . . . Fortunately the fire had not extended to the immediate neighbourhood of our camp, and the wind drove it in a different direction.

From Jaraicejo the army marched on over country parched dry by the sun. On 22 August General Hill's division encamped at a village called Santa Cruz de la Sierra above which rose a mountain covered with myrtles, vines, mulberry and fig-trees. Brushwood at the base caught alight. The unfortunate peasants, trying to save their livelihoods, failed to control the fire which reduced what Andrew described as 'a beautiful mountain garden' to a blackened wilderness.

Reaching the valley of the Guadiana, they found themselves in country which had once been inhabited by Romans and later occupied by Moors. On 23 August they encamped at Medellin, a town crowned by a Moorish castle, on the south side of the Guadiana, where the river was spanned by a bridge of twenty arches. From there, on a day of broiling heat, the division continued to Merida.

This city, the Emerita Augusta of the Romans and capital of ancient Lusitania, also on the north bank of the Guadiana, was here crossed by a bridge of fifty-four arches built by the Emperor Trajan. Andrew describes the walled town as having 'the appearance of great antiquity'. The ruins of the Roman aqueduct were, he thought, much superior to a newer construction built for the same purpose. Much of the Temple of Mars was still standing, although only the foundations of the Temple of Minerva remained. Particularly impressive, in its magnitude and the beauty of its form, was the arch, the 'Arco de St Jago', which, despite its great antiquity, appeared both stable and undamaged. The Temple of Diana, however, patched up with modern masonry, had become the arena for the bullfights.

On 3 September, still following the river, the division marched across the plain which stretched from Merida to Badajoz, the headquarters of the division.

The first view of the city of Badajoz from the Talavera road is very striking. Placed on an elevated situation, the castle rises immediately above the Guadiana, that stream washing the

MERIDA

northern base of the rock on which it stands. The fortifications
descend gradually on the low ground to the south-east of the
town. The Guadiana, even in summer, is, under the walls of
Badajoz, a fine river. It seems to have forced an unwilling
passage between the castle rock and below Fort San
Christobal. Another Roman bridge adorns the Guadiana at
Badajoz, near to which is the Alameda, or public walk.
Nothing that I have ever experienced in this delightful climate
equalled the calm, placid, glowing genial feeling during the
twilight of a September evening on the Alameda at Badajoz.

Little did Andrew guess, at this point, that this peaceful fortress on
the Spanish border would become the scene of a slaughter on a so
far unpremeditated scale.

Continuing his story, he describes how the road to Portugal led
out through the walls of Badajoz by the Puerta de las Palmas. It then
crossed a bridge, six hundred yards in length, which was 'protected
by a *tête de pont*, and also by the guns of Fort San Christobal.'

Once on the north bank of the Guadiana the Portuguese fortified
town of Elvas could be clearly seen. The River Caya, between
Badajoz and Elvas, was the frontier between the two countries.
Andrew, writing in retrospect, thought it extraordinary that the two

73

fortified towns, only three leagues [nine miles] apart, should, during the course of the Peninsular War, have known such very different fates. Badajoz was besieged no less than four times. Elvas was never seriously attacked.

Once across the frontier, he was immediately struck with the difference between the two races.

> The high bearing of the Spaniard, which has survived ages of misrule and degradation, is not to be met with in his Lusitanian neighbour. The Castilian and Moorish blood flowing in his veins still give him an external that belies the insignificance which despotism and ignorance have too frequently rendered triumphant in his character.

The British army encamped on the low-lying plains of Estremadura, only to be decimated by disease. The soldiers succumbed to dysentery and malaria and in particular to typhus, the infection spread by lice, being so contagious that it rapidly became an epidemic. The hospitals were crowded. Elvas became one great receptacle of disease. The doctors, bewildered by lack of knowledge, the relationship between mosquitoes and malaria being as yet unknown, struggled to cope with medicines such as mercury and nitric acid to try to ease the suffering of so many seriously ill men. Soon there were ten thousand sick. Regimental hospitals were overflowing. Each day added to the list.

> The month of September passed with no movement of the troops, no approach of the enemy, no prospect of departure from the sandy plains, on which we appeared fixed to witness only the ignoble death of the bravest of our soldiers. It is for historians to detail the reasons for this waste of life . . . it is sufficient to state that, neither then nor since . . . have I ever been enabled to discover a sufficient reason for Lord Wellington's subjecting his army to this mortal and apparently unnecessary infliction.

While the British army remained inactive in Estremadura, the Spanish generals were attempting to attack the crack regiments of the French army, commanded by Marshal Soult. On 18 October the Spanish General del Parque did win a victory at Tamames, but on

19 November the largest Spanish force ever collected in one army during the war, commanded by General Ariezaga – a man equally incapable, presumptuous, and rash – was totally overthrown at Ocaña.[13]

At this point Andrew himself became seriously ill with typhus fever. A medical board recommended that he be sent to Lisbon. Leave of absence was given, whereupon, together with his friend Captain Tucker, who had also had the disease, he began the journey to Lisbon for a period of convalescence.

9

SHADOWING THE FRENCH

On 9 December 1809 Lord Wellington, with the main body of the army, marched towards the Douro, Later, towards the end of the month, General Hill established the headquarters of his Division at Abrantes on the Tagus where Andrew, by now recovered from his illness, rejoined his regiment.

He describes how the fortifications of the old Portuguese city, surrounded as it was by a ruined wall, had been repaired by the British engineers. Standing in a strategic position, it overlooked the

ABRANTES

76

PUNHETE

important crossing of the river over which a bridge of boats had been constructed. The town itself contained a large population. There were, however, only a few good houses and the streets were narrow and steep. Moreover, thanks to being built on a hilltop, it was open to the winds from all directions, so that during the winter months it proved to be bitterly cold.

On the 5th of January General Richard Stewart's brigade marched to Punhete, a small town beautifully situated at the junction of the Zezere with the Tagus. The scenery is wild and romantic, the adjacent country being covered with wood.

Punhete is built upon a Peninsula. Abrantes, although two leagues distant, forms a fine feature in the prospect. The Tagus winds majestically through the valley, while the large white sails of the boats, passing in rapid succession, and appearing at intervals from among the trees, give life and gaiety to the scene.

At the distance of a league from Punhete, on a rock in the centre of the Tagus, stands the ruined castle of Almiroh. From the gardens of the convent of San Antonio, situated on the banks of the river, the castle has a picturesque and striking effect.

THE CASTLE OF ALMIROH

Andrew, however, had little time to sketch it, more important things being on hand. The weather had improved, giving Marshal Soult the chance to advance his army into the plains of Estremadura. The French were now in force at Mérida on the Guadiana, where Hill's division had encamped in the heat of August only five months before. From there troops who had already moved forward into neighbouing villages were now threatening Badajoz and the Portuguese frontier.

Wellington, realizing the gravity of the situation, sent orders to General Hill to cross the Tagus and occupy Portalegre, in the province of that name, just north-west of Badajoz, which borders with Spain. General Tilson's brigade left Abrantes, crossing the bridge of boats, on 15 January, with Generals Stewart's and Catlin Craufurd's following on the 16th so that, by the 18th, the whole division was assembled at Portalegre.

On the morning of the 19th General Hill ordered me to proceed to the Spanish army, from thence to communicate the movements of the enemy to his front. It was late in the afternoon when I arrived at Arronches, on the road to Albuquerque, where the

ALBUQUERQUE

2nd division of the Marques de Romana's army was then quartered. The route from Arronches leads through a wild, uncultivated country, overgrown with gum-cistus and intersected with innumerable paths, branching off in all directions. Not having adopted the precaution of taking a guide, the tracts that beset me became bewildering – even the bold, rocky, not to be mistaken site of the Castle of Albuquerque, did not assist in directing a selection; for the road which appeared to be leading towards it frequently turned abruptly to either side, penetrating into the interior of the luxuriant brushwood. For two hours no human being, or habitation of any description, appeared. It became dark, nor did there seem a prospect of extrication from this wilderness, when fortunately a light glimmered through the thicket. It came from the habitation of some goatherds, who, astonished at that hour to see a stranger in the unfrequented vicinity of their hut, became for a time uncommunicative. At last, however, one of their number, influenced by bribery, agreed to conduct me on the road leading to Albuquerque.

There he found General Carlos O'Donnell, who, with his division consisting of 4500 infantry, 700 cavalry and some artillery, occupied the town and the neighbourhood.

The following day I accompanied General O'Donnell to his advance upon the Aliseda road. This post was commanded by Don Carlos de España, then Colonel of the Tiradores de Catilla.

Don Carlos, a Frenchman by birth, of the ancient family of Foix, and brother to the Marques d'Espagne, had, on the outbreak of war between France and Spain, altered his name to España. Active, intelligent, and brave, he had rapidly achieved promotion in the Spanish army.

On the 23rd General O'Donnell and myself rode to Villar del Rey [a few miles north of Badajoz] where we remained some hours with the brigadier commanding. When about two leagues advanced on our return, a dragoon overtook the General, with information that the enemy had entered soon after our departure, that the Spaniards had been driven out, and that the town was in possession of the French cavalry.

It turned out that this had been one of the frequent foraging expeditions of the enemy, who, in typical style, had ruthlessly demanded contributions in the form of clothes and money, as well as seizing food and drink without giving any form of payment. Having occupied Villar del Rey for the night, the French soldiers took as much as was possible from the unfortunate inhabitants before threatening to come back for more. They had left on the following morning when 700 Spanish infantry, with a squadron of dragoons, had again taken over the town.

At this point the 2nd *corps d'armée* had troops in many villages close to Badajoz. They included Montijo, just north of the Guadiana, and La Roca, which was only six miles from Villa del Rey.

Meanwhile the Marques de la Romana's army had crossed the Tagus and was marching to occupy a line along the frontier to the west of Alburquerque with Campo Mayor as its headquarters. Romana, by this time, however, was, in reality a leader of partisans.

He successfully maintained this system in Galicia, where, though frequently a fugitive and never enabled to keep his ground when formidably attacked, he contrived to support a

80

guerrilla species of warfare more fatal to the French armies than any they had yet encountered.

On 5 February the weather suddenly became much colder and rain poured down almost ceaselessly for several days. Soon the rivers flooded, the Guadiana becoming so high that it was impossible even to ride across any of the normally shallow fords. The French, as a result, moved their troops further from Albuquerque.

On the 9th and 10th, however, the weather again changed, this time for the better. A dry period set in when, as the floods subsided, the fords became passable once more.[14] A French detachment, 1000 strong, then crossed the River Aljucen and marched upon Caceres to levy contributions on the richest town of Spanish Estremadura.

General O'Donnell, hearing of this, decided to seize on the chance of making a surprise attack. Advancing with 2,500 infantry and 300 cavalry, he encamped two days later at one'o'clock in the morning within six miles of Caceres.

Thanks to the inefficiency of the French intelligence Marshal Foy was in total ignorance of the danger in which he now stood. As the Spanish cavalry reached the French outposts, their soldiers, both mounted and on foot, were seen taking to the hills. Don Carlos de España pushed on as quickly as possible over rough ground. A sharp skirmish ensued, but the main body of the French army, descending from the sierra, escaped across the plain.

Ahead lay the River Salor, which could be crossed by a narrow bridge, but Foy's men were saved from what might have been anni-hilation at this point, by the cowardice of the Spanish troops.

Not all Don Carlos's exertions, nor his animating example, while the drums beat and *'vivas'* resounded, could induce the Spaniards to close with the enemy . . . . At length he [Foy] reached the bank of the Salor. Don Carlos perceived that the moment had arrived when he could, by vigorously pressing on his rear, seriously inconvenience the enemy. He therefore renewed his efforts to accelerate the pursuit and ordered the Spanish cavalry to charge the French when in the act of filing across the bridge. They advanced a short distance but the enemy's chasseurs soon checked their ardour by appearing in line to receive them.

Marshal Foy restored his original formation the moment he

had passed the river. After having persevered in the pursuit for a distance of three leagues, Don Carlos requested I would return to General O'Donnell, report to him what had occurred, and receive instructions as to future movements.

The next day Don Carlos, having requested a meeting of the Junta of Caceres, asked Andrew to accompany him to the council. Don Carlos, having stated that, without the support of the towns, in particular Caceres, the Spanish armies could not carry on the war of resistance, then asked for shoes, accoutrements and money. The councilors denied having any of these necessities, saying they could not afford them, but, after much argument, it was agreed that 30,000 reals should be issued from the coffers the following morning.

Andrew had left Caceres to rejoin the Spanish division near Aliseda, when, only a week later, eight hundred French cavalry arrived to plunder the town, this being the fate of almost every city in Spain.

Riding to General Hill's headquarters at Portalegre, only a few miles away, he was able to receive orders and to report on the whereabouts of the whole of the second corps of the French army, which had been quartered in Caceres, or the towns in its immediate neighbourhood.

On the 30th I joined Don Carlos in his camp on the heights above Aliseda. At daybreak we were on horseback to reconnoitre. Nothing appeared except some cavalry patrols who retreated on being fired at. At nine o'clock the peasants brought information of the cavalry having left Arroyo, and about midday it was ascertained that the second corps had marched from Caceres in the direction of Merida . . . .

It was not satisfactorily ascertained that the whole of the second corps d'armée had quitted the right bank of the Guadiana, but in pursuance of orders and relying upon the information of those by whom they had been given, we followed the track of the French troops accompanied by a squadron of cavalry in whose steadiness it would have been folly to have placed great reliance.

The night was dark and cold. At three in the morning we reached Zangana. At daybreak were again on horseback, and at La Roca found General O'Donnell, who had advanced to the ford of La Lamia with three regiments of infantry and four pieces of cannon to support the movement of Montijo.' [Montijo, a town of strategic importance to the north of the Guadiana, midway between Merida and Badajoz, was then held by the French.]

General O'Donnell had just been told that advanced posts of the French army, now ensconced at Merida, were only two miles from Montijo where a skirmish had taken place that morning. It now became imperative to know the exact position of the army, so Don Carlos's detachment of cavalry, increased to two hundred and fifty, were sent out to reconnoitre. Reaching Montijo, they found the place to be quiet for the present, while the people waited in terror for another French raid.

It then transpired that the Spanish army, asleep on the open plain, had been taken completely by surprise. Andrew could only marvel at the disproportional aspects of their character.

In such a state of apathy or unconcern were they, that thrusts of the Polish lancers broke their slumbers. They were apparently as regardless of danger as the best and most experienced troops, and must have known that danger was near, yet adopted no precaution to avert it. They retired out of reach of observation, but quietly and contentedly slept upon the plain, until trampled on by the enemy's horsemen! These same men, showing this disregard of peril and recklessness of safety, would probably have turned their backs and fled if assailed by their opponents face to face, a proof that the inhabitants of some countries can sleep away their fears.

For some days Andrew remained with Don Carlos at Montijo. Always they sent out scouts to give warning of the approach of the enemy. They themselves were on horseback, and when the breath from the horses' nostrils blew white in the faint light of dawn, they rode in near silence, exchanging. when knee to knee, just a few muffled words. Only hoofbeats, and the occasional creak of a saddle, made the odd small sounds. From vantage points, such as hilltops, where, through telescopes, they could get a clear view, they watched the movements of the enemy, calculating what they

83

foretold. Meanwhile, from Montijo, sharp-eyed patrols watched the roads in every direction.

At last came news that Marshal Soult, having crossed the Guadiana, had established his headquarters at Villa Nueva de la Serena. This meant that no French troops continued to be stationed on the north bank of the Guadiana between Medellin and Badajoz. With the whole of the province of Estremadura now in Spanish hands, Badajoz became the headquarters of the Marques de la Romana.

At this point Andrew was summoned to Lisbon by General Leith, who had recently returned from sick leave to resume his command of the 5th division of the British army. Therefore, leaving the Spanish army, he again became his uncle's ADC.[15]

10

SPANISH LADIES; THE SMUGGLERS OF ANDALUSIA; THE SIEGE OF CADIZ

At the beginning of December 1809 Lieut General Sir Stapleton Cotton, commander-in chief of the cavalry, had to return home on business. He asked Charles Somers Cocks if he would like to go with him as far as Cadiz from where he could make a further exploration of southern Spain.

Charles leapt at the chance. It was now the time of Advent, and, stopping in Seville, they went to a candlelit concert in the great cathedral where the music and singing were exquisite. The next day, when they reached Xeres, a Mr Gordon took them over his farm and into his wine vaults to taste his sherry. Later they went to a Carthusian convent to see a famous collection of Murillos.

On 9 December Charles notes in his diary that they 'embarked at Puerto Santa Maria for Cadiz, crossing the bay which is about two leagues over.'

He then describes the town above the harbour wherein the French Admiral Villeneuve's fleet had been blockaded before the Battle of Trafalgar. The country beyond the isthmus, which connects Cadiz to the mainland, was mostly salt marshes 'not unlike the bogs of Ireland', so that 'Cadiz ought never to be taken as long as herself or her allies are in possession of the sea'.

From Cadiz, where he parted from the General, Charles proceeded to Gibraltar. He stayed in an inn called *The Three Anchors* from where he sent his sister a most amusing account of an uproar during the night:

> If all the devils in pandemonium had regaled themselves in this house last night it would probably have been quieter than it actually was

It turned out that some Irish shipowners and masters, who were drinking in the next room, had fallen out because one of them had pulled a chair from beneath another. He heard them talking of pistols and expected 'the appearance of a ball through the thin, deal boards'. Fortunately however, they then became so drunk that they fell asleep, so 'I turned in my bed and snored at my leisure'.

He returned to Cadiz where he spent Christmas enjoying himself enormously. Not many women can resist a uniform, particularly when it is worn by a tall, handsome young man. 'I have lived a most Cyprian life,' he confided to his cousin Thomas, no doubt making him envious as he toiled away at his ledgers in the family bank in London.

Nonetheless, despite all these distractions, he still managed to send his sister a good description of Cadiz.

> There is a gaiety and neatness in the houses which is very different from anything I have seen in other parts of the Peninsula. The streets are scrupulously clean, I know no city in England which equals it in this respect. The walk round the ramparts, which are washed by the sea, is delightful. *He describes the handsome public buildings and the very good theatre where* the front of the boxes is formed by balustrades. *More importantly he tells her that* There is no part of Spain where the British interest is more fairly established. Nothing goes down but what is English

No wonder he had such a good time!

Charles left Cadiz on 31 December. His destination was the Headquarters of the Spanish Army of the Centre at La Carolina, a town adjacent to the main road which runs across Spain from Madrid to Seville. Taking his time, he explored every town and village as he went. He describes the Spanish army in his diary, writing that its commander, Don Carlos de Areizaga, is:

A man as presumptuous in safety as timid and irresolute in danger. He has thirty leagues, or upwards of one hundred miles, of mountain to guard, crossed by four roads practicable for artillery and by innumerable paths practicable for cavalry and infantry, and turned by a road which goes round the end of the Sierra on the right. I have dined with Areizaga and conversed with him, and under these circumstances, he expressed himself perfectly confident that he should be able to defend his position.

Alas for Areizaga's confidence. The following day, 15 January 1810, Marshal Victor was to lead 20,000 men across the Sierra Morena to Cordoba before, only a few days later, Napoleon's brother Joseph, the King of Spain, was to attack Areizaga and defeat him before joining up with Victor to descend on Seville.

When this happened Charles saw his big chance of proving his worth to Wellington by sending him first-hand news of what was taking place. Accordingly, he bought a horse from a Colonel Roche, a British liaison officer with the Spanish, on which he set out, in pouring rain, with two dragoons of a Spanish regiment, to follow the movements of the French on the left end of their line. On the way he again moved from village to village, noting every detail of the country and the condition of the roads. He had reached a place called Venta de Sarzozo when he decided that, if his information was to be useful, he must report to Wellington immediately. Told that the French were occupying Torrecampo, on the route which he had meant to take, he decided to go a different way:

I left the Venta at midnight in company of some smugglers who were pursuing the same route. It froze very hard and was dreadfully cold. After proceeding a league, on arriving at the summit of a hill, I saw the fires of the French encampment at Torrecampo.

Undeterred, he set off with the two dragoons (the smugglers having vanished into the mountains) on a rough track which he hoped would lead them round the camp. After a mile, however, they met someone who told them that 2000 cavalry were in the camp and that every little hamlet in the valley was full of billeted French soldiers. Disappointed, they returned to the Venta to find a man of villainous appearance drinking as much wine as he could manage before the French laid their hands on it. However, the drink having made him mellow, he sent for a local peasant who knew every inch of the country.

A robust young man appeared, with a countenance pleasing and lively, nor did it belie him, for he proved both active and intelligent. We again left the Venta about an hour after daybreak. I had procured two days' barley for my horses. We had three leagues to the road by which the French were marching; our guide led us by an unfrequented path through a wood. Half a league short of the road we met some peasants who informed us some of the enemy were actually marching down the road. We concealed ourselves in the wood and sent our guide forth to reconnoitre.

After about an hour the man returned with the news that all was now clear of the enemy. Emerging from the trees they continued until, in darkness, they at last reached a small village called Guadalmez, half way between Almoden and Cabeza del Buey. By now they were exhausted, having been travelling, with only a brief rest while they hid in the wood, for about twenty hours.

On 21 January Charles, with his two companions, set out again, heading for Cabeza del Buey. They followed a bridle path along a river and then over a mountain pass. 'The day was dreadful, the snow fell the whole march and when we arrived was some inches deep.' From this town, on 21 January, he wrote to Lord Wellington.

Having told him in great detail of the topography of the country and the directions and state of the roads in Andalusia, he explained:'I feel mortified that I cannot give your Lordship more certain accounts of the enemy, but no dependence can be placed on the flying rumours in circulation . . . . Comparing, however, the various accounts I have received in the different towns where the enemy has passed, I do not think his force on the 20th, south of Almoden, exceeded 20,000 . . . . Had I left La Carolina two days sooner I might have concealed myself 3 leagues from Almoden in a point which commands the road and seen the whole of his left column defile at the distance of 400 yards.

He continues to inform Wellington that the Duke of Albuquerque is marching towards Cordoba:

> I shall overtake the Duke of Albuquerque's army and, in case I meet no other British officer, remain with it until I receive your Lordship's orders. As the British army is now in cantonments and as I speak and write Spanish, I should be most happy should your Lordship think to continue me upon this service.
> The peasantry of the Sierra Morena are bold, active and intelligent and there are among them men who might be made extremely useful in gaining accurate information'.

On 26 January Charles, by this time in Seville, noted in his diary that, after crossing the Guadalquivir by a ferry, he had found himself on a surprisingly good road which ran through very wild country. He had also discovered that the Duke of Albuquerque had established his headquarters at Brenes, about three miles from Cantillana. The Spanish general had led his army through Estremadura and the Sierra Morena so successfully that Charles, who had been following him for several days, had not seen even as many as twenty stragglers.

On 27 January he wrote again to Wellington, praising Albuquerque, but telling him that:

> It is, however, with regret that I inform your lordship that he has done this without the least hope of effectually defending or covering the city.

He then describes the revolution which had just taken place in Seville where most of the members of the Central Junta had been placed under arrest. Three of the Spanish aristocracy, including the Marques de la Romana, had assumed power in their place. Romana, had, however, then left to take charge of his army, leaving the inhabitants of Sevilla to escape the town as best they might.

All too soon he saw the chaos which occurred. On 31 January, having left Xeres for Puerto Santa Maria, the entry in his journal reads:

> The alarm had now become general and men, women and children were flying in all directions. At first they tried to cross the water to Cadiz but, it becoming impracticable to obtain boats

and some having been sunk from being overloaded, the fugitives pushed on towards the Isla by land. The gates of Cadiz presented an affecting spectacle, so many people wished to seek refuge in the city that a contagious fever must have been the certain consequence of a siege. It became necessary to shut them and crowds were in vain entreating to be admitted . . . . Fort Catharina and the fort at Matagorda, the two principle batteries on the north side of the Bay of Cadiz, were given up to our navy to be destroyed. This duty was entrusted to Captain Lindsay of the *Triumph* but it was performed very imperfectly, particularly at Fort Catharina where only the embrasures at the front were thrown open. The Spanish ships and hulks with French prisoners were moved out into the outer harbour among the British squadron.

1 February. Went back to Puerto Santa Maria for my horses but was unable to cross the bar.

2 February. Went to the Isla de Leon. Castaños had established himself here. Albuquerque, who had arrived the day before, had brought about 11,000 men. I went on to Cadiz 1,000 are expected from Gibraltar.

3 February. Went to Headquarters and took possession of my billet. Headquarters were established in the town of Isla. It is considered that the French can only attempt the passage of the River Santa Petri in three points, namely by the Puente Zuarza, by the Point to Santa Petri, and the right of the Carraca and to the left. Between these points the river is so boggy that it is inaccessible on each side . . . .

But there was one firm beach for on 5 February Charles wrote that:

The French entered Seville on the 1st and had about 24,000 in the neighbourhood. *He goes on to say:* The servant of O'Farrell who deserted to Carmona left his master at Cordoba. He was a spy employed by the Spaniards and only entered O'Farrell's service that he might learn all he could. Among the papers he brought away was a plan of [Marta's] to disembark on the Isla near Santa Petri and between that point and Torregorda the strand there is perfectly good. The man says the French have now received 10,000 reinforcements, a number not sufficient to compensate for the loss in the various actions since

Talavera'. [O'Farrell must have been one of the freelance Irish soldiers who fought for the French.]

Charles spent the next few days travelling through the area surrounding Cadiz, noting all the details of the country and the defences, most of which he thought inadequate to repel a strong French attack. He mentions typical incidents of Spanish inefficiency such as :

10 February. The Spaniards endeavoured this morning to destroy the two ferry houses towards Chiclana but, the enemy firing two cannon shot, they desisted.

11 February. The batteries of the Puente de Zuarza amused themselves this morning by endeavouring to break down the ferry houses and by firing at some straggling parties of French cavalry. This was a shameful waste of ammunition, particularly when the Junta of Seville prevailed on Mr Frere [still British Minister in Spain] to apply yesterday to Gibraltar for 500 quintels of powder.

On 12 February General Stewart's brigade arrived from Lisbon. It consisted of the 79th, 87th and 94th regiments with two companies of artillery.

Charles then learnt from Colonel Samford Whittingham, who commanded the Spanish cavalry at Cadiz, that 'the enemy were on the borders of Portugal and that the British army were in motion'. On hearing this, he decided to seize the chance of returning to Lisbon on HMS Sloop of War the *Myrtle,* which sailed on 19 February.

From Lisbon on the 24th his servant Boverick wrote home to a Mrs Gardner, who must have been one of the staff at Charles's home at Castleditch, saying that:

Yesterday I had the pleasure to see the Captain arrive safe and well in Lisbon, in fact I never saw him look so well. It was an agreeable surprise to me and everyone, for Captain Swetenham had told me about three hours before that there was not one of the regiment knew where he was and he thought I should not see him for a month; indeed I find he has had many narrow escapes . . . . The dragoon that was with the Captain tells me that when the Captain was ill of a fever after the battle of

Talavera he was so weak for some time that the man was obliged to carry him about on his back, but he has the character of having done more for the service in the time than any officer in the army.

He then adds intriguingly, He has been more than once selling gin, etc amongst the French lines, but I have not had time to get any particulars as we are so busy preparing for our departure'.[16]

11

THE SUMMER CAMPAIGN OF 1810

Drive the British leopards into the sea
Napoleon to Marshal André Masséna

The Spring of 1810 was a time of great anxiety for Wellington. Napoleon, having defeated Austria at the Battle of Wagram, sent an estimated 100,000 men to the Peninsula, bringing his force of highly trained soldiers to a total of 325,000 in all. Marshal Masséna, who, at fifty-two was his senior marshal, was given supreme command. Napoleon gave him orders to 'drive the British leopards into the sea'.[17/18]

Masséna started his campaign in May by advancing on the Spanish border fortress of Ciudad Rodrigo. The town was held by a garrison of 5, 500 Spanish soldiers who were commanded by the gallant, seventy-year-old General Andreas Herrasti.

It was June before the brigade, which included Charles's regiment, the 16th Light Dragoons, moved up to join General Craufurd's Light Division, stationed between the Agueda and Coa Rivers, opposite the beleaguered citadel of Ciudad Rodrigo. The town was by now besieged by the French, but Wellington did not have enough men or guns to challenge them with any hope of success. Charles wrote:

> It is a bitter pill to us to sit with crossed arms and view this rich prey fall into the hands of the enemy, but our corps is much too small to attempt anything of itself and though the army is within two days' march Lord Wellington does not seem

inclined to attempt anything and I believe circumstances justify him in this cruel inaction.

The situation within the besieged fortress of Ciudad Rodrigo became increasingly desperate. On 26 June it was known that that General Andreas Herrasti had lost 150 killed and had 500 men wounded, On the 29th a Spaniard who had managed to pass the French posts brought General Carrera a scribbled note 'O *venir lugo!lugo!lugo! a secorrer esta plaza*' (Oh! Come now!now! now! to the rescue of this place).[19]

But Carrera retired to the River Dos Casas, leaving the beleaguered garrison to its fate.

The siege, directed by Mashal Masséna, then intensified.

Wellington, ignoring the taunts of Masséna, who told him that the sails were flapping on his ships to take him away, refused to be drawn into an action which, thanks to the French supremacy in numbers, he knew he must lose.

General Craufurd, however, did try to deceive the enemy into thinking that reinforcements were on hand. On the evening of 2 July, having sent some cavalry behind to raise the dust, he marched his troops in single file on high ground in full view of the French in the hopes that this would delude them into thinking that the whole British army was coming to the aid of Ciudad Rodrigo.

The ruse gave a short respite but, two days later, on 4 July, a strong detachment of the enemy crossed the Agueda, forcing the British to retire to Almeida. Their retreat was covered by some of the 16th Light Dragoons and a troop of German Hussars. The English captain, without orders, said that he dared not charge, whereupon the gallant German, Captain Krauchenberg, leading his single troop, rode full speed against the advancing columns, killed the leading officers, scattered the front ranks and drove the rest off in confusion.

General Craufurd then stationed his infantry and guns in a wood near Fort Conception. His cavalry, joined by divisions of the Spanish General Carrera and the guerrilla leader Julian Sanchez, were higher up on the Dos Casas River. The French then withdrew behind the Azava, leaving only a piquet at Gallegos.[20]

From his new position Charles noted in his diary, on 8 July, that 'Ciudad Rodrigo appeared on fire at midnight and from nine or ten there was heavy firing at intervals'.

The next day he wrote to his cousin Thomas, heading his letter, 9 July, Encampment near Fuente de la Conception.

My dear Thomas,

With a beard of four days' growth and a shirt resembling Queen Isabella's shift, I mean to fill up the time till it grows hot enough to bath in writing letters. The quiet of our situation is particularly calculated for any sedate operation of this nature, for except the eternal squealing and fighting of mules and the thundering of the batteries, pro and con, at Ciudad Rodrigo there is scarce any noise to interrupt me, unless indeed anything else like a horse should break loose and run over my hut or the enemy should make a movement in which case our cat-like General Crauford is sure to turn us out.

You see by my mention of the batteries at Ciudad Rodrigo that that resolute town still holds out. For sixteen days has it been bombarded, yet, as far as we can observe, its fire is still kept up with the same alacrity, yet it is very ill-provided with artillerymen or with officers of any description.

Two circumstances only were in its favour. The first is that the enemy, aware of its weakness and ignorant of the disposition of its intrepid governor [the Spanish General Andreas Herrasti] held it in too great contempt and only brought down against it 18 or 20-pounders and 9 mortars, with a scant supply of ammunition. The other circumstance is common to all Spanish towns. From their construction it is scarcely possible to set them on fire. It is a heartbreaking thing for us to remain inactive spectators of this gallant defence, especially as some of the prettiest girls in Spain are in the town. What care would we take of them if we had them here. We would build them such nice huts! And keep them so warm at night! And now these French foutres [devils] will have them all. I am very glad I never was in Ciudad Rodrigo or I should be ten times more.

We are on very good terms with the French. The night before they attacked us at Gallegos I had a long conversation with a French officer, a little brook only divided us. Both parties made a point of never firing on single officers in this way without calling to them first. The French are very badly off for rations, a mess of four men only receive 1lb of bread and $\frac{1}{2}$ lb of flesh per day; we are capitally off. The French desert by every opportunity, even native Frenchmen. We are acting here with some of the German Hussars. Though I have not a very high opinion of the infantry belonging to the German legion, yet I must bear the most unqualified testimony to the courage, skill, zeal and marked good conduct of the cavalry – the fact is, the first are foreigners of all descriptions and exactly the same species of troops except being finer men, as the French armies – the cavalry are old Hussars, almost all Hanoverians, and many of them men of great respectability. These men are perfectly to be depended on and understand outpost duty better, and take more care of their horses than British dragoons.

We are living here almost at free quarters; as we know the enemy will be here before long we make a point of conscience to leave him as little as possible. Since we were driven in on the 4th ultimo from Gallegos we have been much quieter and have been allowed to have our baggage with us and we get hot breakfasts. But our clothes are never off our backs or our saddles off our horses. I must confess I enjoy this sort of life. There is a wildness and continual occupation of mind and body which delights me.

Two days after writing this, on 11 July, he notes in his diary, 'Ciudad Rodrigo preserved a dead silence and it became more and more apparent that it had surrendered.'

The Portuguese border fortress of Almeida was now threatened by the French, making it increasingly important to the Commander-in-Chief to know how the French would advance. Should they come down the Mondego valley, as seemed probable, they would have a choice of roads: a good one on the south side of the river, a bad one on the north. Because it was so essential for him to know which Masséna was most likely to take, Wellington ordered Charles Cocks to go in person to the guerrilla leader to ask for his opinion on which was the most likely route.

Julian Sanchez, one of the most intrepid of the guerrilla leaders, had escaped from Ciudad Rodrigo on 23 June. A former soldier, he was a fund of local knowledge of enormous importance to Wellington.

The Spaniard, small, short-legged and dark-skinned, made a

GUARDA

strange contrast to the tall, lean figure of the British commander. A contemporary, watching them walking up and down together in the market at Freieda, left a humorous description of Sanchez, with his cloak flapping about, hopping along with short steps like a jackdaw, in his effort to keep up with Wellington's easy stride. [21]

> 22 July Went to Don Julian Sanchez's encampment and agreed with him mutually to communicate intelligence.[22]

Don Julian in fact did more than this by sending practical help.

A week later, on the 29th, Charles had just bivouacked under some chestnut trees at the junction of the roads from Castel Mendo and the Ponte de Sedeira to Guarda, when, with a clatter of hooves, a few ferocious-looking men appeared. Dark-skinned and moustached, they were dressed as described by Andrew Leith-Hay:

> The flaring scarlet and light-blue jacket of an Estremaduran hussar, the shakos of a French *chasseur à cheval,* pistols and saddle of English manufacture, the long straight sword of the enemy's dragoon, the brown Spanish sash and leather cartouche belt, and an Aragonese or Catalan *escopeta* [shotgun].[23]

Thus, or similarly accoutred, they announced that Sanchez had sent them to assist his English friend.

Charles makes frequent reference to Sanchez who, by the beginning of May 1811 had no less than 500 cavalry and 1,000 infantry under his command. Little did he realize at that point that he would shortly become involved on a personal basis, as a rival in love, with the brave, but utterly merciless leader of the guerrillas.

The British retreated as the French advanced. Charles wrote in his diary, on 25 July, 'The Royals and the Fusiliers who were on the bank of the Coa have fallen back. Captain La Motte of the former writes me word that General Craufurd has passed that river'.

On 29 July Charles moved to a new camp at a place called Richioso. With him was his great friend William Tomkinson, who, having been wounded and sent back to England earlier in the campaign, was now once more on active service. William, who also kept a diary, wrote:

> It was a most excellent camp, the trees affording capital shade, and from the length of time we had been there each man had a good hut and the encampment wore the appearance of a small village. We were much safer from any sudden attack; the men and horses both continued healthy from having plenty to eat and something to employ themselves with. The men got as much rye bread, mutton, potatoes, and wheat flour from the adjacent mills as they wanted, and the horses as much rye in the ear and thrashed as they could eat, and now and then some wheat, nearly ripe. Cocks and myself had nothing with us but a change of linen, a pot to boil potatoes, and the same to make coffee in, with a frying pan, which we carried on his led horse . . . . We could always march in five minutes, never slept out of our clothes and never enjoyed better health, half past two in the morning was the hour we got up.

Nonetheless they were always surrounded by enemies, not all of them French. Wellington had ordered a scorched-earth policy to prevent anything that was edible and moveable being left to fall into French hands. Naturally this was resented by the Portuguese peasants who saw their growing crops and precious stocks of grain disappearing and some of their mills destroyed. On 1 August Charles wrote:

For some time I have observed increasing symptoms of neglect and dislike in the Portuguese peasantry towards us; they think we are retreating and deserting them and conceive this a proper moment to show all the rancour which has long been brooding in their breasts. I do not blame them for disliking us, the contempt with which Englishmen treat them is a sufficient excuse for it, but I despise them for the manner with which they have hitherto fawned on us and not dared to show their dislike till they think they are getting rid of us. Today, two of my patrols were attacked in two separate villages, a man of each is badly wounded. I immediately visited each village with a party, seized some of the inhabitants whom I considered as culprits and have sent them on to General Cole at Guarda.

Charles does not mention how he himself rode out and rescued one of the men, a soldier called Thompson, who had been wounded. William Tomkinson, however, tells how the man's companion, a dragoon, staggered back into the camp with the awful story that Thompson had been shot through the lungs by the Portuguese peasants and left to die. The dragoon himself had been tied to a tree, but for some reason had been freed in the evening and had managed to return to the camp. Charles found Thompson in time to save his life but his fury is understandable. The man had not only been shot, but, lying wounded and helpless, had been cruelly stoned.

This, however, seems to have been a single example of conflict with the local people whom he usually put to good use. In the early hours of 16 August about eighty to a hundred of them destroyed no less than five mills. Wellington, informed by telegraph from Guarda (by the system of signals invented by the Naval Captain Home Popham), wrote to Stapleton Cotton that 'Cocks and his detachment, and the Ordenanza, [the Portuguese Home Guard] have destroyed the mills near Castel Mendo'.

The Portuguese fortress of Almeida had now withstood the French besiegers for nearly a month. Tragically for the heroic garrison, on 26 August a trail of gunpowder from a leaking barrel was set on fire by a shell. The whole magazine exploded. Five hundred men were killed and the commander found himself with no alternative other than to surrender. [24]

On the day of its happening, 28 August, Charles heard of what had occurred. On 2 September he wrote:

All the cavalry near Guarda was called in and the infantry evacuated that place. The heavy cavalry, 2 squadrons of the Royals, marched with them. My party only occupied the town.

3 September. I received orders to retire on Prados, leaving a small party in Guarda.

Wellington wrote to Sir Stapleton Cotton at the early hour of 8 am:

Captain Cocks is upon Prados with a piquet of observation upon Guarda . . . . He will retire upon Linhares . . . . It might be advisable to strengthen him a little so as to enable him to strengthen his post at, and so patrol from, Guarda, to obtain better intelligence of the enemy's movements I believe [General] Cole has left the English key of the telegraph at Guarda with Cocks; if he has not I shall desire him to send it to him.[25]

Beacons warning of the approach of the enemy were now set alight. The British soldiers, constantly on the alert, had to be ready to move at any moment. Charles's friend William Tomkinson wrote:

We slept in the street, not thinking it safe to put under cover. From lighting the beacon, several houses had taken fire; and, there not being an inhabitant in the town, two or three were burnt down. I was too tired to get up and see the fire.

The alarm at Guarda proved to be unfounded. The French did not advance in that direction and on 4 September Charles received orders to re-occupy the town. The following day, however, Wellington wrote to Stapleton Cotton:

I wish you would strengthen the party upon Guarda and get Cocks to go out to the front towards Sabugal and discover what they are about, whether they have really moved cannon from Almeida by Sabugal; whether it is cannon of a heavy caliber; whether the troops of Ney's corps have moved that way; and let me know the number of any regiment that has marched and I shall know to what corps it belongs.

Charles did as he was ordered, questioning the local people and sending back reports of all that he heard and seen.

100

SABUGAL

On 10 September Wellington wrote again to Stapleton Cotton
enclosing a letter from Charles whom he always referred to as Cocks.

Charles, when he wrote, had been 'about a league from Guarda
towards what he called Mantagua, which Wellington took to be
Manteigas. He told Cotton:

> You will observe that he retired by the road to Manteigas, to
> which I see no objection when he shall retire again. But if he
> does so, there should be likewise a post on Prados to observe
> the enemy and also one at Linhares, otherwise they would be
> on the great road before you would know it . . . . Desire Cocks
> to have the road from Guarda to Manteigas examined and let
> me know what kind of one it is.[26]

Charles's information on the state and direction of the roads was
soon to be of vital importance as events would prove. He was shortly
to tell Wellington that the French were not advancing as expected
by way of Manteigas, up the good road on the south side of the
Mondego, but on the bad road on the north side of the river which
no one dreamt they would attempt.

At about 9 o'clock in the morning on 15 September Charles, on
the hill of Guarda, said to be the highest town in Europe, as he told

101

his sister, spied through his telescope a large number of French soldiers, both cavalry and infantry, in the woods below. He reported this to Wellington, who in turn told Stapleton Cotton: 'I have heard from Captain Cocks . . . that the enemy were passing down Guarda hill.' Thus the whole plan of the French advance into Portugal became clear, as Wellington put it, 'by the northern and most atrocious road'.

The French troops who had briefly occupied Guarda were part of General Reynier's division. Once in the valley of the Mondego they were joined by the 6th Corps and General Montbrun's cavalry. The whole force then crossed the river, marched beyond Celorico and drove back the mounted outposts of the allies to a village called Cortico. Here, however, the first German Hussars attacked them, defeating the leading squadrons and taking some prisoners.

It is at this point that Colonel John Waters, one of the most intrepid of Wellington's Intelligence Officers, again achieved what can only be described as another of his amazing coups. Part of a French brigade, by heading for a bridge across the river, attempted a feint to cover the continuing advance of the main army along the north bank of the Mondego.

Waters, watching undetected, was undeceived. Having reported to Wellington that the divergence was only a feint, he then, together with some of the German Hussars, rode boldly to the rear of the main column, took several prisoners and captured the baggage of a French general.

Waters himself had been taken prisoner shortly before this incident occurred. Forced to work as a groom, he had escaped by the simple method of feeding all the corn to one horse, on which he galloped away, leaving his captors, on grass-fed animals, trailing hopelessly behind.

Thanks to his information, Wellington, now convinced which way the French were heading, placed the First, Third and Fourth Divisions on the Alva and the Light Division at St Ramao in the Estrella to protect his headquarters which, on the night of 16 September, he transferred to Cea.[27]

On 17 September Charles Cocks wrote:

Last night our cavalry fell back on Pinhancos and the army is
in full retreat to occupy the position of the Ponte de Murcella
18 September. Last night there were no fires at Guarda; the

rest of the enemy has passed that place and he appears to be concentrated round Celerico . . . . It is evident that the principal part of the army is marching on Viseu.

Sir William Napier describes how, on the 18th, the French advance guard reached the deserted city of Viseu. Pack's Portuguese brigade immediately crossed the Mondego and General Pakenham, with a brigade of the first division, entered Coimbra to protect it against the French scouting parties. On the 19th Captain Somers Cocks, commanding the cavalry post which had been driven from Guarda, came down from the Estrella and, following the enemy through Celorico, discovered that neither sick men nor stores had been left behind. Thus he could report to Wellington that Masséna, forsaking his line of communication, had directed his cavalry, infantry, artillery and even the hospital wagons to head south-west on the worst road in Portugal.[28]

On 20 September Wellington wrote to Sir Stapleton Cotton.

You see that the enemy have all crossed the Mondego and I propose that you should cross tomorrow . . . . Be so kind as to leave on this side of the Mondego an intelligence officer, either Krauchenberg or Cordemann or Cocks, with about a squadron to observe the enemy's movements between the Dao and the Mondego and do you take care to keep up a communication with him.[29]

The same day, in dispatches to the Earl of Liverpool, Secretary of State, he wrote:

It is but justice to mention the zeal and intelligence with which the duty of the outposts has been performed by Captain Krauchenberg and Cornet Cordemann of the 1st Hussars and by Captain the Hon. C. Cocks of the 16th Light Dragoons.

On 21 September Charles received orders to march to Galizes, near Ponte de Murcella. Riding along the good road, on the south side of the Mondego, he reached his destination in only eleven hours. On 25 September, from Ponte de Murcella, on the Alva, a tributary of the Mondego, he wrote to his sister Margaret, telling her how he had spotted the French army assembling in the woods below Guarda:

103

I had a most interesting duty. The road of the enemy lay through a large plain, on one side of which is an immense mountain. On the mountain lay I, and very much at my ease counted the divisions which marched at the foot. Unfortunately their principal force did not take this route but I, one day, saw 5,000 infantry and 2,000 cavalry perfectly, with all their baggage and etcs.

This advance has caused most horrible confusion. The Portuguese have such a dread of the French, they desert the villages for leagues on each side of their route. Though one must feel for these unfortunate people, driven from their homes and their habits of indolence, into mountains and activity, yet sometimes in these gangs of fugitives one meets with such curious combinations and such extraordinary demonstrations of dread that it is impossible to help laughing.

Fancy to yourself, but first recollect that the scene lies in a grove of pine trees, with firs and brambles about knee high. Fancy to yourself an elderly, fat woman in a flowered satin petticoat trudging away, in one hand a parasol, in the other a lapdog. Then two boys, knock-kneed and trembling, with countenance devoid of every colour but a pasty yellow; a footman, like an old English serving man, with his shoes in his hand, then to two misses with fans, crying 'Jesu Maria'; three serving-maids, with bundles, howling; two bullocks, lowing; a car with the wheels squeaking and a peasant in a cocked hat and a long gun, more frightened than the whole party. Fancy all this trudging through the firs taking *me* for a Frenchman and setting off in every direction.

I believe Marshal Masséna, Prince d'Essling, is in a scrape and I flatter myself we are likely soon to give him, with all his titles, a sound drubbing. He has tried to outmanoeuvre our gallant Wellington and he has hitherto taken in the Frenchman.[30]

Long before his letter reached Margaret at Castleditch. Charles's prophesy had proved to be correct.

Andrew Leith-Hay describes how Wellington lured Marshal Masséna into fighting him in what has been described as one of the best defensive positions in Europe.[31]

104

PEÑA COVA

So well-timed was the junction of the different corps of the British army that Lord Wellington's third division, under General Picton, occupied quarters of Foriera on the 20th [September], these becoming next day the cantonments of the corps from Thomar, commanded by General Leith, while at the distance of a day's march was General Hill, all moving to the same point without interference, confusion or delay.

On the 22nd General Leith's corps was stationed at Sobriera and Casa Nova. On the following morning he crossed the Mondego at the Barca de Conselha, halting at Peña Cova for the night. Having during the 24th encamped near the church of Nuestra Señora de Monte Alto, he moved into the position of Busaco on the morning of the 25th, occupying the extreme right of the ridge, with his flank on the Mondego, on the opposite bank of which was the whole corps of General Hill, extending to the Ponte de Murcella.

The mountain range called the Busaco Ridge, running due north for about ten miles from the Mondego and rising to a height of 1, 800 feet, forms a natural barrier to an approaching force. The steep hillsides are strewn with rocks and covered in gorse, making them hard to climb.

Wellington, months before, had envisaged that this was the place to bring the enemy to bay. To this purpose he had instructed the engineers to build a road, passable by troops and by gun carriages towed by mules and oxen, along the length of the ridge, although near the top on the western side it was just out of view from men marching from the east across the plain below.

The French pursued as he withdrew across the Mondego. Marshal Masséna, described by Wellington as 'one of the first soldiers of Europe', felt sure of success. 'I cannot persuade myself that Lord Wellington will risk the loss of a reputation by giving battle, but if he does I have him. Tomorrow we shall effect the capture of Portugal, and in a few days I shall drown the leopard'.[32]

But Masséna's informers had let him down. He did not know that Hill had joined Wellington. Neither was he aware that the right flank of Wellington's force was almost in the centre of the ridge. Most importantly, he discounted the Portuguese army as being unable to fight. Convinced that he could push the British back to their ships with a force superior in numbers, he allowed himself to be lured into battle.

12

THE BATTLE OF BUSACO

27 September 1810

The 26th was a beautiful day, with bright sunshine; nor can anything be conceived more enlivening, more interesting, or more varied, than the scene from the heights of Busaco.

So wrote Andrew Leith-Hay, summing up the battlefield as seen with an artist's eye. He continued to explain how the Sierra de Busaco, after the army of Lord Wellington and the Corps from Thomar had extended along the ridge, was still not fully occupied. The commander of the forces therefore directed General Hill to cross the Mondego and form on the extreme right of the position.

To give space for this and also to condense the general alignment General Leith moved one of his brigades towards the centre of the line. Farther left, along the ridge, the Division of General Picton was placed to defend the road which ran from San Antonio de Cantaro, in the Mondego Valley, across the ridge. General Spencer's first Division, the next in line, was succeeded by the Portuguese Brigade of General Pack, placed specifically to guard the other hill road to Coimbra, which passed the Convent of Busaco, now Wellington's command post.

From where Andrew Leith-Hay was stationed, as aide-de-camp to General Leith, he had a clear view to the east. The movements of the French army could be seen very clearly.

Rising grounds were covered with troops, cannon, or equipages; the widely extended country seemed to contain a host moving forward, or gradually condensing into numerous masses, checked in their progress by the grand natural barrier on which we were placed, and at the base of which it became necessary to pause. In imposing appearance as to numerical strength, I have never seen anything comparable to that of the enemy's army from Busaco; it was not alone an army encamped before us, but a multitude; cavalry, infantry, artillery, cars of the country, horses, tribes of mules with their attendants, sutlers,[33] followers of every description, crowded the moving scene upon which Lord Wellington and his army looked down . . . .'

On the forenoon of the 26th, I was directed to advance in front with a squadron of Portuguese cavalry and report the movements of the enemy on the roads close to the right bank of the Mondego, directly communicating with the valley of Larangeira . . . . Passing through a very picturesque and beautiful country, we occasionally descended to the banks of the Mondego, or ascended the eminences, from whence was discernable the enemy's line of march on the right, at intervals enveloped in dust and smoke. To the rear was the imposing line of mountains occupied by the allied army, luxuriant woods, fertile valleys; great excitement, and a brilliant atmosphere added to the effect of the whole.

The evening of the 26th closed upon the allies finally arranged in position. After dark the whole country in front was illuminated by the fires of the French army. The 6th and 8th Corps of the enemy had arrived in front of the position by the routes of Castel de Maria and Mortagoa, the 2nd by that leading to San Antonio de Cantaro.

Despite being warned of the danger and difficulties involved, Masséna, with 65,000 men under his command, was fully confident that he would defeat Wellington, whose force of only 52,000 men was almost half composed of untried Portuguese.[34] The battle was as good as won.

The walkover, which he had expected, totally failed to occur. At a quarter to six the next morning, when a thick mist covered the summit of the ridge, the enemy, as Wellington had predicted, advanced from the valley up the San Antonio road. At six o'clock four French battalions, under Marshal Foy, were confronted by

General Picton, who, still wearing his night-cap, led the charge which drove them down the hill.

Charles Cocks, having joined Hill at the Ponte de Murcella, had then moved on to where the General's two Divisions were stationed at the south end of the Busaco Ridge and saw all that was taking place.

> At daybreak the enemy advanced in two columns to attack the hill. The 2nd *corps d'armée*, Reynier, was principally engaged. General Simon led the column which advanced by the Mortagoa road on General Craufurd, the other column attacked General Picton, who was supported by General Hill.

General Leith, on hearing the sound of firing, realized that Picton's division must be engaged, Therefore, in compliance with Wellington's previous instructions to move north, if not himself attacked, and with Hill's consent, he took his second division along the ridge towards the road from San Antonio de Cantaro. The men, having covered two miles over rough ground, found themselves plunged into a pitched battle as Andrew Leith-Hay describes:

> At this moment the enemy had penetrated the very summit of the mountain; the outnumbered light infantry of General Picton were severely pressed. When the smoke dispelled, that at intervals enveloped the whole extent of the face and crest of the ridge, the highest rocks appeared in possession of the French voltigeurs; one officer was particularly conspicuous on the very highest point; cheering and waving his shako, he urged his comrades then climbing up the ascent.

General Leith ordered the 38th Regiment to try to outflank the right of the French army, but this proved impossible,: the steep drop of the precipice making it too dangerous to advance. At this critical moment, however, Colonel Cameron, of the 9th Regiment, told by a staff officer what was happening, lined up his regiment under fierce fire, and with incredible bravery charged the French.

> The 9th Regiment, commanded by Colonel Cameron, being the leading battalion, when about a hundred yards distant, wheeled into line, firing a volley, the effect of which was

terrific; the ground was covered with dead and dying, not new levies or mercenaries, but the elite of the French army. This destructive fire being followed by an immediate charge, the enemy gave way, rushing down the steep face of the sierra in the utmost confusion; nor did his troops attempt to rally until on the same ground from which they had advanced to this most unsuccessful and murderous attack. On the same space of ground has seldom been seen such destruction as overtook the Division of the 2nd Corps on this occasion.

Previous to this defeat, the other division of General Reynier's Corps, after another brave but hopeless attack, had been driven down from the sierra by the Light Division and General Pack's Portuguese brigade. Thus the battle which had taken place to the left of the Convent of Busaco, the centre from which Wellington directed the whole operation, closed with brilliant success on the part of the allies.

The strategy of Wellington, who had not only placed his own forces so strategically, but had foreseen with great accuracy the routes by which the French would advance, was, without any doubt, the main cause of the victory. An added reason for the achievement, however, was that the Portuguese soldiers had proved themselves consistently brave and efficient under fire.

> The 8th Portuguese Regiment, commanded by Colonel Douglas, was particularly distinguished. By that Corps, in conjunction with the 45th and 88th British Regiments, the most successful attack of the day was repulsed. Placed as they were on very commanding ground, the loss sustained by these regiments, being nearly equal to that of all the other corps of the army combined, proves the serious nature of the contest from which they had acquired such merited distinction.

Then, after the elation of the triumph of the victory, came the anti-climax of the aftermath which Andrew, even twenty years later, could not delete from his mind.

> Before dark, General Leith's Corps removed from the eastern face of the ridge, taking up its bivouac at the commencement of the descent, looking towards Coimbra. But near to the

summit, about a hundred yards lower down the slope, were assembled a considerable number of the French wounded, who although removed from the immediate scene of action, had not yet been transported to the rear. The bright day we had enjoyed closed with a night of extreme cold, rendering the situation of these men much to be commiserated; wounded laid on the heath, without any description of covering, their complaints were loud and incessant, accompanied by entreaties to remove them from the rigour of that bleak mist that now shrouded the sierra, attended by a piercing wind.[35]

1. Sir Andrew Leith-Hay.

2. Colonel Colquhoun Grant.

(Scottish Cultural Press)

3. General Sir John Moore by James Northcote.   (*Scottish National Portrait Gallery*)

4. Sir James Leith by Benjamin Burrell.   *(Scottish National Portrait Gallery)*

5. General Sir David Baird by Sir David Wilkie.   *(Scottish National Portrait Gallery)*

6. Major the Hon Edward Charles Cocks by George Englehart.
(James Hervey-Bathurst, Eastnor Castle, and the Courtauld Institute of Art)

7. Sir James McGregor, Wellington's Surgeon-General during the Peninsular War.
(*A. Adams, FRCS, Honorary Librarian of the Medical and Chirugical Society of Aberdeen*)

8. General De Alava by George Dawe. *(Victoria and Albert Museum)*

9. General Castaños.
   *(Army Medical
   Services Museum,
   Aldershot)*

10. The Marquis de
    La Romaña.
    *(Army Medical
    Services Museum,
    Aldershot)*

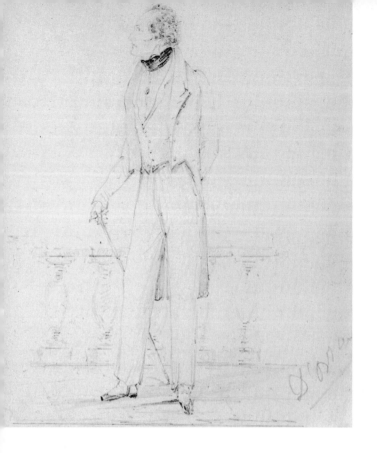

11. A drawing of
Count d'Orsay.
*(Victoria and
Albert Museum)*

12. Napoleon
Bonaparte by
Baron François
Gérard.
*(Victoria and
Albert Museum)*

13. Marshal Soult by
G. P. A. Healy.
*(Victoria and
Albert Museum)*

14. Thomas Graham, Lord Lynedoch,
after Sir George Hayter.
(National Portrait Gallery)

15. A bust of Sir William Napier by G. G,
Adams.
(National Portrait Gallery)

16. Rowland Hill; a
drawing by George
Richmond.
*(National Portrait
Gallery)*

17. The Duke of
Wellington by
Robert Home.
*(National Portrait
Gallery)*

18. Leith Hall.

(National Trust for Scotland)

19. The storming of San Sebastian, 31 August 1813.

20. The Holy Roman Emperor Charles V, who was also Charles I of Spain. Painting by Titian. *(Prado Museum, Madrid)*

21. King Philip III
of Spain.

22. King Philip IV of
Spain.
*(both by Velasquez;
both from Prado
Museum, Madrid)*

23. *The Judgement of Paris* by Sir Peter Paul Rubens.　　　*(Prado Museum, Madrid)*

24. *Judith and Holofernes* by Tintoretto.　　　*(Prado Museum, Madrid)*

PART 3

13

PURSUIT AND RETREAT

September – October 1810.

On the morning of 28 September 1810 word was received that the 6th and 8th Corps of the French army were outflanking the British army. They were heading towards the main highway, linking Lisbon to Oporto, by Boialva and Avelas de Caminho. Charles Cocks was sent out to find if this was true, but in darkness he lost his way and did not reach Boialva in time. However, as dawn broke on the next day, he found out that the head of the enemy's column was actually marching by Boialva.

The enemy continued to advance, and about twelve or thirteen squadrons and 14,000 infantry had descended the mountain when the approach of the enemy's column obliged me to quit the spot where I was reconnoitring. The greater part halted near Boialva while six or eight squadrons, with some infantry, advanced to Avelas de Caminho . . . . the road was so bad that the whole of the French cavalry led their horses down the hill

In the evening I was sent with a patrol to gain intelligence on our left. I found a number of fires at a distance of two leagues, but, hearing a drum in a wood close to me, did not think it prudent to advance; it was clear the enemy had brought infantry to his outposts, which indicates his intention to advance. I rejoined the cavalry at midnight.

1 October. Half an hour after daybreak the enemy attacked our piquets. General Anson's brigade had been imprudently left in a wood from which the only road by which we could

115

retreat was narrow and bad and the enemy came on in force and rather pressed us. Captain Krauchenberg of the Hussars, who was on duty, was wounded so I took command of the rearguard. Eight hussars were nearly cut off but we charged and saved them and although three or four of the enemy were sabred we were ultimately driven back and lost a hussar, besides several being wounded.

Our cavalry formed in the large plain by Coimbra. The enemy's cavalry was checked by our guns but after an interval his infantry advanced on our right by the high road to Coimbra. It became necessary to retreat by the ford in our rear and we experienced the mortification of showing the enemy our line of cavalry without awaiting his attack. Perhaps this would have been imprudent from the beginning because the ground was not very favourable . . . but then we should not have formed line; we should not have shown our teeth unless we meant to bite.[1]

The French army entered Coimbra to find a deserted city. The people, having barred their houses against them, had fled, mostly to hide in the hills. Marshal Masséna established his hospital in the Convent of Santa Clara on the left bank of the Mondego, but left the town poorly garrisoned as events were shortly to prove.

On 5 October Charles became involved in what he called 'a very sharp skirmish'. Napier describes this action as taking place near Leiria, which had just become the headquarters of the army, but Charles, in a letter to his brother, says specifically that it happened 'near Coimbra, at the passage of the Mondego'. According to Napier's account, 'the road was crossed at right angles by a succession of parallel ravines, and Captain Somers Cocks, taking advantage of one, charged the head of the enemy, and checked him until General Anson's brigade of cavalry, and Captain Bull's troop of artillery, arrived to his support.'

The French then attacked the centre of the British line while attempting to outflank it on either side. The accuracy of the British gunners, however, forced them from the ravines on to open ground where, charged by Anson's cavalry, many of them were taken prisoner or killed.

Charles Cocks, writing to his brother admits that

I was more sharply engaged than I have been any time this year; a ball struck my mare but the blanket saved her. We charged the enemy with a few of our rearguard, in the river, and nearly took the colonel of the French dragoons. I hope we shall come across that regiment again. They refused quarter to one of our hussars and we mean to repay them.[2]

Two days after this it was the turn of the French to be surprised when Colonel Trant, a military agent, now commanding a combined force composed largely of Portuguese, sent his cavalry at full gallop through the streets of Coimbra with orders to cross the bridge over the Mondego to isolate the enemy from the town. The daring plan succeeded and Trant's infantry then entered the town. The astonished French put up little resistance and five thousand prisoners were taken, among them a company of the marines of the Imperial Guards.[3]

Andrew Leith-Hay describes how the Portuguese people were fleeing for safety from the French, the roads to Lisbon being crowded with vehicles loaded with possessions of all description. Even churchmen had left their charges, so great was their fear of the French.

> During the process of depopulation which the country at this period underwent, the friars of the great convent of Batalha deserted their residence and when General Leith, with the officers of his staff, arrived, one solitary inhabitant was discovered in charge of the building, and the relics of former ages contained within its splendid walls.

Batalha, founded in 1386 to commemorate the victory of Aljubarotta by the first John, King of Portugal, stood in a valley surrounded by low wooded hills. Andrew describes the old building, rising from amidst a grove of orange trees, as 'very grand and impressive'.

> The long galleries and spacious cloisters of the convent were now seen under peculiar circumstances; the deep obscurity, the deserted aspect of the building, imparted a melancholy feeling.
> The silence that prevailed added to the gloom and solitude of the scene. It was only interrupted by the distant sound of

voices, which at intervals struck the ear, as the British officers, from curiosity, explored the recesses of the building.

The interior of the chapel proved to be very beautiful. Of particular interest was an open coffin, containing the embalmed remains of John II, King of Portugal. The body had survived the centuries so well that his face yielded to the pressure of the hand; the teeth and nails were still perfect and the skin and flesh, which had disappeared from the head and other parts of the face, still looked fresh on the cheeks. Likewise the shroud and robes, in which the body had been buried, had hardly decayed with time, The king appeared to have died quite recently instead of over four hundred years before.

Other interesting relics, including the swords and the helmets of the First and Second John, and the original charter of the monastery, were produced by the one and only brother who was brave enough to stay in the echoing, deserted convent. Because of the danger of these things of such historical importance being either lost or destroyed, General Leith then took them to the San Domingo convent in Lisbon, where many of the fugitive brethren of Batalha had taken refuge.

On 6 October General Leith's corps marched to Quinta de Torres, on the 7th to Ribaldeira. Soon after leaving the first place, in the thick fog of an early morning, they saw macabre figures riding like ghosts from the murk. Only the snorting of horses and men's voices proved them to be alive. They turned out to be a contingent of the Brunswick Oels Regiment, which, on its way to join the British army, had bivouacked on the line of march, a short distance before the town.

The long black clothing of the men – their shakos, bearing in front the emblems of mortality – the waving horse-hair that streamed in the wind, were increased in magnitude and effect by the misty curtain that at times admitted to view these un-usually gaunt figures.[4]

14

THE LINES
OF TORRES VEDRAS

On 14 October Andrew Leith-Hay, in a village called Enexara dos Cavalleros, woke up to a morning of cloudless skies. Seizing the chance of a good day to discover the whereabouts of the enemy he rode to the advanced posts accompanied by Lord George Grenville. Having left their horses concealed in a ravine, they climbed up to where a breastwork had been thrown up to protect a post occupied by the 71st Regiment [a Scottish Regiment.][5] This was only about a hundred and fifty yards away from what Andrew describes as 'a French work, constructed of casks, doors, and planks, brought from Sobral'.

> The French soldiers were observed looking from behind the casks, but not a shot was fired by either party. Our attention was soon after attracted to the road leading from Alenquer into the town of Sobral. A crowd of officers on horseback, detachments of cavalry, dragoons with led horses, and all the cortège of a general-in-chief, appeared upon it. The drums beat; the troops in rear of the village got under arms; still no movement was perceptible in the post to which we were immediately opposed. It was, however, evident that a reconnaissance of some importance was contemplated; nor did it appear probable the troops would be permitted long to continue in their present inactive state. Marshal Masséna, the Duc d'Elchingen [Ney], and General Junot ascended a height a short distance to the north of the town, where they dismounted near a windmill and became seated, apparently reconnoitring the position

opposite. Soon after their arrival a rocket was fired from the cask redoubt, succeeded by the unmasking of some light guns, which were instantaneously discharged against the breastwork of the 71st.

We had previously been kneeling, looking over the embankment, which was struck near its crest by the shot fired. The British detachment continued protected until after the first musketry discharge of the enemy, on receiving which the men started up making a deadly return to the comparatively harmless volley. The French infantry, after this preamble, rushed forward with their usual impetuosity, reaching the embankment unchecked, when the 71st, with Colonel Reynell at their head, springing over the work, not only bayoneted the enemy back to his entrenchment, but drove him from thence into the town . . . .

At this period, some gunboats, manned by the navy, were sent up the Tagus, under the command of Lieutenant Frederick Berkeley. [Fourteen gunboats constantly patrolled the river.] Stationed opposite to Alhandra, firing in all directions whenever an enemy appeared, they harassed and annoyed the parties sent either to reconnoiter or to occupy the villages on the right bank of the river. An accidental shot from one of them killed General St Croix in the act of descending into a road apparently protected from the effects of the cannonade, but where he was nearly cut in two by a recochèt [sic] ball. On many occasions distinguished for his bravery and address, he was much regretted by the French army.

Andrew gives details of the positions of the divisions of the French and allied armies. He concludes by describing the famous plan of defence, devised by Lord Wellington and constructed by Colonel Fletcher and Colonel Jones, the British engineer officers in Portugal, known as the Lines of Torres Vedras. Begun a year earlier, in the autumn of 1809, they were designed for the dual purpose of holding off the enemy and providing cover should embarkation prove necessary as had happened six months earlier at Corunna.[6]

Wellington, with his keen eye for topographical detail, realized that the stretch of land between the Tagus and the Atlantic, to the north of Lisbon, could be defended to protect the city from an advancing force, A low ridge of hills, through which the four main roads ran to the capital, provided a natural barrier to the town. Andrew describes how

> The left of this chain rested on the Atlantic, at the mouth of the Rio Zizandra, which holds its course parallel to, and a short distance in front of, the position between Torres Vedras and the sea. From Torres Vedras, for seven miles in the rear of the valley of Runa, and extending towards Monte Agraca, was the weakest part of this line. There the exertions of the British engineers were unceasingly directed in aid of the natural defences, and to render the country in all respects as impracticable as possible for an invading army.
>
> On the sierra of Monte Agraca, in rear of Sobral, was constructed a redoubt of great magnitude, armed with twenty-five pieces of artillery and prepared for the garrison of a thousand men. The mountain was escarped for nearly two miles, rendering its crest an impenetrable curtain, presenting a natural wall from fifteen to eighteen feet in altitude, not reducible by human assault.
>
> This formidable work, from its commanding and centrical situation, was the constant daily resort of Lord Wellington. [A paved road led to the top.] There he came every morning, and continued until it was ascertained that no hostile movement had taken place, and until light permitted a reconnaissance of the enemy's troops encamped opposite.

From the redoubt on Monte Agraca the line continued, crossing the valleys of Arruda and Calhandriz, until it reached the Tagus at Alhandra. Stretching for twenty-five miles, the sixty-nine defence posts, built on strategic sites along its length, contained three hundred and nineteen guns manned by upwards of 18,000 men.

In addition to this formidable man-made barrier, the engineers had diverted the course of rivers and, by flooding valleys, had turned much of the low-lying country into swamps. Trenches, flanked by guns trained in all directions, had been dug to conceal infantrymen placed to fire at an advancing enemy. Abattis (felled trees with the branches pointing outward so as to repel an attack) of the most formidable description had been dragged up to close the entrance to ravines, or to block roads, made even more inaccessible by being interspersed with yawning gaps. Roads running from the front of the

121

lines had also been made impassable and bridges had been mined, ready to be destroyed by explosion.

The telegraph system, invented by the ingenious but unreliable Captain Sir Home Popham of the Royal Navy, which had radically altered the speed at which messages could be transmitted from one point to another, was now proving to be invaluable.

Telegraphs rapidly communicated information from one extremity of the line to the other. [Messages sent by semaphore along the line of signal stations took only seven minutes to travel twenty-nine miles.[7]] These signal stations were in charge of seamen from the fleet in the Tagus, under the command of Lieutenant Leith of the *Barfleur*. To complete the barriers, palisades, platforms, and planked bridges, leading into the works, fifty thousand trees were placed at the disposal of the engineer department, during the three months ending on 7 October 1810.

The cannon in the works were supplied by the Portuguese Government. Cars drawn by oxen transported twelve-pounders where wheels had never previously rolled. Above 3,000 officers and artillerymen of the country assisted in arming the redoubts, and were variously employed in the lines. At one period, exclusive of the British engineers, artificers, or infantry soldiers, seven thousand peasantry worked as labourers in the completion of an undertaking only to have been accomplished under the most favourable circumstances . . . and above all an intelligence and firmness in command, that could at the same time extract the greatest benefits from these combinations, and urge exertion where it appeared to relax.[8]

Thus did Wellington entrench his army against the onslaught of the French Emperor who had sworn to drive him into the sea.[9]

15

COLQUHOUN GRANT – THE 'LIFTER' OF CATTLE

Marshal Masséna, viewing the lines of Torres Vedras, realized that Wellington had outwitted him. He did not know, however, that the British soldiers, while secure in their position, were also tightening their belts. Storms had delayed the transports which were bringing in supplies. Wellington had 80,000 men to provide for and, in addition to this, the area between the lines and Lisbon was crammed with refugees. Supplies were diminishing rapidly. There was great anxiety all round. It was at this point that Captain Colquhoun Grant first came to the notice of Wellington and many others beside.

Colquhoun Grant, like Andrew Leith-Hay, hailed from the northeast coast of Scotland. Although only twenty-nine, he had served in the army for fourteen years. During this time he had travelled extensively, in the Netherlands, the West Indies, and most recently in Madeira.

Although not noticeably conspicuous, his manner being reserved, he was already renowned for his command of languages for which he had a remarkable flair. Born on a farm near Forres in 1780, he lacked the useful advantages of family status and wealth. The eighth son in a family of ten – which included only two girls – he could, nonetheless, claim ancient Scottish descent. Sent off from home at the age of twelve to a military school near London, he had reputedly learnt French from none other than the French Revolutionary Jean Paul Marat, at that time a refugee in England.

On leaving school at the age of fifteen, his mother had petitioned a relation, old General Grant of Ballindalloch, to get him commissioned as an ensign in the 11th Regiment of Foot. Taken prisoner near Ostend, he had spent a year in a French prison. Frustrating as this had proved to be, he had put his time to good use, learning to speak French fluently and finding out from his jailers how their military system worked.

Once liberated, he had spent the next six years in the West Indies, mercifully escaping the many illnesses for which these islands were called 'the white man's grave'. Subsequently he had been sent to the island of Madeira, surrendered to the British on the orders of Prince John of Portugal, now exiled in Brazil. There he had not only learnt Spanish, but become fluent in Portuguese

Colquhoun Grant was a Highlander whose ancestors had survived by 'lifting' cattle for many hundreds of years. Knowing that he could now save the situation, he conceived a plan. Word of it was taken to Wellington who summoned him to headquarters forthwith. Colquhoun's idea, on the face of it, seemed absolutely absurd. He proposed to slip through the enemy lines and ride up into the mountains, which they could all see in the distance, where he knew that cattle could be found. Essentially he must have money for the Portuguese would not accept letters of credit. They had to have cash in the hand.

Wellington would probably have thought the suggestion ridiculous had anyone proposed it other than Colquhoun. Its sheer audacity amazed him, yet the quiet-spoken Scotsman inspired such confidence that the Commander-in-Chief, with his flair for assessing character, recognized an exceptional man. He had in fact good reasons for doing so. Colquhoun had earned a reputation for bravery and, of even more vital importance, was known to be fluent in both Spanish and Portuguese.

Colquhoun rode out in darkness from the lines of Torres Vedras. He carried a sword and pistols in holsters. Also strapped to his saddle were the moneybags heavy with coin. A thick dark cloak covered the distinctive uniform of the 11th Regiment of Foot, a red coat and white pantaloons. He made his way by moonlight through gaps in the French outposts. His horse's hooves may have been muffled, but thanks to it being a cold night he guessed that he would not be seen. Sure enough the French sentries, terrified of the Portuguese peasants, were huddled round fires or cowering within any shelter they could find. Colquhoun, having successfully avoided them, then rode fast for the hills.

He found himself a billet in a village from where he sent local people to spread the word that he wanted both corn and cattle for which he would pay on demand. He did not have long to wait. The French stole everything and the farmers were only too ready to grab the chance of getting real money for beasts fattened on the summer grass. Soon the sound of lowing cattle, herded by shouting farmers and barking dogs, announced the arrival of the herds.

Colquhoun rode ahead to locate the positions of the French outposts. He then had the herdsmen drive the cattle, in small numbers to escape detection, over carefully planned routes. Nearing the lines of Torres Vedras they used passwords, previously arranged with the sentries of the British army, to prevent them opening fire by mistake. Somehow, by these means, the cattle were driven, mostly at night, over tracks little known to the French, into the British camp.

This, under the very difficult circumstances, was the most extraordinary feat. Wellington, who almost certainly must have wondered if he would ever see his money again, now knew for certain that Colquhoun had unusual qualities which he could put to good use. Having seconded him from his regiment, he made him an intelligence officer while employing him on his staff.[10]

The British and allied soldiers had retired behind the lines of Torres Vedras on 10 October 1810. Almost a month then passed before Masséna began to withdraw his army north towards Santarem. The British units, following in their tracks, found plenty of evidence of the state of near starvation to which their enemies had been reduced. Corpses of men and animals were lying beside the roads. Most gruesome were the burnt-out buildings, set alight by the French in their desperate search for hidden grain. The bodies of Portuguese peasants, many of whom had been tortured, lay beside those of the French.

Masséna took up a strong position at Santarem, where Wellington refused to fight him on the grounds that he might lose too many men. Having once made this decision, he then had to wait for Masséna to make a further withdrawal. During that winter of 1810 the mortality among the French soldiers was appalling. An estimated twenty thousand are said to have died of starvation and exposure. Nonetheless, it was not until the beginning of March 1811 that Masséna did finally start to pull back towards Spain.

Despite this, the French army still held predominance over the British and their allies, the Spanish and Portuguese. On 10 March the Spanish Brigadier-General Imaz surrendered the town of Badajoz to Marshal Soult. This meant that the frontier fortresses of Ciudad Rodrigo, Badajoz and Almeida, were now all in French hands. Wellington, well entrenched in Portugal, was effectually barred from Spain.

His employment of Colquhoun Grant is best described by Grant's brother-in-law, Doctor James McGrigor, himself shortly to come out from England to be Surgeon General on Wellington's staff. By the time of McGrigor's arrival in Portugal, in January 1812, Colquhoun had become chief of the intelligence department of the army and his exploits were already far-famed.

McGrigor, another Scotsman, was not given to eulogizing even his closest friends. Nonetheless he gives a pen-portrait of Colqhoun which betrays his genuine admiration for this greatly talented men.

> Equal to most officers of that army in military capacity, he far surpassed everyone I ever met for the milder virtues of the Christian soldier, and for all that was amiable, kind, and benevolent in disposition. Colonel Grant was devotedly fond of his profession . . . . Along the whole of the Spanish frontier [he] was known, and wherever known, he was held in the greatest esteem.
>
> Of this I cannot here omit to mention a very singular instance. Employed in the same service viz. that of the intelligence department, there was, in singular coincidence, another officer of the same name, and rank, What the peculiar features of his character might have been, I cannot take it upon me to describe, but he and Colonel Colquhoun Grant were at the opposite poles in the estimation of the Spaniards; the latter they designated the *Granto Bueno*, the former the *Granto Malo*.

McGrigor then goes on to describe Colquhoun's talent as a linguist. He was as fluent as any native in the different dialects of at least three of the provinces in Spain. He knew all their customs, their songs and their music, and even their particular prejudices. He was widely read in Spanish literature and joined in their local dances with such perfection of footwork that they might have been Highland reels.

Sensing his interest in all that was Spanish, the local people loved him in return. Among his many friends were the peasant farmers, and the priests who, while welcoming him into their houses, were always forthcoming with news. They were simple people but trust-worthy to the point where, even at the times of greatest danger, when, on his secret missions, he was surrounded by outposts of the French army, he knew that he would never be betrayed.

> In collecting accurate information of the French army, as he informed me, and as was well known to Lord Wellington, he was occasionally in their rear, where he obtained exact intelligence, not only of their numbers and equipment, but of the descriptions of their troops, the manner in which their cavalry was mounted, the number and equipment of their guns, the state of their supplies etc.
>
> He was acquainted not only with the character of each separate officer, but with that of each commandant of battalion. The hairbreadth escapes which he had were numerous; sleeping frequently in the fields under any shelter, or, as it frequently happened, without any, and in all kinds of weather . . . . He said he always felt secure when in Spain, where one padre or peasant passed him on to another . . . however, he did not feel so secure in Portugal.[11]

Colquhoun got most of his information from Spanish and Portuguese patriots. He kept up a close association with the leaders of the guerrillas of whom the French lived in mortal fear. By this time the guerrillas, who had started as bands of peasants marauding the French lines, had become highly organized. Each leader had his own territory rather like the criminal gang lords of the present day. Juan Martin Diaz, a swarthy peasant, was the most famous. Merino, who held sway near Burgos, was in fact a priest; Don Julian Sanchez, with whom Colquhoun kept in close contact, was the former soldier who was also so well known to Charles Cocks.

Colquhoun, thanks to his popularity with the local people, had an enormous advantage over his counterparts in the French army who were universally detested in both Portugal and Spain. 'The French,' wrote Wellington, in May 1811, 'have no knowledge of the position or circumstance in which the other is placed, whereas I have a knowledge of all that passes on both sides.'

Much of this knowledge came from the guerrillas, who killed the French dispatch riders without mercy, before purloining their horses, clothes and weapons and anything else of use. The orders and messages they carried, frequently written in code, were often hidden in secret compartments in the saddles. The guerrillas sold them to the British for ready cash. In January 1810 Wellington had sent £500 to Brigadier General Cox, then Governor of the fortress of Almeida, 'to be expended in procuring intelligence, of which sum I request you to keep a separate account'.[12]

Not all of them were mercenary, however, as the testimony of a contemporary shows. General Sir William Napier, a friend of Colquhoun's and one of his greatest admirers, wrote in his *History of the Peninsular War* that:

> As conductor of the secret intelligence Grant, beside his own personal exploits, displayed a surprising skill. I have seen letters from Alcaldes [mayors] and other agents of his from all parts of Spain, conveying intelligence rare and useful; and it is worth noticing that he told me his best and indeed only sure spies were men who acted from patriotism and would not accept money. His talent in discovering them was not the least of his merits.

16

THE BATTLE OF FUENTES DE ONORO *and* CHARLES AND JOSEPHA

Charles Cocks had to return to England at the beginning of March, summoned home by his father, because his grandfather, the Reverend Doctor Nash, had died and left him a considerable estate. He sailed with the greatest reluctance. His father then tried to make him stay in England to resume his political career – he was Member of Parliament for Reigate – but to no avail. Charles's heart was set on the army and he was very ambitious. Determined to be promoted to major, he used his time in London to search the army lists for vacancies. He could not get back to Portugal quickly enough and returned at the end of April 1811, just in time to take part in the extremely hard-fought battle of Fuentes de Onoro.

Wellington had moved his headquarters to Freineda in the north of Portugal. It was here that news reached him that Masséna was advancing from Ciudad Rodrigo. He decided to confront him, although his army, compared to that of the French, was numerically small. Once again, however, he chose his position with the forethought for which he was already famed.

The village of Fuentes de Onoro, a rambling collection of low houses, stands on the east-facing slope of a low ridge on the Spanish side of the frontier with Portugal. Behind it, as at Busaco, Wellington placed his men out of sight.

On the east side of the village a river called the Dos Casas runs from north to south. In those days, although easy to cross near the village, it formed a natural barrier where it ran through a steep ravine to the north. Wellington visualized that this would protect his left flank. South of the village, however, the open country, where cavalry could charge unimpeded, was a hazard with which he had to contend.

Masséna, who after the débâcle of Busaco, had this time made careful reconnaissance, was soon aware that the right flank of the British army was its most vulnerable point. With his cavalry outnumbering the British, he was in such a strong position that he felt assured of victory.

Charles rejoined his regiment, the 16th Light Dragoons, on 1 May. In a letter to his cousin Thomas he wrote that on that very day:

The enemy made some demonstrations in front of Ciudad Rodrigo and established himself in front of the Agueda. His army . . . consisted of about 30,000 infantry and 1,000 or 1,500 cavalry of the old army and 2 or 3,000 infantry and 3,000 cavalry brought up by Bessières, Duc d'Istria. The latter were all fresh troops from France and brought for the purpose of defeating the British cavalry, very well mounted on Spanish horses. Our force was 32,000 infantry, 1,000 British cavalry, 150 Portuguese and 48 guns. The cavalry horses were very weak as it had been impossible to bring forward stores and they had lived chiefly on grass.

Skirmishing began near the village on 3 May and continued throughout the following day. Then, early in the morning of the 5th 17,000 French infantry and 4,000 cavalry attacked the British right flank. The 7th Division, which held it, supported by Julian Sanchez with his army of guerrillas, was forced to withdraw. Charles wrote that:

[The French] drove in the Spanish cavalry and charged after them. The Spaniards made for the 14th and Royals, with the French pell mell behind them. The Royals and the 14th, or rather part of them, saw only the Spaniards who were in front and almost suffered themselves to be charged by the French. The consequence was a complete confusion: Spaniards, French and British, all mixed, man to man hacking and sabring, At this moment the remains of the two squadrons under Myers got in the rear of the French and charged them.

130

The reserve of the French cavalry behaved in the most dastardly manner; had they come on with the same spirit as the advance the moment would have been critical . . . . Fortunately we kept our people quite steady and ready for whatever might happen. This was not easy as many of the French were in our rear and charging like drunken madmen through our intervals and our men wanted to cut them down, there being no order to give quarter. The result of all this was that the advance of the French cavalry was annihilated.

The retreat of the 7th Division, when the infantry held off the advancing French by forming squares, was one of the most outstanding episodes of the whole Peninsular campaign. The cavalry, outnumbered as they were, fought with magnificence, charging again and again, until their exhausted horses could hardly move. Charles wrote:

The French were said to be drunk but their officers led them bravely. They had never seen British cavalry and rode forward till they were cut down. Many individuals got up to the formed squadrons of our reserve and were there killed . . . . The remains of Myers's squadron got round their flank, charged their rear, and the four squadrons were cut to pieces except for their commanding officer, Colonel la Motte, and forty men, who were taken. The enemy showed no dash.

Colonel Sir William Napier (as he then was) thought otherwise, writing that 'there was not during the war a more dangerous hour for England' and Wellington himself confessed that it was 'a near run thing'.[12]

The French continued to attack until about four o'clock in the afternoon when Masséna, his men discouraged and exhausted by the stubborn British defence, finally ordered a withdrawal. Wellington, unsure of his intentions, then ordered Charles Cocks to shadow the French army and to report to him on their movements:

10 May. This morning I got intelligence that the enemy was retreating on Ciudad Rodrigo. I went to rising ground about two miles from that place and saw him moving in two columns by Carpio and Gallegos.

131

By two o'clock the greater part of the army had crossed the bridge over the river . . . . Most of the columns which crossed the bridge continued their route to Salamanca, whilst the remainder encamped behind Ciudad Rodrigo. At night there was a great light behind the town.

11 May. Don Julian passed the Agueda and followed in observation of them.

12 May. By the information I received today I learnt that the whole of the French army has marched for Salamanca except for 3,000 infantry in Ciudad Rodrigo and 800 cavalry encamped under the walls.

13 May. The French cavalry has moved from Ciudad Rodrigo with about 1,000 infantry, leaving 2,000 in garrison under Renant, mostly foreigners. Don Julian is halfway to Salamanca.

Charles then adds a note of great interest referring to the escape of the French garrison of Almeida for which General Erskine was blamed. Wellington was furious but magnanimously forgave him on the grounds that no man is infallible even when in high command.

This night [10 May] by some unfortunate mistake or neglect the garrison of Almeida under Brennier made their escape, crossing the Agueda at Barba del Puerco . . . previous to their departure they blew up some of the work but all the mines did not take effect; however, the fortifications are still materially injured. Had Lord Wellington's orders been executed not a man would have escaped.

Charles then became Deputy Assistant Quartermaster General to Sir Stapleton Cotton. He persuaded the General to allow him to become a volunteer officer with artillery in the trenches to allow him to extend his knowledge of how a town could be besieged. Wellington was determined to capture Badajoz, before Marshal Marmont, now Duke of Ragusa, who had succeeded Masséna, could bring in reinforcements.

The siege began at the end of May 1811, but because the British did not have enough heavy cannons nothing much was achieved. A breach was made in the garrison wall but the French garrison immediately filled it with *chevaux de frise*, a fence of upturned swords.

On 6 June Charles wrote to his mother, from the 'Trenches before

Badajoz' to tell her, with great jubilation, that he had just been gazetted a major. Four days later, however, he noted in his diary, that, to his enormous annoyance, Wellington had decided to raise the siege.

It was soon common knowledge, however, that the Commander-in-Chief had acted with his usual circumspection. Informed by his intelligence officers that Marshal Marmont had moved south to join up with Marshal Soult who was heading north-west from Andalusia, Wellington realized that, with the combined French force of 60,000 men against him, it would have been madness to continue to lay siege to Badajoz. Playing for safety, he moved his army beyond the Guadiana, where he once more took up a strong defensive position along the Portuguese frontier with Spain. Charles noted in his diary:

17 June. This day the investment of Badajoz was broken up and the whole of the army crossed the Guadiana. The movements commenced at 2 am when the moon rose.

Charles's correspondence at this time is mainly concerned with purchasing the majority which he so greatly desired. Writing to his cousin Thomas he said that he would 'mortgage or sell two thirds of his estate and live on bread and water' rather than lose the promotion on which he had set his mind.

On 30 June he wrote to his sister Margaret telling her that since the siege of Badajoz his regiment had been quietly encamped between Elvas and Campo Major and had hardly seen any action. He feared that such inactivity was bad for the soldiers' health. 'We are too idle here, I think the army will get sickly, but we are perfectly supplied and Anson's Brigade, the 16th and 1st Hussars, are in good condition. My horses are well . . .'

Charles was not left idle for long. On 1 July Wellington sent him off to explore the country round Albuquerque, La Roca and Villa del Rey to reconnoitre enemy movements in the area north of the Guadiana. He set off with about twenty men with whom he rode round the small Spanish villages while gaining information on the movements of the French army from the local people.

You get pretty good information through the peasants, only Spanish peasants sometimes give their guesses for facts and have always some absurd story about artillery.

133

Fit young man as he was, he was scarcely out of the saddle for two weeks and owned up to being exhausted. On 8 July he described how he had slept in a little garden near the town.

> I was heartily tired. For the last forty hours I have been almost constantly on my horse and have not closed my eyes above one hour.

By this time, however, he could report to Wellington that Marshal Marmont was withdrawing further into Spain. Confident of safety, Charles himself rode boldly into Mérida, the old city on the Guadiana, some twenty miles east of Badajoz, where the relics of Roman occupation had so intrigued Andrew Leith-Hay. Two years had now passed since, in 1809, Charles had last seen the town. Nonetheless, he was remembered and welcomed back with acclaim.

> I saw them all and they were delighted to see an old friend, especially as their new friends Messers Marmont & Co had only left them a few hours.

Charles, having carried out his special mission in the district round Albuquerque in Spain, returned to his Regiment, which was now stationed at Monforte, some thirty miles to the south-west in Portugal. Hardly, however, had the 16th Light Dragoons been settled there than, together with most of the rest of the army, they were transported over the Tagus. Wellington ordered this move in an effort to save his men. The valleys of the south of Portugal, infested with mosquitoes, were notoriously unhealthy. More soldiers were dying from diseases such as typhus than were being killed in action. Wellington, although unaware of the real sources of contagion, concurred with the current belief that illness resulted from bad air.

Determined therefore to prevent the sickness which was sapping the strength of his army, to the point where at least one-third of his men were unfit for active service, he moved back to the area around Castelo Branco, north of the Tagus, which was thought to be healthier ground.

Charles was not pleased:

> We have changed for the worst in point of cantonments, *he complained to his sister*, but they say this country is healthier.

I do not think, however, place makes much difference, an idle army is generally less healthy than one on the move if the latter is well fed.

Wellington, however, was already making plans for a forthcoming siege, the capture of the key fortress of Ciudad Rodrigo in Spain being uppermost in his mind. Accordingly, at the end of September, he moved his whole army (with the exception of Hill's division in the south) north-east into the valley of the Agueda.

As in almost any other campaign throughout the centuries, the British soldiers, men and officers alike, soon got heir feet under the tables in the local houses. Charles, on a previous occasion, had written, 'We have balls every night.' Now he was busy organizing dances in the farmhouse barns.

> I borrow two or three clarinets, an octave and a tambourin from some neighbouring infantry regiment and set the girls dancing all night.

Foremost amongst the dancers was Josepha Siego, daughter of a local Portuguese farmer who had leased his large farmhouse to the army. A man of some substance, he also owned property in the nearby town of Fuentes de Onoro on the Spanish side of the frontier with Portugal.

Josepha, aged just sixteen, with 'eyes black as jet, lips ripe as peaches, and teeth white as ivory and limbs for the Venus de Medici', as Charles described her to Thomas, must have been a lovely girl. Aware of her charms, she made use of them to attract every officer in sight. She first set her cap at Augustus Schaumann, commissary to the 1st Hussars, who wrote of her in glowing terms. According to him she was 'an extraordinarily cultivated girl, full of feeling and tender, steadfast, enterprising and passionate, severe but also a faithful character . . . gorgeous, her gait that of a queen, overflowing with vitality and good health [and] wonderfully built.'

In addition to her physical attractions, Josepha had a mind of her own. Her father had betrothed her to none other than Don Julian Sanchez, commander of the guerrilla band. The families seem to have been well acquainted, for Josepha had several brothers who fought in Don Julian's force. Nonetheless she hated *Son brutos* (that ugly man) as she called him and made her plans to escape.

She threw herself at Charles and went to live with him. Charles, however, at that moment, did not want to marry her. A wife would be a hindrance to his career. Frustrated, and probably trying to make him jealous, she returned to Augustus Schaumann but had no better luck with him as far as matrimony was concerned.

Charles, for his part was then distraught.

> Josepha has left me *runs the entry in his diary of 14 September,* though she loved me it was deluded for the love . . . she would not refuse to go . . . when at a word by the man with whom she has lived for one year, poor girl. She regarded me as her husband. Her departure has aroused feelings I thought my emotions had forgot, I could kill myself and everyone I meet. Heaven bless her, poor girl, wherever she is. She deserved a better fate than will now be her lot . . . my bed the scene of so much pleasure, I left on the ground. When she went I shed the first little tears that have wet my eyes since I parted with – I thought I had forgotten this weakness . . . . I shall not easily forget her.

Events, however, took an unexpected turn as her father went to Wellington and told him what had occurred. Wellington sent for Augustus Schaumann who was forced to send her home, but her family then apparently disowned her and back she came to Charles. Their reunion, although rapturous, was marred by the fact that she was now very ill. Suffering from a fever, perhaps picked up from the soldiers, she was delirious with a high temperature, Writing to Thomas he said:

> Josepha, my beautiful girl, is lying a few yards from me, scarcely knowing me from fever. I have been separated once from her but ultimately succeeded in securing her. This letter has been often interrupted by her crying for water and I can even now scarcely proceed while I listen to her heavy and painful respiration.

Then Josepha vanishes. The letter, dated 2 October 1811, is the last mention of her name. Did she die or did she recover? The mystery remains unsolved. All that is known is that Don Julian did not marry her. She may have retired to a convent, a refuge for single women, where her name would not be revealed. In the event that she lived, this would seem the most likely explanation, for Charles, in his state of infatuation, would surely have recorded her death. Their love was doomed to tragedy. He might have taken more care for his own safety had she become his wife.[13]

17

RIVALS IN LOVE AND WAR: THE SIEGE OF CIUDAD RODRIGO

As Josepha vanished, two of the men who had vied for her possession became embroiled in a new military campaign.[14]

Charles, on her departure, obtained a fortnight's leave. He rode north to Oporto which he found extremely dull. All the best families had left for the watering places and would not return until the winter.

> There were no balls, no concerts, no frolics. I dined sometimes with the English merchants who gave me a quantity of hot port, very good perhaps but as strong as the port in England. I was not used to it and it got into my head, which I did not at all approve of.

Riding back to join his squadron he passed by a place called Villa de Ponte, writing that it was

> Four leagues from Lamego where our heavy artillery is, but whether to form the siege of Ciudad Rodrigo in the spring or to throw into Almeida appears doubtful.

Wellington, however, had no doubts. The coming year of 1812 was going to be one of victory when he would drive the French from Portugal, if not into their own country, at least far back into Spain.

His first target was Ciudad Rodrigo, the fortress which a gallant Spanish garrison had finally been forced to surrender in July 1810. Wellington, as Charles reported, had in fact laid siege to the town in June 1811, but, lacking heavy artillery, had been forced to withdraw in the following September.

This time, with a siege train assembled, he was determined to succeed.

The town of Ciudad Rodrigo was first invested by Julian Sanchez, the swarthy leader of the Spanish guerrillas to whom Josepha had been betrothed by her father. With his band he actually captured the Swiss Governor, General Reynaud, who had gone out of the town to look over his herd of cows. On the strength of this success, Wellington, knowing that the enemy would expect a spring campaign, decided to act at once. On 4 January he moved his main force over the frontier into Spain where he established a position round Ciudad Rodrigo within the space of three days.

This achieved, he then publicly organized a 'field sports day', supposedly to entertain the men. In reality it was to make a reconnaissance of the two low ridges, called the Greater and Lower Tesons, just to the north of the town. The Spanish garrison, totally unsuspecting, cheered wildly from the ramparts as 'the mad English' tore up and down on their horses round the low hills.

The Greater Teson, being actually higher than the ramparts of the fortress, was a natural strategic position. The French for this reason had built what they called the Reynaud Redoubt on it, named after the Governor.

Charles had received permission to watch the siege, in which, being a cavalryman, he did not actually take part. He described it in a letter to his father, telling him that

> Ciudad Rodrigo is situated on a rising ground close to the River Agueda which runs at the foot of the hill on which the rampart is situated on the south side. It is surrounded by a strong Moorish wall about twenty feet, forming an irregular oblong without bastions and very few towers. The ditch is seven feet deep . . . . Three hundred yards from the western front is the convent of Santa Cruz and four hundred and fifty yards from the northern front, opposite the Salamanca gate, is the convent of San Francisco . . . . Opposite the north-west angle is a hill called the Tero de San Francisco. This hill commands the town.

139

On the Tero de San Francisco the enemy had erected a sod redoubt. Charles continues;

> Thirty-five 24-pounders and three 18-pounders, all beautiful iron guns belonging to our battering train, had been brought up. We had two companies of British artillery, some German artillery and the Portuguese regiment of artillery number 4. The artillery was under the direction of Major Dickson of the Portuguese service; Colonel Fletcher [architect of the lines of Torres Vedras] was Chief Engineer.
>
> The advantage of approaching within seven or eight hundred yards under cover was so great as to decide Lord Wellington on attacking the place from the Tero de San Francisco. This was the side in which the French attacked it and it was to be expected that the new wall, built where they had breached, would not be so strong as the old one. Lord Wellington was said to direct their works. It is a principle of his to avoid the use of mortars. 'The way to take a place,' I heard him say, 'is to make a hole in the wall by which troops can get in and mortars never do this, they are not worth the expenditure of transport they require.' Well, this is very well against such a place as Ciudad Rodrigo, but it would sacrifice men against a more formidable fortress.

On the night of 8 January three hundred men of the Light Division, the details of the Redoubt imprinted on their minds, stormed the defence. To their utter disgust they found that the scaling ladders with which they had been issued, probably made of green wood, were so rotten that they would not support a man's weight. Cursing, but undeterred, they stuck their bayonets in the sod of the rampart and, having levered themselves to the top, jumped down into the fortress. The garrison of sixty men, bewildered in the darkness and unprepared, were overcome in twenty minutes. It was a brilliant, a daring and a successful coup.

Two days later the convent of Santa Cruz was taken by the British and that of San Francisco on the next. On the 16th a thick fog descended which was an advantage to the sappers. Charles recorded:

> They got on well with the second parallel, 400 yards from the place, and commenced a fourth battery in front of the first

parallel, 500 yards from the place to the left of our other batteries, and much nearer the convent of San Francisco.

The north ramparts had by now been breached in two places which, as the French struggled to rebuild them, the British pounded with shells. Then, as an intelligence officer brought news that Marmont was concentrating his army only fifty miles away Wellington decided to attack. On 19 January he issued the order 'Ciudad Rodrigo must be stormed tonight'.

Charles, describing what happened, wrote:

> Lord Wellington determined to storm at 7pm, that is an hour after dark. The main breach was allotted to the 3rd Division which was on duty, the left breach to the Light Division, the next for duty. Four attacks were made.

General MacKinnon's brigade, the 88th and 45th, were to storm by the main breach. They were to move at seven, had ladders 24 feet long and were preceded by their flank companies as a storming party.

The 500 men of the 'Forlorn Hope', as the storming party was called, belonged to the 88th, the Connaught Rangers. General Picton, sending them into action shouted 'Rangers of Connaught. It is not my intention to expend any powder this evening. We'll do this business with a cauld iron. The men cheered him to the skies.[15]

The main breach, nearly thirty feet wide, was fronted by a steep slope of crumbling earth. The 5th Regiment, together with the 88th and the 45th, took the breach, but then found themselves faced by traverses, cunningly placed by the French to separate what they knew to be the weakest part of the wall from the rest of the rampart. The column, brought to a halt, was thus left without protection from the enemy's guns.

Fortunately they were saved from annihilation by the Light Division which had succeeded in storming the smaller breach by the Salamanca gate. The enemy in the houses opposite the main breach, then finding themselves surrounded, ceased firing and all resistance ended. The battle seemed won. Then tragedy occurred.

> At this moment the commandant of [French] artillery sprung in motion a skit communicating with a magazine in the rampart.

141

The huge explosion shattered the walls, murdering men on both sides. General MacKinnon was killed and General Craufurd died afterwards of wounds. The survivors of the 3rd Division, however, pursued their way into the town. Lieutenant Gurwood, who had led the 'Forlorn Hope' of the Light Brigade, was left unconscious, having been blown off his feet. Coming to his senses in the ditch, he then walked, or rather staggered, into the Castle where he found the Governor at dinner with his staff. Gurwood demanded his surrender whereupon the Governor gave him his sword. The young lieutenant gave it to Wellington, but the Commander-in-Chief was so impressed with his courage that he gave it back to him next day.[16]

18

COLQUHOUN GRANT

'INTELLIGENCE RARE AND USEFUL'

Colquhoun Grant went with Julian Sanchez on many a secret and daring expedition. Colquhoun's brother-in-law, Doctor James McGrigor, vouches for the fact that he knew every detail of the personnel and equipment of the French army even down to the extent of how their cavalry was mounted and the state of their supplies.

Much of his information came from the local Spanish people who, thanks to his fluency in the dialects of at least three provinces, and his knowledge and love of their customs, music and literature, now regarded him as one of their own. Foremost amongst his friends was Leon, a Spanish peasant of more than usual intelligence and perspicacity, whose loathing of the French invaders provided an incentive, not only to attach himself to the British, but to serve the intelligence officer whom he held in such high regard.

Leon's knowledge of the country was invaluable. He knew every track and, more importantly, all the 'safe houses' where they would find food and rest. Frequently, however ,they slept, wrapped in their cloaks, under trees, behind walls or in dry ditches. Their horses, often left saddled, but with loosened girths, were tethered a few paces nearby.

In January 1812, while the greater part of Wellington's army was engaged in taking Ciudad Rodrigo, Colquhoun and Leon were riding through the country between Celorico in Portugal and

Segovia, eighty miles east of Salamanca in Spain. Wellington had instructed him to stay in the country between the two rivers, the Agueda and the Tormes, to discover what Marmont was about.

Most people in the British army expected that the French would try to recapture Ciudad Rodrigo. On 5 March Wellington wrote to General Victor Alten, commander of the 1st German Hussars, giving him detailed orders on the action he should take if the French moved against the town or crossed the River Agueda below it. As a final instruction he wrote: 'I beg you to desire Major Grant of the 11th Regiment who is, I believe, at Tamames, and Lieutenant Blankley of the 23rd Regiment, who is at Bejar, to give you constant intelligence of the enemy's movements.'

Wellington's next objective was Badajoz, another of the fortresses on the Spanish side of the frontier with Portugal. The town, on the Guadiana, lies some hundred and twenty-five miles, as the crow flies, almost directly south of Ciudad Rodrigo. In mid-March two bridges were laid across the river, one about a mile and half above, and the other about ten miles below Badajoz. The siege began on 16 March.

Marmont by this time had heard that, as he had anticipated, Wellington was moving south towards the Guadiana. There was little he could do, however, as Napoleon had instructed him specifically to concentrate his strength round Salamanca, the Spanish city some fifty miles to the north-east of Ciudad Rodrigo. The dispatch riders carrying these orders had been captured by Sanchez's guerrillas, so Colquhoun had first-hand information of where Marmont was to be found. Wellington, above all things, desperately needed to know whether Marmont would obey his Emperor's orders and remain in Salamanca or act on his own initiative and move south to join up with Soult near Badajoz. Colqhuoun was instructed to find out everything he could about what Marmont intended to do.

So on a dark wet night he and Leon rode away from Tamames to Salamanca, a distance of some thirty miles. Avoiding the city, they crossed the River Tormes just as it was getting light and found shelter in the house of a man whom they knew they could trust. Emerging when it seemed safe, the two of them rode round the whole area within which the French were encamped. Colquhoun made a note of everything that could possibly be of interest to Wellington. Details such as the number of transport wagons, supplies, scaling ladders and troop movements never missed his eye. He reported all that he found in brief messages both to General Alten and to Wellington himself.

Always he and Leon were alert, glancing over their shoulders to see if they were followed, for both knew only too well what would happen should they fall into French hands. Somehow, however, despite their precautions, Colquhoun was recognized, either by a Frenchman or a traitor, his exploits now being so well known. Fortunately one of his agents got wind of it and brought him a copy of a General Order, issued by General de Lamartinière, Marmont's Chief of Staff, saying that 'the notorious Grant' had been seen in the area and ordering his arrest.

It soon became common knowledge that the whole area around Salamanca was under constant supervision by both sentries and mounted patrols. Colquhoun, aware of this and knowing himself to be trapped, turned for advice to the Spanish friends who were sheltering him as to how he could possibly escape. Even if he could avoid detection, slipping past enemies unseen in darkness as he had done many times before, he still had to get across the Tormes. This at first sight seemed impossible. The river was so deep near the town that it could only be crossed by a bridge.

The Spaniards, however, told him of a ford at a place called Huerta, about six miles east of the town. Here he might be able to get across the river in semi-darkness. Nonetheless, they pointed out that one man would have a better chance than two. Therefore it would be advisable for Leon, an ordinary Spanish citizen whose face was not well known, to follow him across the bridge in daylight.

Colquhoun rode to Huerta in near darkness, his horse picking its way along the road. Reaching the village, he hid in the house of some local people whom he trusted and who told him exactly what he should do. Once across the river he would see a wood ahead of him. If he followed a path, which ran through the trees, he would, on his good horse, stand a fair chance of escaping all pursuit.

Waiting within the little village house, through what seemed like an interminable night, Colquhoun heard hoofbeats as sentries rode up and down the river bank. Then, at first light, the men of a French infantry battalion quartered in the village paraded at their alarm posts.

At this moment the Spaniards moved. Taking advantage of the noise made by shouting orders and stamping feet, they led Colquhoun on his horse to a place by the ford where, fortuitously, the low gable of a house hid him from the soldiers' view. The two mounted sentries, riding back and forth from the ford patrolling the river bank, presented a greater threat. But the Spaniards had planned every move.

Waiting until the riders were well apart, some of them climbed onto a low wall and began shaking their large cloaks as if airing them after using them as blankets during the night. They flapped away with great gusto until, as the sentries reached the furthest point of their beat, they signalled to Colquhoun to move. Instantly, putting his spurs to his horse, he dashed into the ford.

The sentries, alarmed by the splashing of hooves, swung round in their saddles. Levelling their own guns, they yelled at the foot soldiers to fire. Bullets hissed into the water but, within minutes, Colquhoun was out of range. The sentries charged into the river, pursuing him to the far bank, but, as the wood loomed dark in front of them, the thought of an ambush by the guerrillas, made them turn back.

Later, in full daylight, Leon, insignificant amongst a crowd of people, jostled his way across the bridge over the Tormes where no one looked at him twice. By nightfall he had reached Tamames where to his joy he found Colquhoun.

Colquhoun knew that it was vitally important for Wellington to have at least some idea of Marmont's intentions. While scouting round near Salamanca he had heard rumours that a major campaign was planned. This seemed the more likely when, from a place of concealment, he had seen scaling ladders being built.

Marmont crossed the Tormes with a force of about 25,000 men on 29 March. Colquhoun and Leon, told by their friends in Tamames that the French army was on the move, hid themselves among trees on a hill to the south-west of the village. Below them they clearly saw the junction from which one road ran due west, to Ciudad Rodrigo, while another headed for Perales and the valley of the Tagus in the south. Hidden as he was, Colquhoun had a 'bird's-eye view' of the whole force tramping by. So clear was his vision that he was able not only to identify the regiments but actually to count the number of men, horses and guns that passed below. Most importantly, he realized that the scaling ladders, which he had expected to see, were not there. He was even more surprised when, firstly the van, and then the whole army, took the road west to Ciudad Rodrigo, rather than as he had surmised, the one to the south.

As soon as the last of the French soldiers were out of sight Colquhoun rejoined Leon who was waiting with the horses somewhere well concealed from view. They rode back to Tamames over the ruts in the road made by the gun-carriages. On the outskirts of the village they parted, Leon going ahead to make certain that all the French had gone. It proved a wise precaution. Some indeed had stayed behind, but all were now sheltering within buildings thanks to the drenching rain.

Colquhoun, himself, soaked to the skin despite the protection of his cloak, rode to within sight of a building where, to his amazement, he saw the scaling ladders propped against the walls. Now he had the proof that he needed. He could report to Wellington that Marmont, obeying his Emperor's orders, was not heading for Badajoz. Instead, in an attempt to lure Wellington away from besieging that fortress, which Napoleon rightly guessed to be his next objective, he was heading towards Ciudad Rodrigo, where, upon arrival, he plainly did not intend to attempt to re-capture the town by scaling the defending walls.[17]

19

BADAJOZ

Ciudad Rodrigo had hardly fallen before Wellington decided to lay siege to Badajoz. He did so secure in the knowledge that the two frontier fortresses, Ciudad Rodrigo and Almeida, although still in need of repair, were now strong enough to protect Portugal from invasion by the French.[18] Also the battering train of the French army had been captured at the former place.

The army began to move towards the Tagus on 6 March. Great precautions were taken to conceal its direction from the enemy but nonetheless the governor of Badajoz, General Phillipon, sent an urgent message to Marshal Soult telling him that he was preparing for an imminent siege.

To make matters more difficult for the allied army the weather was cold and wet. The engineers struggled to make trenches in drenching rain, while the misery of the foot soldiers, forced to march and sleep on damp ground, steadily increased. On 22 March the Guadiana rose to such a height that the bridges, erected with such difficulty, were destroyed. The pontoon bridge was washed away, while the strength of the current tore the bridge of boats apart.

This was a serious setback, supplies of both food and ammunition being unobtainable across the river. However, Wellington's luck held good. The level of the water fell and preparations for the siege went ahead.

On 24 March the 5th Division [commanded by General Leith] having captured the outlying fort of San Christobal, trained its batteries on the other outlying defences of Fort Picurina, the Lunette of San Roque, and the bastions of La Trinidad, San Pedro and Santa Maria. These were the outlying defences, cited to protect the citadel, that Andrew Leith-Hay in the twilight of that peaceful evening of

September 1809 had so lyrically described. Then they had been manned by Spanish allies. Now, in such different weather, garrisoned by the French, they menaced the approach of the allied army, intent on recapturing the important guardian of the frontier of south-west Spain.

The same night, in darkness, General Kempt, commanding in the trenches, took Fort Picurina by storm. From there no less than thirty-eight guns were trained on the walls of the fortressed town. Three breaches were made. They were not large enough to assure a successful assault, but Wellington, told that Soult with a large force was approaching from the south and hearing, probably from Colquhoun Grant, that Marmont was advancing from the north, had to press home his attack.

Andrew Leith-Hay, an eye-witness, described what then occurred.

> On the 5th April the 5th Division bivouac'd in the rear of the Sierra del Viento. On the following morning [Easter Sunday] four divisions of the allied army were destined to mount the walls of Badajoz, and triumphantly accomplish a service, only to have been achieved by the best soldiers and the bravest men.

For various reasons, however, one being that the storming ladders were not complete, the attack was postponed until ten o'clock at night. The batteries, as pre-arranged, ceased firing at half past seven so that the French garrison had time to repair the breaches with impedimenta of every kind, surmounted by the vicious *chevaux de frise* of sword blades like shark's teeth waiting to rip a man apart.

The Light and 4th Divisions, attacking the citadel from the south, were virtually cut to pieces.

> Passive, immovable, unshrinking, and determined, the brave officers and soldiers of the 4th and Light Divisions continued for a length of time, under these annihilating circumstances, occasionally in small numbers mounting the breach, until they grappled with the sword blades, in the act of endeavouring to remove which, the bravest men were either bayoneted, killed by the musketry fire, or rolled back into the ditch upon their less adventurous but gallant comrades.[19]

149

During this time General Picton, with the 3rd Division, was struggling to gain possession of the castle at the north-east end of the town. For over an hour they had been trying to force an entrance over the walls.

> The ladders were placed and ascended, but death met the successive officers or soldiers that reached the parapet. At length, by the personal exertions of General Picton, with the leading officers of his division, and the constant succession of fresh assailants that undauntedly ascended, an entrance was forced from the summit of one ladder, and lodgement being at last effected, the troops rushed forward in support. Resistance became less determined, and the 3rd Division remained in possession of the castle.

In just over an hour, after forty failed assaults, over two thousand men were lying dead or wounded in the ditch before the walls. Wellington, appalled by the slaughter, as witnesses recalled, was about to call off the attack when a messenger galloped up with the never forgotten words 'My Lord, the castle is your own.'[20]

But the battle was far from over, as Andrew vividly recalls.

> An officer conducting the party with the scaling ladders from the engineers park to the bivouac of the 5th Division, lost his way. General Leith, in consequence, had the mortification of being delayed until past eleven o'clock, before he could move to carry the escalade of the bastion of San Vincente into execution.

At last, as the ladders appeared, General Leith, having been instructed to take San Vincente with one brigade and to support the attack with other regiments of his division, ordered General Walker, with the 4th, 30th, and 44th, to mount the wall.

The troops, seen by the French garrison, came under heavy fire before they could even force the barrier gate. But nothing could stop General Walker and the battalions under his orders until they reached the towering wall. Above them they saw marksmen waiting to shoot them as they scrambled singly up ladders at least thirty feet high.

Some of the ladders were thrown back into the ditch. Others, made of green wood, split apart, while some proved to be too short. Yet somehow, by near super-human efforts, the men of the 5th Division, in the face of heavy gunfire, scaled that apparently impenetrable wall. Many fell in the struggle but others reached the ramparts where General Walker formed up his brigade. He then, as previously planned, moved forward into the town to come in from behind to attack the enemy's troops defending the breaches.

Meanwhile other regiments of the 5th Division climbed up and over the wall. General Leith, himself narrowly missed being precipitated into the ditch by the fall of a soldier, shot dead on the upper part of the ladder he was mounting. Reaching the top in safety, he at once dispatched a message to Lord Wellington that the 5th Division was in the town.

> His bugles sounded the advance in all directions, distracting the enemy's attention, and inducing him to believe he was to be assailed from all quarters . . . . The 5th Division drove everything before it, and having opened the communication with the bastions of La Trinidad and Santa Maria, the [survivors of] the 4th and Light Divisions, which had been withdrawn, again advanced and marched into the town by the breaches.

Andrew Leith-Hay, perhaps in deference to the military commanders, most of whom were alive at the time of his publication in 1831, makes no mention of how, after capturing the city, the British troops went wild, causing dreadful devastation. Neither does he describe how Wellington, when handed the list of casualties on the day following the battle, actually broke down and wept. It was left to his Surgeon General, Doctor James McGrigor, to record that the 'Iron Duke' had a softer side to his character.[21]

20

CONSTRUCTION AND DESTRUCTION

It was at Villafranca, on 8 April that Marshal the Duke of Dalmatia [Soult] received information of Badajoz being in possession of the allies. The object of his march being thus frustrated, he put his army in retreat on the following day and returned to Seville.

Lord Wellington, having directed the necessary repairs to the works of Badajoz, and ordered Sir Richard Fletcher to see them completed, marched his army to the north, with the exception of Sir Rowland Hill's corps, left to manoeuvre on the Guadiana, and to observe the motions of Comte d'Erlon, who continued in Estremadura with his division of the army of the South.

The allied headquarters were established at Fuenteguinaldo on 25 April 1812. From there Wellington sent Colonel Sturgeon of the staff corps to Badajoz and Elvas to superintend a very ingenious repair to the gap of the bridge at Alcantara (on the Tagus near its confluence with its tributary the Alagon) which had been blown apart with gunpowder by the French.

The arch destroyed was of so extensive a span, and the parapet of the bridge so great a height from the bed of the river, that no repair by using timber was practicable; the gap to be passed over being ninety [feet] wide, and the height of the bridge one hundred and eighty from the bed of the river. Colonel Sturgeon selected the pontoon house, in the arsenal at Elvas, as the place

152

for forming the net of ropes destined to afford a secure passage for troops, artillery and carriages of every description across the chasm.

The work was commenced by placing two beams on supporters four foot high and ninety feet asunder. These were secured to the side and end walls of the building by braces and tackles, to prevent their approximating by the straining of the ropes. Eighteen cables were then stretched round them, extending from end to end. Eight pieces of timber, six inches square at equal distances, were placed upon the ropes, with notches, one foot asunder, cut on their surface to secure them. These notches were seared with hot irons to prevent the ropes from chafing. The cables were then lashed to the beams, they were netted together by rope yarn, and chains of sleepers were bolted and laid on the network and secured to the two beams originally placed at the extremities of the work. Planks were cut and prepared for being laid across, bored at the end so as to receive a line destined to secure them to the sleepers and to each other.

This effective but extremely portable bridge was, on being completed, packed up for removal. The great net beams and transverse bearers were rolled up like a web of canvas and placed on one of the pontoon carriages, which conveyed them to Alcantara. The next point was to prepare the edge of the fractured part of the bridge and to cut channels in the masonry for the reception of the purchases.

When on the spot four strong ropes were stretched from side to side as conductors for passing the cable bridge across. The beam on the south side having been previously sunk into the masonry, the whole was then stretched by windlasses erected on the opposite pier, by which means it was so tightly drawn as to prevent any sinking even when heavy weights were passed over, or the vibration which might render it insecure and dangerous.

The bridge, simple and ingenious in its construction, for the first time in Europe established the fact that, by cables drawn to their utmost tension, without any support whatever, the whole equipments of an army could be transported, without difficulty or danger, over a great river, and very extensive chasm, while, on the approach of an enemy, the apparatus

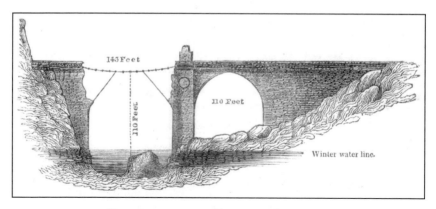

BRIDGE OVER THE TAGUS AT ALMARAZ

could be withdrawn and transported to safety without the slightest inconvenience.

I cannot close the description of what has ever appeared to me a very eminent application of scientific knowledge without noticing the person to whose varied intelligence and superior qualities more competent authorities have borne testimony. Colonel Sturgeon possessed extensive and scientific information, sound judgement, unwearied assiduity and undaunted courage.

Wellington, his own bridge now secure, determined to make it impossible for the French Marshals Soult and Marmont to cross the river by destroying the bridge at Almaraz. To this purpose he sent Sir Rowland Hill, with heavy cannon from Elvas, via Trujillo to the banks of the Tagus.

Almaraz, on the great route from Madrid to Badajoz, was the focal point where the French armies, to the north and south of the Tagus, could cross the river. Most essentially reinforcements from Andalusia or Spanish Estremadura, if unable to cross here, would be forced to take a great detour at the cost of much valuable time. The French, in view of its importance, had built a temporary bridge of pontoons, guarded by what Andrew describes as a *tête-de-pont*, and two formidable redoubts, armed with eighteen pieces of cannon, against attack by the regular Spanish troops and guerrillas. Fort Napoleon, manned by a garrison of four hundred and fifty men, stood on the right bank and Fort Ragusa, with a defending force of four hundred on the left.

Sir Rowland Hill, with great promptitude and judgement, reduced these works, without sustaining a very severe loss. Having ascertained that the pass of Miravete, by which alone artillery could be transported, was not to be forced without considerable difficulty and delay, he resolved to leave his guns on the mountain, and adopting a path only practicable for infantry, to carry the *tête-de-pont* and Fort Napoleon by escalade.

This was immediately accomplished by General Howard's brigade. The 50th, under Colonel Stewart, one of the most distinguished regimental officers in the army, accompanied by a wing of the 71st Regiment, placed ladders and carried the fort. They then rushed with the fugitive garrison, *pêle-mêle* into the *tête-de-pont*, not giving the enemy a moment to rally or to organize any systematic defence. The French infantry crowded towards the bridge, hoping to receive shelter and protection from their companions in Fort Ragusa.

Those [of the British] who first succeeded in gaining the right bank cut away the three boats nearest to that end of the bridge, by which means the survivors of the garrisons of Fort Napoleon and the *tête-de-pont* were prevented escaping. Many had been drowned in the bustle and confusion, but two hundred and fifty officers and men were secured. The commander of Fort Ragusa, panic-struck, abandoned the work without an attempt at resistance, and marched his garrison in the direction of Navalmoral, for which dastardly action he was shot at Talavera de la Reyna.[22]

Sir Rowland Hill, who by destroying the bridge had effectively cut off Marmont's army from that of Soult, then returned to Mérida.[23]

21

THE SPY WHO WALKED INTO THE NIGHT

The amazing story of one of Colquhoun Grant's greatest adventures is related by his brother-in-law, Doctor McGrigor, in his autobiography, many years after the event. McGrigor, who had by then become Sir James, wrote:

> It was during the siege of Badajoz, that, for the last time for a long period, I saw my late much lamented brother-in-law, Colonel Colquhoun Grant, who was chief of the intelligence department of the army, and by no means the least distinguished for military talents of the many distinguished men who served in the Peninsular army. [24]

Marmont, when Colquhoun had last seen him from his perch on the hilltop near Tamames, had been heading for Ciudad Rodrigo as he had rightly assumed. He did not, however, remain there, but instead moved over the frontier and went south-west into Portugal to Sabugal. Colquhoun had been dogging Marmont's army every since he had left Salamanca. He had seen for himself that there was scarcely any forage, the country in that area being very bare. Nearly all stocks of provisions, as well as fodder for horses, had been consumed. Marmont, if he remained there, would see his army starve. Colquhoun, therefore, foresaw the probability that the Marshal would withdraw from Portugal and return to Spain.

Wellington was determined to pursue him, but the knowledge of the Marshal's exact movements were essential to his plans. Colquhoun, when he left Badajoz, rode round to the east, over the

Sierra de Gata, so that he could obtain first-hand news from his Spanish friends as to Marmont's movements when he left Portugal and moved back into Spain. He is known to have reached Castelo Branco from which place, on 15 April, he and Leon rode away just before darkness fell.

From there they headed north-east for about fifteen miles to a village called Idanha Nova, on the River Ponsol, where they stopped for the night in what they believed to be a safe house. Alas they were mistaken. Marmont had offered a reward for the capture of Colquhoun and someone, almost certainly a Portuguese, betrayed them. As Colquhoun told McGrigor, 'it would never have happened in Spain.'

He and Leon went to bed believing they were secure, but the unknown informer had already left the village and was riding or running to the village of Pedrogao, eleven miles to the north, where he knew he would find a French patrol. The officer in command was intelligent. He realized that if he searched the houses in Idanha Nova in darkness Colquhoun would slip out of a back door or a window and vanish into the night as he had done so many times before. Therefore he made his plans most carefully. Leading his party of mounted men and foot soldiers to the edge of Idanha Nova, he threw a cordon round the village. Then in the dawn he advanced with a party to search the houses one by one.

Colquhoun and Leon were woken by the terrified people who had housed them with the news that the French were searching the northern end of the village. Having, as usual, slept fully dressed, they were on their feet within seconds, at the same time buckling on their swords The horses were in the stable below. They led them out, mounted and rode at a gallop down the street. The men of the cordon tried to stop them, but leapt out of their way to avoid being run down. Colquhoun and Leon passed them, jumped a stone wall, then a brook and were away.

But their luck at last had failed. Another French officer was leading a patrol round the village, who, seeing the fugitives, pursued them, followed by his men. Nonetheless they out-rode them, heading for the hills to the west. It seemed they would get away, but a party of French soldiers, who had been foraging, suddenly appeared in front of them.

Colquhoun and Leon, wheeling their horses, made for a clump of oaks, but Colquhoun's scarlet coat and white breeches were all too easily seen. Riding into a copse, they left the horses and ran, scrambling over the walls of small enclosed fields. It was rough ground and waterlogged after heavy rain. Leon either tripped or slid and fell. The French pounced on him, hallooing with delight. Colquhoun implored them for mercy, but the first men to reach him killed Leon with bestial savagery. Colquhoun, held bound and helpless, was forced to watch his friend die.

Speechless with fury and misery, he had no alternative, when his horse, found by his captors, was led up to him, other than to mount it as they demanded. Then, with his reins held by a sergeant and closely surrounded by French troopers, he was escorted up the road to Sabugal, his triumphant captors knowing that when they reached Marmont's headquarters they would be the heroes of the hour.

Colquhoun was led into the castle of Sabugal. He was then taken before General de Lamartinière, the Marshal's Chief of Staff. Lamartinière, known for his bad temper and hatred of the English, shouted and swore at him when he refused to say anything beyond giving his name. Then, as the fat little general became almost apoplectic with rage, a soldier came in with orders from Marshal Marmont to say that he wished to interview Colonel Grant.

Marmont's headquarters were at Salamanca and thither Colquhoun was transferred over a distance, to the north-east, of more than fifty miles. The French Marshal received him most graciously and asked him to dinner. Colqhoun accepted because he thought that he might pick up some hints as to the Marshal's intentions during the course of conversation. Marmont, of course, had issued the invitation for the same reason. They dined in great magnificence, Marmont, one of the few high-ranking officers in Napoleon's army who was of noble birth, travelled with a contingent of cooks and powdered footmen who handed round the dishes of solid silver conveyed to the front in a wagon train.

Despite the pressure put upon him, Colquhoun refused to divulge anything about what the French commander so desperately needed to know. Was Wellington heading north from Badajoz? How many divisions did he have? What had been the casualties during the storming of the town? Colquhoun parried the questions, refusing to answer directly anything that he was asked. Marmont, increasingly frustrated, eventually desisted and ordered that Colquhoun be held under close observation in a room used as a cell.

The next morning he was interviewed again. This time Marmont, rather to Colquhoun's surprise, asked for his parole. Colquhoun agreed unwillingly, knowing that in doing so he was giving his sworn word that he would not attempt to escape.

Once he had done so the Marshal said to him 'It is fortunate for you, sir, that you have that bit of red over your shoulders [the red coat of the British officer]. If you had not, I would have hung you on a gallows twenty foot high.'

Colquhoun answered, 'Marshal, you know I am your prisoner; and recollect I have given you my parole, but hitherto I have not been treated as an officer on parole.'

He had, in fact, good reason to complain. Ever since arriving at Salamanca he had been confined within a room where he was watched night and day. Not only was a sentinel posted at his door but an officer stayed permanently in his room. Colquhoun regarded this as an insult, protesting that it was not within the rules which governed his parole. Nonetheless the French were taking no chances. They had captured the most wanted spy in Europe. They were not going to let him go.

Nevertheless, despite its inconvenience, this form of imprisonment did have its advantages in that he succeeded in creating a genuine friendship with his guards. As a result the officer who happened to be in charge of him usually tactfully departed when he had a visitor from the town.

In fact the whole population of Salamanca and its neighbour-hood admired his deeds, *wrote Doctor McGrigor*, his hairbreadth escapes, and of all things, the annoyance he had been to the French, whom they cordially hated. One of his most frequent visitors was Doctor Curtis*, head of the Irish College at Salamanca, from whom I had particulars which I now detail.

The frequent visits of Doctor Curtis to Colonel Grant gave great offence to Marshal Marmont, who sent for the reverend gentleman. As Doctor Curtis related to me, the Marshal behaved very harshly to him and threatened him much if he did not reveal the secrets he was in possession of, i.e. the secrets of Colonel Grant. He said, 'You frequently visit the English

* Doctor Curtis, the, principal of the Irish College of Salamanca, was by now a near legendary figure, famed not only on account of his scholarship but for his network of intelligence throughout both France and Spain.

159

colonel.' He replied, 'I do.' 'How is it possible, sir, that you do so without having some purpose, some business therein?' He replied, 'The Holy Catholic religion, which you, Marshal, and I, profess, enjoins us to succour the distressed, to visit the sick and the prisoner, and to administer comfort and consolation to them.' The Marshal rejoined, 'He is not of your religion, he is a heretic, a Protestant.' Doctor Curtis replied, 'We are both Christians, we follow the precepts of our Saviour, and he is my countryman.' The Marshal said, 'That is false, he is an Écossais, and you an Irishman, and you shall immediately go to prison unless you reveal me secrets which I am informed the English colonel has confided to you, and which it is material to the interests of the Emperor that I should be put in possession of.

He did not throw Doctor Curtis into prison, but treated him very harshly, expelled him from his college and took possession of his furniture, and a valuable library.

Even at this time, in Salamanca, Colonel Grant continued to convey much valuable information to Lord Wellington, and in this manner. Whenever the weather was favourable, he was permitted to walk out. On such occasions, some of the Spanish peasants who had long been employed by him got near to him and he put into their hands, in small twisted bits of paper, such information as he had collected; and they, as Lord Wellington afterwards informed me, carried these to headquarters, where they always received handsome rewards. I have reason to believe that the priests organized these messengers, trust-worthy, hardy fellows, for this very dangerous vocation.

Doctor McGrigor continues to tell how, 'Having completed the arrangements for the wounded at Elvas and Badajoz, so as to leave them tolerably comfortable in the hospitals, I, according to his orders, followed the Commander-in Chief.'

At my first interview with him [Lord Wellington] he immedi-ately entered upon the subject of Grant's capture and blamed him much for having given his parole; as he told me, that before he had learned his having done so, he had offered a high reward to the guerrilla chiefs for his rescue, if they brought him in alive.

160

Two days afterwards, Lord Wellington again entered into the subject with me, which appeared much to engross him. He lamented his capture extremely and said that the want of the valuable information with which Grant was wont to furnish him was an incalculable loss to him. He added, 'Sir, the loss of a brigade could scarcely have been more felt by me; I am quite in the dark about the movements of the enemy, and as to the reinforcements which they expected.'

The day after this, and after my daily visit, when I reported to him the state of all the hospitals, he desired me to walk out with him. He then said, 'Grant is a very extraordinary fellow, a very remarkable character. What think you of him, at this moment, when a prisoner, sending me information?'

He showed me two twisted bits of paper, which he said a Spanish peasant had brought in that morning, and he added, 'The information coming from Grant, I know it is correct, and is most valuable.' He then read me a courteous reply to a letter which he had written to Marshal Marmont requesting the exchange of Colonel Grant, for whom he had offered any officer of the rank of colonel, of whom he had several as prisoners. In his reply, the Marshal promised it should be done and expatiated on the inexpressible pleasure it would give him to have an opportunity of doing anything that might be agreeable to such an illustrious character as Lord Wellington, of whom, of all others, he was the greatest admirer. I expressed great joy at this, when he said sarcastically, 'Do you believe this? There is not a word of truth in his promise, for here I hold a French despatch from Marmont to the minister of war at Paris, which has been intercepted by Don Julian.'

The despatch of the Marshal to the minister of war expressed great joy at the capture of Colonel Grant, whom the Marshal described as a singular man, who had for so long a period done infinite mischief; to whom the Spanish priests and peasantry were devotedly attached, and who could be deterred by no threats or punishments from communicating with him and supplying him with every information for Lord Wellington. He added that he had sent him off with a strong escort, and recommended him to the strictest surveillance of the minister of the interior and police at Paris.

To the best of my knowledge the despatch bore the same date

as his letter to Lord Wellington, informing him of the pleasure he would have in sending Colonel Grant to his lordship in change for a French colonel.[25]

Marmont was in fact so terrified of losing Grant that he sent him off from Salamanca to Bayonne with an escort of three hundred men and six guns. The journey was a long one of 320 miles, taking in all about three weeks. As they toiled over the road to France Colquhoun made friends with the officers, who greatly admired the courage of this now famous man. Persuaded by them to tell of some of his exploits, the journey, at least for the French, went merrily enough.

At last they reached Bayonne. It was evening and the light was failing as the party entered the town square. Then, with what seems under the circumstances to have been amazing negligence, the officers and soldiers of the escort apparently went off in different directions searching for billets for the night.

The fact that they left Colquhoun alone in the square, even for a few minutes, appears, in retrospect, to be beyond comprehension. These men were guarding a most important prisoner, who Marmont himself had ordered to be strictly watched at all times. In taking their eyes off him even for a few minutes they were risking, as they well knew, not only their reputations and careers but probably their lives as well. Execution was, as the officers at least must have known, the likely outcome of carelessness in allowing their prisoner to escape. The only possible explanation for their laxity is that they trusted the man whom they had got to know so intimately because he had given his parole.

Yet escape he did. There in the town square, which was probably crowded with spectators come to gape at the newly arrived party of soldiery escorting an important captive, Colquhoun simply slipped away. Did one or more of the escort, who are known to have admired him greatly, perhaps by secret arrangement, merely turn a blind eye? Only one thing is certain and that is that we shall never know. Colquhoun, tight-lipped and loyal, would never, under any circumstances, have betrayed the identity of anyone who had helped him even to his dying day.

As it was, on that memorable evening, he made his way into the centre of the town, where he boldly strode into several hotels to ask if any French officer was leaving for Paris. Amazingly, his luck was in, for in one of them he learned that General Souham, the Divisional

162

Commander of the Army of Portugal, who had been granted leave to attend to urgent family business, was departing almost at once. Colquhoun, who had lived so long with danger, now risked everything in the biggest gamble of his life. Asking to speak to the General, he introduced himself as an American officer.

Souham, amazingly, took him at his word. His naivety, in fact, is not quite so extraordinary as it might initially seem when it is remembered that America was about to declare war on Britain, for which reason soldiers of that nationality were now appearing in France. Souham, with problems of his own uppermost on his mind, seems to have ignored the fact, or else to have been totally unaware of the improbability, that this so called Yankee officer was wearing a faded red coat. Americans were reputedly wealthy and this one, true to form, belied his shabby appearance by offering to share the cost of what he presumed must be a private coach. (The French must have allowed him to keep whatever money he had been carrying when he was captured and when he gave his parole.) The General, however, informed him that he was travelling in the public diligence, in which, so he declared, he would be delighted to have the American gentleman's company to lessen the tedium of the journey which lay ahead. It then being quickly discovered that there was an empty seat, the two travellers, French and Scottish, boarded the waiting stage coach.

They rattled off in the gathering darkness, carriage lamps lighting the road ahead, as the strong team of horses carried them away from Bayonne.

Behind they left chaos, as Colquhoun was afterwards to learn. Search parties roamed the country, never guessing for an instant the direction in which their quarry had gone. The fate of the officers of his escort remains unknown. One can only hope that their punishment was mitigated by the fact that the prisoner they escorted had given his parole.[26]

22

AN AMERICAN IN PARIS

Colquhoun is known to have been taken prisoner between the capture of Badajoz, on 6 April 1812 and 17 June, when Wellington entered Salamanca. We have it on the word of Doctor McGrigor that 'It was during the siege of Badajoz that, for the last time for a long period, I saw my brother-in-law, Colonel Colquhoun Grant.'

Likewise we know from the same source that he was kept prisoner in Salamanca when held by the French army. So Wellington must have reached Salamanca only a few weeks after the day when Colquhoun, under a strong guard, had been taken off to Bayonne.

Wellington must have questioned Doctor Curtis minutely, both on the ways and means of his escape and, in particular, to have asked him whether he had any further news. It is problematical, however, whether in such a short space of time the doctor had received any definite information as to what had actually occurred.

Colquhoun, following his escape from Bayonne, had not, in fact, gone immediately to Paris. Instead, having given a plausible reason for doing so to Marshal Souham, he had left the coach at Orléans.

There he had gone at once into the town to seek out a secret agent with whom Doctor Curtis kept in touch. The Roman Catholic priests had no cause to love the Government of the Republic, which, having nationalized their land, had reduced their status to that of civil servants. The great majority of the clerics, while remaining loyal to the French monarchy, were hostile to the new government over which Napoleon held sway.

The friend of Doctor Curtis in Orléans, his name unknown, had advised Colquhoun to go to Paris where he had told him that a Mr McPherson, a fellow Scot, would find him a safe house.

McPherson himself had known much danger during an eventful

life. As a Jacobite, he had fled from Scotland after the defeat of Prince Charles Edward in 1746. Once established in Paris, he had become a jeweller and was held in high repute. Much involved with his fellow émigrés from Scotland, he had frequented the Scots College in Paris. This institution, founded originally for the education of the sons of Scottish Catholics, had, since the failure of the Risings in Scotland of 1715 and 1745, become a haven for Scottish refugees. The College itself, however, had been seized by the French Revolutionaries in 1793.

Shortly after this McPherson had been thrown into a dungeon by Robespierre and had only escaped the guillotine by the latter's death. He was probably related to Abbé Paul MacPherson who rescued the Stewart papers and the archives of the Scots College at the height of the Terror in 1794. This would also explain the old jeweller's association with Doctor Curtis, for many books from the now closed institution in Paris were taken to the Irish College in Salamanca, of which Doctor Curtis was the principal.

Suffice it to say that the jeweller found Colquhoun not only lodgings but an American passport and enough money to live in the style of the American officer whose identity he had assumed. Presumably he also gave him a uniform which such a man might wear. Paris was now so full of soldiers that a young man in civilian clothes would have been much more conspicuous than his counterpart in military dress. McGrigor vouches for the following, amazing as it may seem:

While with Mr McPherson, as an American with an American passport, Grant moved freely about Paris, made it a point to be present at all the reviews and, by entering into conversation with various individuals, whom he met out of doors and at Mr McPherson's table, got correct information of the reinforcements sent to all the armies, particularly that of Portugal.

At Mr McPherson's he frequently met a gentleman with whom he contracted some degree of intimacy. These two gentlemen, as acquaintances, became most acceptable to each other and Grant gained much very valuable information from him; and, extraordinary as it may appear, he continued to convey that information to Lord Wellington which came to my knowledge in the following manner:

I do not exactly recollect where the British army was at this time in Spain, but one day, when I was with Lord Wellington on business, a day on which the mail for England was being made up at headquarters, Lord Wellington, addressing me, said, 'Your brother-in-law is certainly one of the most extraordinary men I ever met with; even now when in Paris he contrives to send me information of the greatest moment to our government. I am now sending information of his to ministers of the utmost value about the French armies in every quarter; information which will surprise them, and which they cannot by any possibility get in any other way and, what is more, which I am quite sure is perfectly correct. Go into the next room and desire Fitzroy [Lord Fitzroy Somerset, Wellington's A.D.C.] to show you the information from Grant enclosed in the despatch to Lord Bathurst.'

Tantalizingly, McGrigor does not give a date for this happening, but it seems likely that it occurred in the following winter when the army were in winter quarters in Freineda. The reason for supposing this is that Colqhoun, by this time, would have been well established in Paris, living as an American and using a false name. He is known to have spent about eighteen months in the French capital before, being warned of danger, he had, yet again, to make furtive and hurried escape.

23

SALAMANCA

The capture of Badajoz meant that the allied army now held the two most important fortresses on the frontier between Spain and Portugal. Wellington was in the strongest position that he had been in since his arrival in Spain. Sir Rowland Hill, by destroying the bridge at Almaraz, had made it virtually impossible for the French armies, commanded by Marshals Soult and Marmont, to unite. Nonetheless, the danger that Marmont might try to recapture Ciudad Rodrigo remained,

He knew that Marmont was heading west for Ciudad Rodrigo because Colquhoun Grant, hiding on a hilltop, had seen the French army take the road in that direction on that day of pouring rain. Also, in what must have one of his last messages before being captured by the French, he had sent minute details of the strength of his force and equipment, mentioning in particular the absence of scaling ladders, an indication that, however he meant to take the fortress, it was not by escalading the walls.

Wellington, from this information, had concluded that Marshal Marmont, by marching towards Ciudad Rodrigo, was attempting to lure him away from the siege of Badajoz which at that time was just about to begin. Nonetheless, the possibility that he might attempt to recapture the town could not be discounted and, for this reason, the British army marched up and down the frontier between Spain and Portugal keeping a constant watch.

On 15 April Charles Cocks wrote to his mother telling her how, on 11 April, 'Young Soult', the Marshal's brother, who commanded the French cavalry, had attempted to make a stand between Villa Garcia and Llerena. Fortunately he had underestimated the British strength. Charles wrote:

We had two brigades up and drove him 2 or 3 miles over a plain till he got under the protection of his infantry and guns . . . . I had no personal adventure except that coming in contact with a French hussar we rolled over each other. I was on my legs first and with a coup de sabre invited him to surrender. *Then on a sad note he adds,* But I lost the best dragoon in my old squadron, a man who loved me as if he had been bred up with me. He died of his wounds the next morning.

The frontier patrols continued. On 3 May Charles noted in his diary:

In the last 32 days my horse and I have marched upwards of 500 miles with only two days halt.

His brother James, who was also by that time serving in Portugal, reported to their mother that Charles had become very thin.

While he rode over the rough mountain roads the beauty of the scenery seems to have barely impressed him. He certainly did not describe it, his mind it seems being preoccupied in gaining his much-longed-for promotion. The strength of his ambition reveals itself in his letters. Nothing must stand in his way. As was then common practice, commissions in the army, with rare exceptions, were bought and sold. Men, weapons and horses changed hands in a way that seems not only extraordinary but quite immoral today.

Promotion he believed would be faster in a Scottish Regiment. Therefore he transferred to the Queen's Own Cameron Highlanders, the 79th Highland Regiment.

On 22 May he wrote to his mother from Lisbon where the festivities were once again in full swing.

Dearest Madam,

Here I am in the capital of Portugal diverting myself with sea-bathing, eating strawberries and visiting senhoras and going to balls. In a few days I join the 79th. It is a Highland Regiment and I assure you I make a very respectable figure with the bonnet and tartan. We look forward to something very active this year though we are still in suspense exactly what it will be.

Then in another letter to Thomas, written on the same day, he said:

I am now at Lisbon equipping for the Highlanders, having got leave to join the battalion here, I shall be with them in a week or so . . . . I do not regret leaving the cavalry at this period, no man is fit to rise to command who does not know both arms . . . . I have shaved off my moustaches and most of my beard and turn out a smooth regular infantryman!

In June Wellington moved out of Portugal and headed towards Salamanca in Spain. Charles's Highland Regiment was part of the 1st Division under General Graham and to his fury did not take much part in the ensuing campaign. 'My cursed division not engaged,' he fumed in a letter to Thomas. Nonetheless he recorded in his diary a day-to-day description of events.

Andrew Leith-Hay who was also there, gives a first-hand account:

The 5th Division [General Leith's] marched from its cantonments in Portugal on the 5th of June [1812] halting at Trancoso until the 8th, on which day it arrived at Freixedas and Alverca. From Alverca the division advanced to Castel Mendo, situated on an eminence overhanging the Coa, a river accompanied by one general character of scenery along the whole extent of its course; bold rocky banks invariably confine this rapid, wild, and picturesque stream.

On 10 June they left Castel Mendo and marched to Poza Velha, where they encamped in a beautiful valley, shaded by lofty trees. On the 11th, having passed through Espeja and Carpio, they reached the left bank of the Agueda. Here they were joined by the 4th division, which, together with two brigades of cavalry, formed the centre column of the army. The right consisted of the 1st, 6th and 7th Divisions. The left the 3rd Division, comprising the Portuguese brigades of Generals Pack and Bradford, and one brigade of cavalry. The Light Division, with the German hussars, horse artillery, and detachments of British light cavalry, were on the right bank of the Agueda, near to the convent of La Caridad.

Never, since the start of the campaign in the Peninsula, four years before, had the army been more efficient. Every section of the force was both serviceable and well equipped. The cavalry horses, well fed with corn and grazing on summer grass, had recovered their condition. The weather was beautiful. The soldiers, forgetting the misery of the winter, elated by recent victories, had found new confidence both in their commander and themselves. Morale in Wellington's army had never been so high.

Andrew describes how all remained quiet until the morning of 16 June when he rode forward to join the patrols of the 1st Hussars on the Carneiro road. About six miles from Salamanca, at sight of the advance of the French cavalry, they charged. The French stood firm, exchanging shots with the hussars until, as the main body of the regiment emerged from a wood, they retreated back to Salamanca. Much skirmishing followed until, when the enemy was finally driven to within two miles of Salamanca, Wellington gave orders to desist from farther pursuit.

At first light on the 17th, however, the army was again on the march towards the city. Andrew, riding on ahead to gather information, having passed the allied advance posts, rode to the bridge of Salamanca, where he found some of Don Julian Sanchez's guerrillas and a patrol of the 11th Dragoons. The French, on seeing them, began shooting from forts, hitherto unnoticed, on the right bank of the Tormes.

> Next to the bridge I met Major Brotherton, who had been in the town, where he ascertained the fact of the enemy having retired during the night, leaving garrisons in the forts; that the bridge was not destroyed and that the houses in the immediate neighbourhood of the fortified convents having been set on fire, were then burning, which accounted for the smoke that occasionally enveloped the place.
>
> Returning with this information, I met Lord Wellington who sent me to General Leith with directions that he should halt until further orders. I then followed the commander of the forces and overtook him before he reached the Tormes. The bridge being in possession of the enemy, the only means of getting across to the town was by proceeding up the river and passing across at the nearest practicable spot. In the act of attempting what appeared to be a ford, a discharge of grape from Fort La Merced wounded the horse I rode. A ball entering his back, close to the saddle, he immediately drooped, and appeared in the act of falling, but recovered himself, and was, notwithstanding the injury received, enabled to go on. The river became so deep, that abandoning the attempt to pass, I

170

returned to the left bank, and with the whole of the staff crossed a considerable distance higher up the stream.

Lord Wellington entered Salamanca about ten o'clock in the forenoon: the avenues to it were filled with people clamorous in their expressions of joy; nothing could be more animating than the scene. The day was brilliant, presenting all the luxuriance of the southern climate. Upwards of fifty staff officers accompanied the British general; they were immediately followed by the 14th Dragoons and a brigade of artillery; the streets were crowded to excess; signals of enthusiasm and friendship waved from the balconies. The entrance to the Plaza was similar to a triumph; every window and balcony was filled with persons welcoming the distinguished officers to whom they looked up for liberation and permanent relief.

Lord Wellington dismounted and was immediately surrounded by the municipality, and the higher orders of the inhabitants, all eager to pay him respects and homage. At the same moment the 6th Division of British infantry entered the south-west angle of the square. It is impossible to describe the electric effect produced under these circumstances by the music; as the bands of the regiments burst in full tones on the ear of the people, a shout of enthusiastic feeling burst from the crowd, all ranks seeming perfectly inebriated with exultation.

From this scene so calculated to distract the attention of ordinary men, Lord Wellington retired to make immediate arrangements for reducing the forts. A plan of them having been produced and placed in his hands by the Spaniards, he left the adulating crowd, escaping from the almost overwhelming demonstrations of friendship and respect with which he was greeted; and before the town had recovered from its confusion and its joy, or the 'vivas' had ceased to resound, his system of attack was decided upon, and the necessary orders for its execution issued to the troops.

Andrew then describes how the French had used Salamanca as the depot for the Army of Portugal. Many of the monasteries and colleges, for which the town was so famous, had been damaged in previous attacks. Thirteen of the convents were in ruins and twenty-two buildings of the university had been destroyed.

The French had then converted three of the most substantial of the convents into forts. The largest was San Vincente. Standing directly between the great convent of San Francisco and the river, it rose from the old wall of the town, which, at that particular point, was built high on the summit of a precipice above the Tormes. From San Vincente, in the direction of the bridge over the river, the ground ran down into a valley, on the opposite side of which, at a distance of two hundred and fifty yards from San Vincente, stood the two other convents of Gayetano and La Merced, which had also been turned into forts.

The 6th Division, under General Clinton, was ordered to destroy these defences, which, on being thoroughly investigated, were discovered to be more formidable than had been imagined. The Division did not have guns powerful enough, to knock down such well-built, heavily fortified walls. Nonetheless Wellington ordered the assault to begin and on the night of the 17th ground was broken before San Vincente.

The forts under attack could clearly be seen from the high spire of the cathedral. The convents, which had been loop-holed for musketry, kept up a heavy fire, but a battalion of the German Legion, stationed in the neighbouring buildings, returned it with rifles, which were not only more accurate but of longer range.

The next day (the 19th) two more batteries were brought in which did severe damage to the convents. Part of San Vincente collapsed, but the French pulled out burning material so quickly that the fires, started by explosions, did not spread throughout the building.

There was then a period of stalemate until, on the 20th, it was known that Marshal Marmont, the Duke of Ragusa, was approaching at the head of a considerable force.

Wellington, on hearing this, moved his army, with the exception of the men laying siege to the forts, to the heights of San Cristobal. On the following morning General Leith's Division was also moved to the fine position covering Salamanca. The enemy then appeared in force, bivouacking directly in front of the allies on the plain below.

Early in the morning of the 22nd Marshal Marmont attempted to reconnoitre the right of the allied position but was driven back with the loss of a hundred men. Later in the morning, when he tried to discover the position of the allied left, he was nearly captured. Wellington, spying through his telescope, seeing the chance of taking him prisoner, immediately sent his aide-de-camp, Captain Burgh, to order two squadrons of the 12th Dragoons to mount and set off in pursuit. Andrew Leith-Hay was among them.

> Nothing could be more congenial to the feelings of Colonel Ponsonby than this chase.* The men and horses were lightened of every encumbrance and, being formed without delay, he placed himself at their head, and at a quick pace sallied forth from the village . . . . it was a species of a great tournament, the lists of which were peopled by 50,000 men.

They tore through the huts of the enemy encampment where the men leapt out of their huts and stared in amazement at what they seemed to think was a race taking place within the cannon-shot of either army. The Marshal and his staff, alarmed by the thunder of hoofs, realized their danger just in time. Some voltigeurs who were with them covered the plain on their left. They checked the charge of the dragoons with a 'warm tiraillade', keeping them at bay just long enough for the Marshal to turn tail and spur his horse to the safety of his own lines.

The 12th, their chargers blown, returned to their quarters, as the French infantry, shaking their heads in confusion as to what had actually occurred, made their way back to their huts and all was quiet as before.

The next day the French were on the move and it was realized that Marshal Marmont now intended to station his army to the right of his former position. Wellington then heard that some of the French troops had crossed the Tormes, whereupon he sent Sir Thomas Graham to cross the river at the Santa Marta ford with the 1st and 7th Divisions of infantry to cut them off from the town of Salamanca.

On the day after this [the 24th] Wellington ordered the 6th Division, commanded by Generals Hulse and Bowes, to storm the two smaller forts of Gayetano and La Merced. Andrew had a clear view.

> From the spire of the cathedral I witnessed the scene that ensued . . . . The enemy was on the alert; the moon shone

* Major Frederick Ponsonby had already taken part in the heroic charge, led by Colonel Elley, at Talavera. Now Colonel of the 12th Dragoons, he was in his element once more.

bright, rendering the slightest movement discernible. The moment the British troops debouched, an uninterrupted and vigorous fire burst forth from the artillery of the forts, accompanied by incessant discharges of musketry; the valley presented one continuous blaze of light. General Hulse attacked La Merced. General Bowes succeeded in rearing some ladders against Gayetano, but could not force an entrance. Unfortunately he fell and the column under his orders lost upward of 120 killed and wounded. Of the former was Captain Sir George Colquhoun of the Queen's Regiment.

The attack by General Hulse proved equally unsuccessful, and hopes of gaining immediate possession were consequently abandoned.

However, all was not lost for on the 26th a new supply of ammunition reached the British army. The batteries at once resumed firing, this time with heated shot, and, as the sun set, the roof of San Vincente was seen to have been set alight. All night the old timbers blazed with such intensity that even a torrential downpour failed to douse the flames. At ten o' clock the next morning the whole range of the building was seen to be on fire.

The commandants of the forts of San Vincente and Gayetano now realized that the buildings were too damaged to hold out against the pulverizing force of British guns. White flags of truce appeared as offers of surrender were made. Then, as the French prevaricated, Wellington gave them five minutes, at the end of which, when there was no sign of the imperial flag being lowered, he ordered the batteries to recommence their deadly fire. Under cover of the cannon the troops advanced to the assault, carrying Gayetano by its gorge and San Vincente from the fascine battery at its southernmost front.

The garrisons made such slight resistance that the allies suffered few casualties in the final capture of the forts. The French, however, lost not only thirty-six cannon and a large quantity of stores and ammunition, but no less than eight hundred prisoners, who were captured in the forts.

Salamanca went wild. In the evening the town was illuminated, and rejoicings were heard in every direction. People crowded the streets and music, cheering, dancing and singing disrupted the peace of a quiet and beautiful night.

Early on the 28th the Duke of Ragusa, knowing that the forts had surrendered, left his position before Salamanca, sending one of his columns marching on to Valladolid and another down the Toro road.

When it was ascertained that Marshal Marmont had retired, *wrote Andrew,* a Te Deum was performed in the cathedral, at which Lord Wellington, accompanied by a numerous body of the officers of his army, attended. The scene was grand and impressive, the spacious noble building, crowded to excess, and the ceremony performed with all the pomp and splendour of Catholic worship. The pealing organ never poured its tones over a more brilliant, varied, or chivalrous audience.

All the pomp of a great Episcopal seat was displayed on the occasion. Contrasted with the sombre dresses of the numerous unofficiating clergy, the scarlet uniforms of the British were held in relief by the dark Spanish or Portuguese costume. The Spanish peasant, in all the simplicity and cleanliness of his dress, appeared by the mustached and fierce-looking guerrilla; while the numerous mantillas and waving fans of the Spanish ladies attracted attention to the dark, voluptuous beauties of Castile. It was an enthusiastic and imposing scene; nor was its least impressive effect produced by the quiet, unassuming presence of the great man, who, in the career of his glory, knew that by showing respect to the religious institutions of other countries, he best secured for himself those feelings which are only to be substantially acquired by deference to the customs of a people having an equal right with ourselves to adopt the persuasion or the forms most congenial to their minds and most consistent with their conscientious views.

Of the clergy present on this occasion, one of the most dignified in manner and appearance was Doctor Curtis, whose perfect knowledge of the language and customs of both kingdoms enabled him to become essentially useful in all communications with the civil or ecclesiastical authorities of Salamanca.

In the evening the town was again illuminated and a ball given by the magistracy to Lord Wellington and his officers, at which the sounds of music had not ceased when the allied army marched in pursuit of the enemy.[27]

175

24

THE BATTLE OF
SALAMANCA

Madrid is at our mercy
Charles Cocks to his father, Lord Somers, 6 August 1812.

Wellington's army, having finally captured the town of Salamanca on 27 June, spent the next few weeks in manoevering back and forth against the French,

> We have amused ourselves with plenty of marching lately *wrote Charles to his sister Margaret,* very little fighting but a good deal of chess-playing with the enemy. I expect the next fortnight will bring us to hard blows. The two armies are close to each other today; we get plenty of lemon ice-cream and I received yesterday a strong reinforcement of claret but am still badly off for champagne. Very little game or poultry is stirring. At Medina del Campo we were encamped eight days, we had a ball every evening.

The long-predicted battle took place on 22 July. Wellington, aware that Marmont was trying to cut him off from Portugal, had to make up his mind whether to fight or retire. South of Salamanca two ridges called the Greater and Lesser Arapile ran almost parallel. The French seized the Greater Arapile, a height of about 400 feet, in the early morning and Wellington then took the Lesser Arapile only about a mile away. In mid-morning it appeared that Marmont was about to launch an attack on the nearby village of Los Arapiles. Wellington then ordered two divisions to move to the north of the hamlet and another two divisions to the south.

As this happened, Marmont, believing his chance had come to cut the British off from Portugal, ordered his leading division on the Greater Arapile to push forward to the west. In doing so he made the fatal error of overextending his line. Wellington, watching through his telescope, seeing the gap extend to a mile between the First Division and the next, cried out 'By God. That will do', and set spurs to his horse.

He rode at a mad gallop to a village called Aldea Tejada where he had stationed the Third Division in anticipation of what Marmont might attempt. The leading French division fell into the pre-arranged trap. Marmont, seeing his men slaughtered, realized, to his horror, the enormity of his mistake. Even as he tried to comprehend what was happening he was badly wounded by a shell.

Wellington, in the meanwhile, had galloped back to Los Arapiles to order his 5th Division to attack the main body of the French. The battle was over in forty minutes. The French, totally defeated, broke their ranks and fled.

Beat the enemy yesterday, *wrote Charles on 23 July,* in the action and pursuit took 5,000. Our loss 1,500 killed and wounded. Generals shot out of all proportion. The enemy apparently retiring towards Madrid, Marmont said to have lost an arm. We have taken 12 guns, 2 eagles and a general. We pursued by moonlight.

To his father he was more explicit. Dating his letter 6 August, he wrote:

The 3rd Division turned Marmont's left and in less than two hours 45,000 men were in a state of complete rout. Marmont and ten generals, wildly endeavouring to restore order, were killed or wounded . . . . But for the darkness I believe the battle of Salamanca would have completely dispersed the enemy's army, but night and darkness impeded our pursuit. Not a peasant could be met with for a guide, the enemy fled through woods where we blundered till midnight. However, the battle and its consequences have deprived the enemy of 17,000 men and 25 pieces of artillery, which we have taken or he has

177

buried. He only got off his wounded by dismounting part of his cavalry and loading the carriages of his guns. This broke all Marmont's measures; his army, inferior in number, heart-broken, without stores, many regiments without officers and many individuals without arms, could no longer come near us. He never stopped till he had crossed the Duero. Eight grenadiers supported the unfortunate Marmont, once the favourite aide de camp of Buonaparte and the handsomest man in Paris, in a litter they use in Spain for carrying corpses to interment.

We are, with 40,000 men, in high spirits and tolerably healthy twenty leagues north of Madrid. Hill has 20,000 watching Soult. General Maitland is daily expected to land in some part of Spain with 8,000 British troops and an army of Spaniards disciplined by Whittingham and other British officers. Madrid is at our mercy.

And so it proved to be.[28]

25

THE SIEGE OF BURGOS

Ten days later, on 16 August, Charles told his sister Margaret of how Wellington, created an earl after the capture of Ciudad Rodrigo, made his triumphal entry into the Spanish capital of Madrid.

> The Earl made his entry into this place on the 12th. I think he could not have paid the Prince Regent a more noble compliment than in thus associating his birthday with an event so proud for England. Our arrival produced a joy far beyond description; indeed, anyone accustomed to the cold manners of England can scarcely conceive what on such an occasion a character lively as the Spanish is capable of doing. I was never kissed by so many pretty girls in a day in all my life, or ever expect to be again. If we moved on horseback the animals were pulled one way and we were hauled and caressed the other. On foot it was impossible to make your way, this ebullition of enthusiasm was kept up all day.'[29]

The Peninsular army remained in Madrid for less than three weeks. On 31 August Wellington left the capital to march north with his army of 35,000 men to lay siege to Burgos. He looked forward to this next challenge with quiet confidence. At Salamanca he had defeated 40,000 French soldiers in forty minutes and was justified in believing that Napoleon's power in Spain was on the wane. Events were to prove, however, that, as with the forts at Salamanca, he had underestimated the strength of the French defences at Burgos, which, with insufficient power of gunfire, he was about to attack.

179

Lord Wellington left the capital on the 1st September [Andrew's date] and the headquarters were at Valladolid on the 9th, *wrote Andrew Leith-Hay*. At Palencia, on his route to the north, Lord Wellington was joined by the army of Galicia, commanded by General Castaños; and on the 9th September he entered Burgos . . . .'

The artillery provided for the siege of the castle of Burgos was the same that had been in battery against the forts at Salamanca; and if defective in numbers and force upon the former occasion, it became doubly inefficient when brought against a much more formidable work, ably and skillfully defended.

Everything, including the forces of nature, now seemed to conspire against the allies. The weather was dreadful. Rain, driven on before violent gales, added to the misery of the troops as they struggled to escalade the walls of the fortress under constant and heavy fire.

The city of Burgos, the capital of Old Castile, was a centre of communications. On the approach of the allies the main body of the French army had withdrawn, but a garrison, of about 2,000 men, had been left to hold the strongly fortified castle, standing, as though defiant of attack, on a hill above the cathedral.

The castle itself was surrounded by two lines of defence and above it, on the ridge of San Miguel, the French had built an outwork known as the Hornwork.[30]

Wellington was short of both guns and ammunition to the point where he had to collect and re-use the discarded French cannon-balls. Also, remembering the terrible losses at Badajoz, he was reluctant to risk any more men than was absolutely necessary in an assault on the fortress. Nonetheless, on the night of the 19/20 September, he ordered a detachment of the 1st Division to make an assault on the Hornwork.

Charles Cocks led his men behind the enemy lines. They crept up on the fort in silence, but, in the bright moonlight, they were seen. The French, fighting valiantly, were finally overpowered, but 421 British soldiers died in the capture of this outwork.

Charles noted in his diary on 20 September that 'A lodgement [a small area gained and held in enemy territory] had been formed in the Hornwork.' Guns were then installed in the batteries and approaches to the walls of the fortress improved, until, on 23 September he wrote:

At midnight the town wall was attacked. 200 of the 1st Division, supported by as many men, were to escalade in front while a Regiment of Cacadores, supported by two Portuguese companies of the line, were to force the palisading [a strong fence made of stakes driven into the ground] which joined the left extremity of the wall with the other works. They would thus have cut off the troops defending the wall, as the only retreat of the latter to the lower enclosure was by a gate, near the point where the two Portuguese [brigades] if successful, should have entered. There was cover for both of these parties to have assembled within 50 or 60 yards of the points to be attacked; nevertheless they both failed.[31]

An attempt was then made to destroy part of the city wall with mines. The engineers, working continuously in four-hour shifts, struggled to lay a gallery, a subterranean trench, fifty feet long, which was to pass under the ditch surrounding the wall. On 25 September another gallery, to the right of the first, was begun. The first one had now progressed to a point where, at a distance of forty feet underground, the candles started guttering from lack of oxygen. Work then had to be suspended until the air had purified itself enough so that it was safe to continue.

On 27 September Charles sat down to write what would prove to be his last letter to his sister. Heading it Camp before Burgos, he wrote:

In what a different situation do I write and you read this letter. I am sitting in a very small bad tent . . . . My table is rickety, one leg being too short, and whenever the stone slips away, which I shove under to keep it steady, down rolls the ink. The said table is covered by a blanket instead of green baize, which identical blanket, in the course of half an hour with an addition of a bearskin and a cloak will form my bed, bedstead and bedding. So much for the inside. Outside three mules belonging to my nearest neighbour are occasionally whinnying.

Note. The whinny of mules is between the bray of an ass and the neigh of a horse, more unharmonious than either. A little further some drunken Portuguese have got some music and are singing, playing and huzzaing much to their satisfaction.

181

Further still is heard the continual firing of the siege and if I chance to look out, the chances are I see a shell or two in the air; all round are camp fires.

The most magnificent part of my writing equipage is *my wax candle in a silver candlestick*. You will receive this in a room so closely shut that everything like free air, when it accidentally approaches you, is denominated a 'thorough draught' and voted dangerous, being supposed impregnated with cold, rheumatics, etc. In this close room you will be further warmed by a large coal fire, there will be a dozen tables and *soft* chairs – these I envy you – your bed, instead of being handy and convenient, eighteen inches off, is God knows where, at the other side of the house and when you get to it you must be at the trouble of undressing instead of just lying down ready prepared for breakfast in the morning.

You will probably see by the papers that I was engaged in a rather sharp affair the other day; however, I got well out of it and it has got me a lieut-colonelcy. Whenever I see my name in the gazette for that rank, which I hope you will about the time or soon after receiving this letter, I shall begin to feel settled as my promotion is then secure and cannot be accelerated except by some great piece of good fortune.

As soon as I get command of my regiment, which I expect to do in a few days, I shall be much more comfortable than I have been in this campaign, which I have been obliged to spend in rather stupid society. However, it has turned out most fortunate for me that I have adopted the line that I have. I received a slight wound by a musket ball the day of the storm, but it was so trifling I did not return it. When will Thomas and Agatha be noosed? I was much pleased with *Childe Harold* though I must despise the prejudiced liberality of some of the sentiments.

An odd incident occurred to me; it was represented one night in the trenches, apparently from authority which left no doubt, that I was killed. Next morning it was my turn for duty. The first groups I met were those of other regiments. 'What news, lords?' say I. 'Nothing sir but Major Cocks is killed.' One man actually argued the matter with me. A little further were my own men and some of my friends, consoling over my fate. The surprise on their faces was very whimsical and it [was] not a little gratifying to observe how one's death took. The last of all was Colonel Guise, whom I was coming to relieve and who was the very man through whose mistake the report had originated. He had half a mind to run away and when he came to himself his stammering apology for killing me almost did kill me with laughing.[32]

The digging of tunnels continued, but, thanks to the obstruction of rock, the first gallery, as it was termed, now sixty feet long, had scarcely reached the bottom of the city wall. The French defenders, aware of what the British were up to, brought down two howitzers behind the wall immediately opposite to where the tunnels were directed. Charles wrote, however, that 'they failed to break into the galleries and did not materially inconvenience the firing parties of the 6th Division'.

On 30 September, when the first gallery had reached the wall, a chamber was hollowed out in which 400lbs of powder was exploded at midnight. It brought down the wall but not the earth, built up as a bulwark in support. At the same time an attack by the 6th Division was driven off by the defenders.

The second gallery, now also 60 feet long, extended to the bottom of the ditch. A trench was dug in zigzag form down the face of the hill below the Hornwork with the object of giving protection to the marksmen, but the enemy fire was so dangerous to the working party that little progress was made.

On 2 October Charles wrote to his cousin Thomas asking him to find the money, some £2,400, to purchase his colonelcy and telling him that 'We are getting on slowly with our siege'.

By nine on the morning of 4 October the second gallery had passed the city wall by seven feet. The chamber was filled with 1,000 lbs of powder and the miners began to stop the mine. At three o'clock in the afternoon, the mine was reported ready and two hundred men of the 24th Regiment were ordered into the trenches, termed parallels, which had been dug before the city wall.

At half past five in the evening all was ready. The signal was given and a slow match, drawn from a tinder-box, put to the fuse. Men held their breath and watched as flames shot up from below the wall, followed by a pall of smoke. Then the wall seemed to rock backwards and forwards before, in two places, part of it collapsed.

The forlorn hopes, led by two lieutenants, rushed forward into the breaches which had been made. Parties of the 24th Regiment, protected by a tremendous fire, then followed them into the town. Twenty-four hours later, however, the French garrison from the castle took the Portuguese, who were holding the breach on the right, by surprise, before driving the men of the 24th Regiment back through the main breach in the wall.

It was a costly failure. Two hundred and forty-five allied soldiers had been killed. Wellington, who from the start had doubted that he had enough heavy guns to take the castle, nonetheless, with typical stubbornness, refused to abandon the attempt.

Two days later, on 7 October, on a night of heavy rain, Charles took over as field officer in the trenches. Just after three in the morning a party of the French garrison attacked, driving out both the workmen, who were making it more stable, and the soldiers protecting them, to the foot of the breach.

Charles reformed his men and led them, running up the slope, to the gap in the wall which stood before a covered way. As always he was careless of danger, his tall figure, even in semi-darkness, being a target hard to miss. He had just scrambled to the top of the fallen masonry when a French soldier, waiting in shadow, shot him at point-blank range. The ball, severing the main artery above his heart, killed him instantly as it struck.

Andrew Leith-Hay, recording what took place on that dark and awful night, pays his own tribute to Charles:

> At three o'clock on the morning of the 8th October the sortie took place, rendered memorable by the fall of Major Cocks, commanding the trenches, and who, with his accustomed energy, had assembled the guard and workmen to force the enemy back into the covered way . . . . During the future operations against the place, previous to the night of the 8th October, no opportunity of distinguishing himself was permitted to escape; his name carried with it the assurance of service being brilliantly executed wherever it became his duty to be present.

The following morning Charles's body was brought out of the castle under a flag of truce. He was buried with full military honours under a cork tree in the ground of the 79th Regiment at Bellina. His friend William Tomkinson wrote: 'He is regretted by the whole army and

184

in those regiments in which he has been, not a man can lament a brother more than they do him.'

It was Tomkinson who wrote to his brother, John Somers.

We have this day done our last duty to him and I derived what little satisfaction I could on so mournful an occasion by seeing Lord Wellington, the Prince [of Orange] and the whole Head-quarters with a list of sorrowful friends attending the funeral. I have taken upon myself to settle his affairs, disposing of his favourite mare to the Prince, who wished to take her, not allowing any little thing to be sold, distributing them to his numerous friends and kept his journal and notes to proceed to you.[33]

Wellington, who stood ashen-faced beside the grave, was for some time unapproachable in his grief. He wrote in despatches, 'I consider his loss as one of the greatest importance to this army, and to his majesty's service.' Later he was to say that had Charles but survived he would certainly, in his estimation, have reached the highest of military commands.[34]

PART 4

26

THE RETREAT FROM BURGOS

Nothing is so unmanageable as a British army in retreat, or when foiled

On the night of 20 October 1812 the siege of Burgos was raised. The whole of Wellington's army then marched for the Douro. The French 'Army of Portugal' now outnumbered the British. On the arrival of Soult (the Duke of Dalmatia) from the south, no less than 70,000 men were assembled at Valencia.[1]

On 23 October Soult appeared on the bank of the Tagus and became united with the Army of the Centre. The British force on the left bank of the river was then withdrawn while Sir Rowland Hill placed troops on the River Jarama to cover Madrid. On the night of 21 October Wellington crossed the Arlanzon and at five o'clock on the morning of the 22nd the rearguards were retired.

The enemy pressed forward relentlessly on the retiring British. At one point the guerrillas of Don Sanchez were so hotly pursued that the French actually mingled with the rearguard of General Anson's cavalry before they were recognized and, with the help of the German Legion, driven off.

On 30 October Wellington placed his army in position on the heights between Rueda and Tordesillas, thus securing his retreat to Salamanca.

On 31 October the British army left Madrid by the Puerta de San Vicente on the great route towards the Escorial. During a halt on 1 November Andrew went with General Pakenham to visit the palace, 'the most extensive building we had ever seen, rendered more

189

impressive from being surrounded with all the gloom of the wildest mountain scenery.'

The Escorial, seated at the base of the Sierra de Malagon, forming a bold and rugged portion of the line of mountain embracing the chain extending from the Sierra de Avila to that of Carpentanos, is very romantically situated: the venerable trees, growing in luxuriance and displaying their natural beauties, are in majesty corresponding to the magnificent edifice which they surround and adorn.

The desolation which had overtaken the Convent Palace and the wild aspect of the deserted and neglected grounds added to the solemn grandeur of the scene. Nothing could be more impressive than were, at this time, both the exterior and the innumerable spacious apartments of the ruined Escorial. The proud trappings of the Bourbon Palace; the rich and gorgeous spoils of South America; the decorations of the great convent chapel, the well-stored refectory; the splendid gallery containing the noblest specimens of the Italian and Spanish schools; all had vanished. The Madonna of Rafaelle, the Sebastian del Piombo, the Venus of Velasquez, no longer graced its walls.

The mausoleum of the royal family alone remained perfect. We descended into this splendid pantheon, and stood by the sarcophagus containing the ashes of the Emperor Charles V. The remains of the Spanish monarchs are deposited in urns composed of black marble, supported on claws of bronze; these are formed with great simplicity and plainness, the name of the personage whose ashes it contains being inscribed on the front of each in golden characters. The wantonness of French spoliation had not visited the grand cemetery.

Passing from the pantheon, we visited the galleries, the cells, apartments of state, the cloisters, terraces, the chapels, and spacious courts, of this imposing edifice – all had been appropriated to the accommodation of troops. Cavalry horses had occupied the lower portion of the building, while the blackened walls and scathed floorings of the apartments, proved the frequent fires lighted within them to cheer the sojourns of French infantry.

On 2 November the army from Madrid resumed its march to the north. The whole force, now in one column, proceeded to ascend the Guadarrama Mountain. The French were in hot pursuit. Soult, on discovering that the British had left, told his army to circumvent the city and to follow the banks of the Manzanares, the quickest route to Guadarrama.

Andrew, now aide-de-camp to General Hill, was told to ride with all speed to Wellington to tell him of what was taking place.

> I was immediately on horseback, and from Villa-nueva de Gomez, passing through Arevalo, arrived at ten o'clock, after travelling a distance of fifty-two miles.
>
> I found Lord Wellington inhabiting a very indifferent quarter in the village of Rueda, but notwithstanding the reverse he had sustained, apparently in the same excellent spirits, the same collected, clear, distinct frame of mind, that never varied or forsook him during the numberless embarrassing events and anxious occasions that naturally occurred to agitate a commander during the long and arduous struggle which he conducted with such firmness and judgement.

The Commander-in-Chief, having questioned Andrew minutely as to the positions of the several divisions of Sir Rowland Hill's Corps and on the places to which the enemy had advanced, quickly wrote a despatch. Then, almost before the ink was dry, he handed it to Andrew, telling him to deliver it with all possible speed.

Andrew, knowing that Hill's headquarters would be at Fontiveros by nightfall, then rode on hired post horses, by Medina del Campo (on the River Zapardi, a tributary of the Duera, as the Douro is called in Spain) to arrive at Fontiveros by the evening. Stiff with exhaustion, he dismounted. He had ridden for fifteen hours almost without stopping except to change horses over a distance of eighty-eight miles.

On the morning of 8 November, during a storm of wind and rain, the Light, 3rd and 4th Divisions, the guards and Colonel Skerret's brigade from Cadiz, with Sir William Erskine's Division of Cavalry, marched in single file over the bridge at Alba de Tormes. On the same day Wellington's army from Burgos reached the San Christobal position in front of Salamanca, the two armies thus being divided by a distance of just a few miles.

The allied army, now assembled on the Tormes, with its head-quarters in Salamanca, was the most numerous Lord Wellington had yet collected under his immediate command during the war. It was composed of nine divisions of infantry, exclusive of the Spanish corps acting with it, of about six thousand cavalry, and from sixty to seventy pieces of cannon.

To this numerous and brilliant force was opposed the united troops of the enemy, composing the armies of the 'South' under the Duke of Dalmatia [Soult]; that of the 'Centre,' commanded by Marshal Jourdan; and of 'Portugal' and the 'North,' by Generals Souham and Caffarelli; the whole being under the nominal control of Joseph Bonaparte, ninety thousand strong, including ten thousand cavalry, and accompanied by two hundred pieces of artillery.

In the course of the 10th the enemy's whole army appeared on the Tormes; on his left was Marshal Soult, who pressed forward to force the allies from Alba and obtain possession of the bridge.

The unfortunate citizens of Alba then endured a heavy bombardment. Parties of French voltigeurs tried to storm the town but were 'bayoneted back' by three British regiments, the 50th, the 71st and the 92nd, under the command of General Hamilton. Andrew Leith-Hay, sent into Alba to report on what was happening, found the soldiers using the shells of ruined houses to protect them from enemy fire. Assured by General Hamilton that he could continue to hold the town, Andrew rejoined General Hill on the heights above Carpio.

From there on the next day (11th) he watched the arrival of King Joseph (Napoleon's brother, the *soi-disant* King of Spain) in the French camp. 'The bands played, the troops got under arms and rolls of drums honoured Joseph and his commanders.'

The following day, 12 November, Wellington arrived on the heights opposite the bridge of Alba from where he summed up the situation of the French army. From the town of Alba the right bank of the Tormes was covered in a dense forest in which it was perfectly possible that large numbers of troops might be concealed. Wellington therefore sent Andrew, with a patrol of the 13th Light Dragoons, to ride up the left bank of the Tormes as far as a place called Salvatierra. From there he was to cross the river and make his

192

way through the forest to get as near to the enemy's bivouacs as was possible without being seen.

Andrew set off on his mission. The people at Salvatierra knew nothing. No French troops had been near them, so they said. He therefore crossed the Tormes as instructed and followed a road through the forest to a place called Galinduste. There he met a peasant who declared that that he had seen French cavalry in the morning, but that they had since disappeared. Andrew, however, was taking no chances, so he sent the peasant into the town to find out if the coast was clear. Meanwhile he and his dragoons hid themselves in the trees amongst which, should the man return with a party of French soldiers, they could hastily disappear.

Nothing of the sort occurred. The man returned alone saying that the French had left Galinduste and were heading towards Alba.

> From the alcalde [mayor] I learned that no French force had passed through this town, nor had any troops moved towards the upper line of the Tormes . . . . Taking a guide from Galinduste, we pushed forward in the direction of Alba, without obstruction or meeting any of the enemy's patrols until arrived within two leagues of that place and consequently at a short distance from the left of the French army. It was neither safe nor necessary to advance farther; therefore, in the middle of the night, I forded the Tormes and, having left my escort at the quarters of General Long, rode direct for Salamanca there to inform Lord Wellington as to the result of my observations.

The French army did cross the Tormes on 14 November. Wellington, aware that an attempt to confront it in that position could only result in huge loss of life, then gave orders for his army to leave Salamanca and march towards the Valmusa.

Having crossed the Valmusa by different routes, the allied army, on the night of the 15th, bivouacked in the woods on its northern bank. The soldiers had to sleep on the ground without any kind of cover to shield them from drenching rain. The following morning, when the march was resumed, a large body of French infantry and cavalry were seen to be following in their tracks. Surprisingly, however, even the men in the rearguard were not seriously attacked.

The troops were now marching in two divisions along a road surrounded by ilex trees which stretched like a dark green curtain down to the very verge. Days and nights of successive rain had turned the surface into mud. Gun carriages and carts, dragged by mules and oxen, became stuck, slowing up the march of the Second Division, which soon lagged behind the First.

General Sir Edward Paget was spurring his horse ahead to the rear of the First Division, to instruct it to slow down and close the gap when a detachment of light cavalry dashed out from the wood and carried him off, disappearing back into the trees. In fact his captors were only three dragoons, but General Paget, who had lost an arm in the crossing of the Douro in 1809, could not defend himself properly and was carried away into the depths of the forest before anyone realized what had occurred.[2]

Andrew describes the hardships which the British army endured during the retreat from Burgos:

> It was not so much from the excessive length of the marches as the particularly unfavourable state of the weather, the scarcity of provisions, and wretched quality of the roads, rendered by the violent rains and numerous carriages of every description passing along them, almost impassable.

To make matters worse the commissariat had become so disorganized that the men were on the verge of starvation, living largely off Spanish chestnuts and acorns and the occasional wild pig which they managed to kill in the woods. Likewise the horses, mules and oxen suffered from lack of fodder because now, in late November, not even grass could be found. The beautiful Andalusians, which Andrew had brought from Madrid, could hardly be ridden, their ribs staring through dry coats.

Andrew, a veteran of the retreat to Corunna in 1809, comparing it to that of 1812, wrote that, while the cold was less intense:

> The country through which Lord Wellington moved was incomparably more dangerous . . . lateral roads branched off in every direction; cavalry could act in all parts of the country; there were no mountain positions to defend; nor were the flanks of the retiring columns ever secure.[3]

We have it on the word of Doctor McGrigor that Wellington himself was at this time greatly despondent over the state of drunkenness and disorder which now affected the army, which, but a few months previously, he had led with so much pride. In the first interview that he had with him after arriving at Ciudad Rodrigo Wellington said to him:

> I never knew till now, nor believed, how unjustly poor Moore had been dealt with in the outcry raised against him in England about his retreat. I consider him the worst used man that ever lived. Nothing is so unmanageable as a British army in retreat, or when foiled.[4]

27

THE CONSEQUENCES
OF MOSCOW

By the end of November 1812 both the British and French armies were in cantonments. Wellington's headquarters were at Fuenteguinaldo on the left bank of the Agueda. Valladolid had become the principal station of the French Army of Portugal, the Army of the Centre, commanded by Count D'Erlon was at Arganda. Marshal Soult, with the Army of the South cantoned in the valley of the Tagus and in La Mancha, had his headquarters in Toledo and King Joseph was back in Madrid.

Sir Rowland Hill's headquarters was at Coria on the Alagon, a very dull place, according to Andrew, who, after six weeks of kicking his heels, was sent off to La Mancha to find out what he could about the movements of Joseph Bonaparte and Soult.

Heading due south, he crossed the Tagus and the following morning arrived at Brozas, the headquarters of the cavalry division commanded by Sir William Erskine. From there he rode on through Caceres to Trujillo, where he met the rough old Spanish General Morillo, a man devoted to General Hill, who gave him letters to prove his identity to the Spanish authorities, who, on his journey, he was likely to come across.

From Trujillo he rode south to Castelo Branco and then east to Anchuras in the mountains of Toledo, before riding back over 'many intricate bad roads in the dreary mountains of Toledo, ' to Castelo Branco in Estremadura.

There he was sitting, presumably in the local hostelry, with the cura [priest] of Anchuras, 'discussing the popular topics of the day' when, to his great delight, in walked no lesser a person than Lord

Tweedale.[5] It turned out that Tweedale had also got bored with the monotony of camp life at Coria and had decided to explore 'the neighbouring quarters of the enemy'.

Accordingly, on 23 January, they both returned to Guadalupe to visit the famous monastery where the shrine of Nuestra Señora de Guadalupe, in the convent chapel, drew pilgrims from all over Europe.

Realizing, however, that they were too far away from the scene of action to be of any practical use, they decided to get closer to Marshal Soult and his army on the Tagus. Thus they set off towards a place called Corral de Calatrava to search out the partisan officer who had been told by the Spanish General Morillo to give details of the movements of the enemy troops.

Approaching the village, they were warned that it was occupied by a party of French cavalry. Looking in all directions and constantly turning in their saddles, they then left the main road and followed mountain tracks to the castle of Calavassos, perched high on a cliff overhanging the Guadiana River. Here they spent the night in safety, before riding next morning to a hill above the town of Corral from where the departure of the French soldiers could clearly be seen.

Emboldened, they rode down into the town, but hardly had they reached it before a party of the *chasseurs à cheval* came thundering into the main street firing pistols in all directions. These men, however, having questioned the local people regarding the detachment that had spent the night in their town and been told that it had consisted of French soldiers, departed and were seen no more.

Nonetheless, warned that the French foraging parties were now everywhere, they had to be constantly on their guard. Fortunately, the country was so wooded that, watching and waiting on vantage points usually hidden among trees, they could count the detachments of cavalry riding back and forth. Also by hanging about in the neighbourhood of the army quarters, they managed to make fairly accurate guesses as to the number of men stationed in the district and also as to how, in the near future, they were likely to be deployed.

Lord Tweedale departed to visit Andalusia while Andrew went on to Cordoba. Told that the enemy's troops had left Ciudad Real, he rode into the town, the capital of the district, surrounded by an old Moorish wall.

Surprisingly, he was met with a coldness amounting to hostility.

197

which, considering how the Spanish loved the British, was hard to understand. A Spaniard who was with him, however, explained that the French, who were still in the neighbourhood, would, should they hear of it, take revenge not only on a named individual but on the families of anyone known to have entertained a British officer in their home.

Andrew, nonetheless, managed to question the chief magistrate, who gave him the information, which he needed, as to what was happening in the district. Also, he told him where it was at least comparatively safe for him to go. Subsequently he rode to a village called Miguelturra, less than a mile away, which was, in fact, a suburb of Cordoba,

From there he was able to explore the province of La Mancha, one of the richest agricultural areas in Spain. Thanks to the abundance of corn and olive oil and, in particular, of wine, it had become a favourite quarter of the French army (renowned for living off the land) commanded by Marshal Soult.

Andrew then moved on to Piedrabuena, a town just north of the Guadiana and about twenty miles to the west of the city of Ciudad Real. Here he was safer, being some distance to the west of the line of country usually raided by the foraging parties. From there he rode out into the surrounding country where he greased the palms of the local people to bring him any information of what was taking place in the French quarters.

Returning one afternoon to Piedrabuena, Andrew was warned that the French were in the town. Faced then with the alternative of retracing his steps or of trying to get past the town, he chose the latter.

> Favoured by the obscurity of the night, I followed a route down the ravine between the town and the ruined castle of Miraflores . . . . Fortunately we passed unnoticed and at Luciana I found my horses and servants, who had made a precipitate and not very orderly retreat on the approach of the enemy's detachment . . .
>
> A Spaniard placed on the Cuidad Real road to give me information, returned to Piedrabuena early on the morning of the 24th with a report that a detachment [of the enemy] had passed the river during the night and were marching direct to the town . . . .

198

In a few minutes the people were perceived running in all directions, in great agitation and alarm, while the cry of 'Los Franceses! Los Franceses!' echoed from every quarter.

The consternation of my host, Don Vencislaus, was extreme. The crisis was to him overpowering, his mind wavered under the circumstances of anxiety and alarm. Instead of being active in forwarding the removal of evidences that a British officer had been received beneath his roof, he bewailed the fate that awaited him and I left him pacing from one apartment to another apparently reduced to helpless childishness. His family, assisted by their constant visitor, the Sangrado* of the village, showed greater presence of mind and the moment I had departed closed the front gateway, thereby occasioning some delay in parleying with the French officer who was kept thundering for admittance until the apartment I had deserted no longer appeared to have been recently occupied. When, on the following day, I returned to Piedrabuena, Don Vencislaus claimed for himself great praise in having effected the speedy removal of my baggage from French observation, and I was too happy in having it restored in safety to question the agency by which it had been accomplished.

After the alarm they had received, it would not have been surprising that this family should have expressed some degree of reluctance at again admitting so dangerous a visitor; but, on the contrary, I was welcomed with, if possible, greater kindness than formerly; nor was a repetition of the late scene either anticipated or dreaded.

On 7 March Andrew heard through his informants that the French had left their cantonments in Almagro, a town just over twenty miles away to the south-east. To get there he must, in all probability, have ridden along the main road which ran through Ciudad Real, the town where, only a month before, the inhabitants had been too terrified to acknowledge him for fear of retribution from the French.

Now it was a different story, both there and in nearby Almagro, where, at sight of a British uniform, the people welcomed him with joy.

* This is what Andrew wrote; possibly *sagrado* or holy [man].

Its inhabitants appeared delighted at the departure of the enemy; the streets were crowded with musicians and people dancing; guitars sounded in every direction, the sprightly 'seguidilla' of La Mancha being in accordance with the cheerfulness that seemed to pervade all ranks.

It soon transpired that it was because of his disastrous defeat in Russia that Napoleon had ordered Marshal Soult to move the Army of the South, composed largely of veteran soldiers, to reinforce his new levies in Saxony.

Soult, having handed over command of the detachments left in Spain to Count Gazan, left Toledo on 1 March. He reached Madrid on the 2nd and then, in a series of forced marches, went north to Valladolid and from thence into France, before crossing the frontier into Germany.

Once confident that this had happened, Andrew decided to head north, across the mountains of Toledo, so that once again, by scouting round, he could discover the positions and the strength of the divisions of the French army now commanded by Count Gazan.

Having passed through Alcoba and Retuerta, after travelling a steep and intricate mountain road, I descended to Navalucillos, there establishing a direct communication for intelligence with the capital. This was carried on through the medium of the *Madrid Gazette*, the circulation of which to the provinces had not been interrupted by the French authorities; and on its margin, written with invisible characters, until subjected to the process by which they became legible, were conveyed the remarkable events occurring at the court of Joseph Bonaparte.

A *Gazette* received on the morning of the 19th [March] communicated the final departure of the Court having taken place on the 17th, on which day King Joseph, attended by the ministers O'Farrel, Urquijo and Azanza, and escorted by his guards, several regiments of cavalry, with a numerous convoy of persons of the French interest, left Madrid . . . .'

The enemy's troops evacuated Talavera de la Reyna on the 3rd of April . . . . Not a French soldier remained upon the immediate bank of the Tagus, with the exception of the *12me légère* and one hundred and fifty *chasseurs à cheval* that accompanied General Maransin, and still lingered in Toledo.

There appeared a great reluctance in abandoning the fertile country in the neighbourhood of that city; nor were the French detachments within its walls without serious apprehension of being subjected to attacks by the numerous guerrilla parties that infested the whole country. To prevent the possibility of surprise the gates of the bridge of San Martin, and that of Alcantara, were barricaded.

Andrew now based himself in the town of Polan. He rode daily to the heights, about half a mile from the town, from where he could clearly observe the movements of the French soldiers confined within the walls. Eventually, on 10 April, General Maransin left Toledo and, at daylight on the 11th, Andrew rode across the Tagus and entered the old cathedral town. He found the inhabitants so over-joyed at the departure of the French that the chance of inciting local resistance with a propaganda campaign sprang to his mind.

> Having received intelligence of the events passing in the north of Europe, detailing the successes of the allied powers and decadence of the French Imperial influence, I considered it important to communicate to the inhabitants of New Castile, as extensively as possible, information so much calculated to inspire hopes of a successful termination to the war of resistance which they had so long waged with varied and doubtful advantage.
>
> For this purpose, having procured a translation of the most important paragraphs, a proclamation [was] issued from the Toledo press and thousands of copies were put into immediate circulation. They were read with avidity and, to prevent the possibility of a doubt as to the author, I dispatched copies in my own name to General Maransin, General Leval at Madrid and to the headquarters of the 'Army of the South'.

Andrew seems to have been unaware, or else contemptuous of the fact, that he was, in a literal sense, putting his head into the dragon's mouth. General Maransin was absolutely furious. Fulminating against the impertinence of a junior officer, albeit one of the enemy, who had dared to impugn against the Emperor, he swore to take him prisoner by any possible means. He did not waste time. On the evening of 27 April Andrew was warned by a local man that the French were returning, Hastily leaving Toledo, he rode back across the Tagus to Polan. Here he received a copy of General Maransin's reply to his own proclamation, in which the General flatly denied that the French had fallen back before the Russians, causing loss of imperial prestige.

Andrew, having added his own retort to several copies of this diatribe, then prevailed upon a Spaniard to place them on the gates of Toledo. He was now involved in a vendetta in which, by further provoking Maransin, he actually relished the danger in which he stood:

> This mode of life was extremely interesting. The constant sight of, and almost communication with, the enemy, produced excitement; while the fact that an officer, removed one hundred and fifty miles from the nearest troops of his country, being enabled to continue in safety close to the quarters of the enemy's army for months, proved the current of popular opinion to be decidedly in favour of the cause of which he was the partisan.
>
> On the 6th May the muleteers, travelling the route towards Polan, informed me that the French troops were preparing for departure. Subsequent travellers from Toledo communicated the march of General Maransin, when I immediately pro-ceeded to occupy his quarters.

The guerrilla bands in the locality then wanted to bar the gates of the town against the French. A meeting of the Junta was summoned, Andrew being bidden to attend. It was decided, however, that because the partisans had neither the means nor equipment to defend the town successfully, the enemy would only take revenge on the unfortunate inhabitants.

On the morning of 9 April a detachment of the French Army was seen to be marching towards the gate under a flag of truce. On reaching the town walls the Frenchmen reined up their horses to begin a lengthy parley with some of the Spanish officials. While this was happening a Spanish peasant came running to Andrew, who was waiting in the upper part of the town, to ask him to come down and talk with them.

This I had no hesitation in doing and upon reaching the barrier, with difficulty penetrating the crowd collected, I checked my horse close to those of two officers of the 2nd, or Chamborin Hussars. Civilities having passed, I was anxious to become acquainted with the object of their visit, but it being made apparently from pure curiousity, and to ascertain whether a British officer really was in Toledo, I put a stop to the communication, bade them adieu, returned to the town and they speedily disappeared on the route from whence they came.

Andrew was not to know how eagerly Maransin waited their return. Told what they had learned, he was exultant. He now knew his antagonist's whereabouts and would soon have him in his power. It was only a question of time.

On the morning of 11 May, with the *45me Regiment* and a squadron of cavalry, Maransin entered Toledo. Andrew, by now used to these comings and goings, took little notice. Then, suddenly, he was told that a letter had been intercepted from Maransin to General Leval in which the former declared his intention of making Andrew a prisoner with the least possible delay.

Not considering Polan very safe quarters, I determined to move two leagues farther into the country and, having taken the usual ride to the Sierra de los Palos, proceeded at night to Fuentelcaño, a country house surrounded by woods and at some distance from any of the principal lines of communication. Having left the Intendant of Toledo in this apparently secure retreat, I made daily excursions, returning in the evening, and by my reports restoring that confidence in the mind of the Spanish functionary, which solitude and the lack of cigars had nearly destroyed. In returning from the heights above Toledo on the 16th, I became so unwell as to determine me not to proceed farther than Polan. I consequently sent a messenger with the information to Fuentelcaño and made preparation for securing timely information should the enemy make an excursion in that direction during the night. An Andalusian, who had for some time been employed in procuring information, was stationed on one of the roads, while a Spanish sergeant undertook to watch the only other leading to Toledo . . . . Had this duty been either diligently or

203

honestly executed, there could not have existed the slightest danger.

Relying on these arrangements I retired for the night . . . .

It was past nine o'clock in the evening when General Maransin became acquainted with the circumstance of my having resolved to continue for the night at Polan. He immediately resolved to detach and surprise me. In ignorance as to the force he believed had for some time been hovering about his quarters, and apprehensive of the neighbouring guerrillas, he ordered an unusually numerous detachment to be paraded in marching order.

At the distance of a league from that village is a venta, or inn, whose inhabitants were secured to prevent an alarm being communicated. This accomplished, the troops advanced until near the town, when the cavalry left the road, and in patrols closed the different routes leading from the houses; the infantry marched direct to the street forming the entrance to Toledo.

Having secured the roads by which escape was practicable, the French aide-de-camp, Captain Acoste, impressed a peasant from the first habitation at which he arrived, menacing him with instant death if he did not without delay lead to the quarter I had occupied during my frequent visits to Polan. About two o'clock a violent knocking was heard at the outer gateway, which speedily gave way before the force applied to bring it down, and soon after the court was filled with French infantry.

The house, although spacious, was but one story in height, the windows were slightly elevated from the court, which, of considerable extent was surrounded by a lofty wall. There could not for an instant be a doubt as to what had happened. The enemy's troops had succeeded in surprising me, and a last but hopeless effort at escape was the only alternative.

Extinguishing the lamp which burnt in my room, I locked the door, retiring into a chamber at the back of the house, the entrance to which I also secured, and attempted to force through a window, the only one in the apartment, which I had not previously inspected, but which proved to be closely grated with iron bars. My fate became inevitable. The whole range of windows in front of the house gave way with a loud crash, as the butt-ends of the French muskets were directed through them. I heard my bedchamber fully occupied, while noise, confusion and loud conversation marked the progress of rapid and anxious search. At length violent blows, applied in rapid succession, completely demolished the door that obstructed a sight of their prey; when, perceiving no possibility of escape, I walked forward surrendering to Captain Acoste.[6]

28

'MR JONATHAN BUCK OF BOSTON'

With Andrew now a captive and Charles Somers Cocks killed, Wellington had lost two of his most trusted intelligence officers who provided him with the information on which he so greatly relied.

What, however, had happened to Colquhoun Grant in the meantime, last heard of in Paris after his dramatic escape from Bayonne?

Colquhoun, as described by his brother-in-law, Doctor James McGrigor, had been living in the capital city of France, where, passing himself off as an American, he had been allowed to go about almost as he pleased. So little suspicion had been attached to him that he had openly attended all the military reviews and, by asking a few questions in the right quarters, had been able to send Wellington details of the reinforcements being sent to the French armies, in particular that of Portugal.

Then, as it became obvious that information as to the movements of the French army was being leaked to the British Commander-in-Chief, someone in the French hierarchy started putting two and two together, as to the identity of the spy who must be somewhere in their midst.

Perhaps the charming, urbane 'American' who showed so much interest in military matters asked too many questions, or perhaps it was simply through routine enquiry that a man, with no proven identity other than that of his passport, came into the list of suspects who could be termed traitors to France.

About this time, *writes Doctor McGrigor,* his friends, whom he met at Mr McPherson's told that gentleman to desire Grant to desist going to the reviews, and further that he must remain quiet for some time, change his appearance if possible, and get a different passport. All this was accomplished. He assumed a different appearance and got another American passport, that of an American gentleman recently deceased in Paris. But McPherson was further informed that the police were secretly making inquiries about him and it was decided that he must leave Paris.

Colquhoun, according to his new passport, was now a Mr Jonathan Buck of Boston. As such he travelled down the Loire to Orléans to seek out the agent who, on his escape in the stage-coach in the previous autumn, had proved to be such a staunch friend. From there, presumably on the agent's advice, he sailed down the river on a barge until he reached the port of Nantes in Brittany. Here he went boldly into the shipping office to try to obtain a passage on a vessel sailing to America.

This, in the spring of 1813, was not as easy as it sounds. America was now at war with Britain, on the side of France, and the French ports were blockaded by British men-of-war. However, told at the shipping office that a ship was about to sail, he introduced himself to the Captain as Mr Jonathan Buck who was desperately keen to return to Boston from which city he came. The Captain replied that he was perfectly willing to take him but could give no promises as to when that would be. It was not simply a question of waiting for a favourable wind. A British ship-of-the-line, carrying seventy-four guns, was prowling like a hungry tiger back and forth across the harbour mouth.

The Captain, sensing Colquhoun's disappointment, and short of company himself, welcomed him into his cabin where drink of some sort was produced. Colquhoun, sizing him up and recognizing a kindred spirit, once again risked everything in a gamble which could have cost him his life. Trusting his instinct as to his integrity, he confessed to this man, to whom but a short time before he had been a perfect stranger, the truth of his identity.

Once again his knowledge of human nature, plus a measure of sheer audacity, paid off. The Captain, who may well have had Scottish connections, sat down and weighed up the possibilities of the various ways in which Colqhuoun might escape from France. Colquhoun's own idea of heading across the Atlantic in an American ship in the hopes that it might be intercepted by a ship of the British navy, he dismissed as too dangerous. Posing as an American, he might well be shot on sight.

Instead, after much deliberation, he devolved a plan of his own. Colquhoun would be an American sailor. He must go to the American consul in Nantes with whom he would lodge a complaint of ill-treatment on the Captain's ship. From the consul he would then obtain a certificate with which he could go from one French port to another, claiming to be a discharged sailor looking for employment on a ship.

Colquhoun, while almost astounded by the ingenuity of his new friend, was decked out from the ship's slops as an American deck-hand. Then he and the Captain took leave of each other, in what appears to have been a ridiculous charade, parting with curses and a great show of clenched fists, before Colquhoun, his few posses-sions in a ditty-bag, headed back into town.

The American Captain had told him that the British battleships blockading the coast put in for water on the small islands offshore. Most of the inhabitants of these islands, which included Belle Ile and Noirmoutier, were fishermen with small boats. It was probably in the little port of Pornic that Colquhoun found one of these local men who agreed to take him out to an island on which it was known that the crew of a British man-of-war had gone ashore to fill their casks. The price, which he asked, amounted to blackmail, no less than ten gold Napoleons, but Colquhoun, with no alternative, agreed to his demand.

They had almost reached the island and the masts of the British ship were in view when the French fisherman, probably in the hopes of extracting yet more money from his passenger, about whom he may have had doubts, suddenly turned back for the shore.

Colquhoun, frustrated and furious, disappointment clouding his mind, gave him only one of the promised coins telling him that he could go to the police if he wished but that they would be sure to want to know why he had charged so exorbitantly for taking a passenger to the island.

He stumbled ashore feeling desperate. His money was nearly gone. He had come so near to freedom. Now again he was a fugitive, hunted down by an enemy from which there seemed no chance of escape. All that remained was his courage, together with a grim determination that somehow he would get back to Britain.

His chance came in the little town, probably in one of the local inns where gossip was always to be found. Here, in the course of conversation, having probably loosened the tongues of a few of the local worthies with a liberal dispensation of wine, he discovered that he was within walking distance of the house, or chateau, of a French marshal of Scottish descent, whom he knew to be related to his mother. Amazed by this extraordinary coincidence and feeling that, as his last chance of escape it could only be heaven-scnt, he determined to try to find the marshal's abode. Accordingly he set out and, after travelling the whole of that night, he spent the following day in a dry ditch well overhung with weeds. Once it grew dark he again began walking and reached the mansion of the marshal.

According to Doctor McGrigor he slipped into the garden in the early morning where, somewhere close to the house, he once more hid in a ditch. Possibly a dog barked, for a woman came out and cried, 'Qui va là', in an unmistakably Scottish accent. Colquhoun, once more risking everything, emerged from the ditch and said, 'I know by your tongue you're a Scotswoman.'[7]

This story does give a plausible reason for Colquhoun gaining entry to the house. Once coming face to face with him the marshal immediately acknowledged the relationship and ordered his servants to bring him much-needed food and drink. He then told him, however, that he did not think it would be safe for him to stay any longer in his house, but, having said that, he lent him one hundred *louis*.

Thus, with the coins safely hidden in his pocket, Colquhoun returned to the port where he found another fishing boat. Having reached an agreement with the owners and gone aboard, he was actually passing the mouth of the harbour when a shot fired from a shore battery forced the fishermen to stop the way of their vessel by bringing the bow up into the wind.

A number of soldiers then appeared in a boat which put out from the shore. Colquhoun, at sight of them, knew then that he must be found, there being nowhere to hide. It was a dreadful moment when, after all that had happened and at last so near to safety. he realized he must be caught.

But he had reckoned without the presence of mind of the fishermen, for at this critical moment, when the sail was lowered to be coiled round the mast, one of them put him upright against the mast and twisted the sail around him so that he was totally hidden.

The soldiers jumped on board, searched everywhere and prodded with their bayonets. Colquhoun, expecting to be run through, simply held his breath and stayed rigid, his back pressed against the mast. Then, after some talk and laughter, to his utter amazement, he heard shouts of *au revoir* and *bonne chance*, and guessed, as it proved correctly, that the soldiers were leaving the boat.

Once the soldiers were safely out of sight the fishermen told him that they had gone and, having found nothing suspicious, they had been given some fish. They had departed, telling them that they must wait under protection of the battery until night fell, but that then they could put out to sea.

On the following morning the faithful fishermen took Colquhoun out to a British ship of 74 guns. Once on board, as he later told his brother-in-law, he found he could hardly believe that, after all his adventures, he was actually sailing for home.

> Great was my surprise, *wrote Doctor McGrigor,* on receiving a letter from him in London, wherein he complained of the illiberality of the then Transport Board, and the difficulty he had in getting those two poor fishermen released from an English prison who had so faithfully conveyed him from a position of extreme danger.[8]

Colquhoun had in fact gone first to the Commissioners of Transport who had arranged for him to be exchanged for a French major. This had enabled him to serve again as an acting soldier, having now been exchanged for an officer of equivalent rank after giving his parole.

It was after this that he found the French fishermen in the prisoner-of-war hulks lying off Porchester. On leaving them, when they had taken him to the British battleship, he had rewarded them for their bravery with all the money he had left. Also, he had given them a certificate of protection, naming them as saviours of his life to whom freedom should be allowed. Nonetheless, seized by a British warship, they were now prisoners of war.

Colquhoun, having arranged their repatriation, sent them back to France with enough money to cover, not only the cost of a new boat, but to compensate for the internment they had been so wrongly forced to endure.

Meanwhile he himself went back to his home in Forres in Morayshire to take some well-deserved leave.[9]

29

A PRISONER OF THE FRENCH

Andrew's imprisonment began in a farcical manner. Firstly he asked to be allowed to finish dressing. Then there was great hilarity when his English groom was found hiding under a mattress in the dormitory above the stable.

Meanwhile, some of the French soldiers, having plundered the village, returned with a great amount of food, together with numerous animals, which were herded into the courtyard.

> The officers assembled in the room I had previously occupied; conversation commenced; we were no longer enemies and in the course of two hours were seated at a substantial repast of viands prepared for the occasion, and to which ample justice was done before these warriors would move on their return.

The French officers were openly friendly. Not so some of the soldiers, who, as the Spanish white wine elevated their already buoyant spirits, insisted on my unqualified assent to the fact that *'Les Francais sont des braves gens.'*

Andrew had to endure the annoyance of seeing them trying out his horses but he did manage to make the aide-de-camp, Captain Acoste, promise that he would not allow his men to do more damage to the house and furniture of the worthy Spanish farmer who had taken him under his roof.

> The troops again being formed, we sallied forth, and amidst clouds of dust entered upon the road to Toledo . . . . Upon the

211

heights, near to the city, the road is conducted between walls, bounding the orangeries of some villas belonging to the inhabitants of Toledo. It occurred to me as possible, by watching an opportunity when unperceived, to leap one or other of these walls and penetrate into the thicket beyond. But the escort was too vigilant to permit a chance of success in such an attempt, nor did I conceive it, under the circumstances, worthy of a trial, the failure of which would inevitably be accompanied by a shower of musket balls.

On our arrival in the town I was immediately taken to the palace of the archbishop and presented to General Maransin. His manner at first distant and reserved, became softened by degrees, and restored to what appeared his natural and usual demeanour.

Maransin had commanded the vanguard of Marshal Soult's army for some time. Having served for a long time long in Spain, his career had suffered a setback when at the beginning of 1812, he had been attacked and totally defeated by General Ballesteros, near Cartama, when about 3,000 of his soldiers had fled in terror towards Malaga.

Although now approaching middle-age – Andrew thought him to be about forty – he appeared to be both physically active and mentally alert, being very much aware of all that was taking place. Created a baron of the empire by Napoleon, his military rank was that of *Général de brigade*. However, the only soldiers that he now commanded were the light cavalry of General Soult (the Marshal's brother), which were in fact the only French troops left on the banks of the Tagus.

The General, despite his sworn allegiance to his Emperor, was openly critical of the débâcle of the retreat from Russia of which news, exaggerated by rumour, was constantly reaching Toledo.

Accompanied by an officer of the *état major*, I was permitted to pay visits to the town, returning to the palace at six, where the General was attended by several of his officers and a very sumptuous dinner was served up. In the evening, the other members of the family having retired, I had an unconstrained conversation with the French baron. For upwards of an hour we paced along the spacious and elegant salon of the archbishop, discussing the leading topics rendered interesting in the progress of the Spanish warfare, with a frankness that occasioned my surprise . . . .

The campaign in Russia, the frightful sufferings of the grand army, the hopeless state of affairs in the Peninsula, the imbecility of Joseph Bonaparte, or the military talents of Lord Wellington, were alike subjected to the unreserved remark, the eulogium, and occasionally to the bitter invective of the French General. A stranger, overhearing the conversation, would rather have supposed it carried on by officers of the same family than by a person of rank in one army and a prisoner brought to his quarters, after having instigated the inhabitants of the country to rise, and cut off the supplies on which the existence of the other depended.

General Maransin, without hesitation, admitted the difficulties and losses to which the French army in the Peninsula were subjected; the faulty arrangements made under existing circumstance, and the improbability of reinforcements at a time when the guerrilla system was of all others most harassing and destructive. The departure of Marshal Soult he considered an event much to be deplored, and calculated to have a serious effect on the *morale* of his army.

The next morning General Maransin, taking Andrew with him, left Toledo to go to Olias for the purpose of meeting General Soult. For some reason Maransin insisted on walking through Toledo while the horses were led. The population, at sight of him, crowded to their doors and windows, showing such obvious hostility that the General quickened his step and, on reaching the outskirts, hastily mounted his horse.

Arrived at Olias, they were introduced to General Soult, a very different character to Maransin, to whom Andrew took an instant dislike.

Gross and unwieldy in his person, he had all the look of a parvenu of the vulgarest and lowest description. After a *déjeuner à la forchette* of the most substantial kind, I was ushered into the cabinet of the officer acting as the chief of staff, and by him informed that, by giving my parole of honour, I might become immediate master of my motions; that is, in selecting any portion of the French army with which to continue, either

213

accompanying the *5me Chasseurs*, or, by proceeding to Madrid, partake of its society.

When Andrew refused this offer the French officer who was acting as chief-of-staff could hardly believe what he was hearing. Leaping from his seat he went off to find General Soult to tell him of the temerity of the young officer who had actually turned down an offer which most in his position would have thought impossible to refuse

The French then naturally took it for granted that the only possible motive for such extraordinary behaviour was that Andrew was planning to escape. Therefore he was told that special care would be taken to hold him captive and that he would be shot immediately should he even attempt to get free. Subsequently an escort was ordered and, the officer in command having been given strict instructions as to his surveillance, Andrew was ordered to depart.

Emerging from Soult's headquarters, with an armed man on either side, he found about fifty of the *5me*, drawn up in the street. A horse being led forward, he mounted as he was told, whereupon two chasseurs unslung their carbines, placing themselves on either side. With an officer riding near to them and headed by an advance guard, they left Olias behind them as they reached the level and sandy plains leading to Illescas.

Andrew, so used to hours on horseback, now sat uneasily in his saddle.

> The officer in charge of the detachment communicated to me, soon after leaving Olias, that in the event of the slightest deviation from the route on my part, the chasseurs, holding my bridle, were instructed to discharge their carbines into my body and that if any guerrilla party, either from accident or design, appeared to obstruct our passage, I was to be dispatched as a preliminary measure. It is unnecessary to describe the anxious feeling with which I hoped and trusted that no partisans would cross our path; it was decreed that we should pass unmolested.

Mercifully they did reach Illescas without any alarm taking place. Once there, however, thankful as he was to dismount, Andrew found himself forced to sleep in a guardroom under constant supervision. Despite this obvious annoyance, he was, nonetheless, treated most kindly by the French officers, in particular by a Colonel St

Laurent. He was much impressed by the fact that, despite the known failure of the Russian campaign, this officer and most of his compatriots, unlike General Maransin, were unreservedly loyal to Napoleon. Asked by Andrew how, in these disastrous circumstances, the Grand Army could possibly be not only saved but restored, Colonel St Laurent merely replied, *'L'Empereur était là'*.

> His quarter seemed the rallying point of many French officers. In it was constantly assembled a numerous society. The weather was brilliant, and in the garden was placed the superb band of his regiment. On one of these occasions, I had an opportunity of witnessing the constant terror in which the enemy's troops were kept by the guerrillas. The Colonel had passed the forenoon in shooting, and not returning at the accustomed hour, the anxiety expressed was great, the surmises as to what had happened were various, but the predominant feeling was, that he had fallen into the hands of the guerrillas . . . . At length the expected Colonel made his appearance, having seen no guerrillas, and but few partridges.

On 20 May, having said goodbye to the kindly Colonel St Laurent, Andrew, accompanied by a detachment of St Laurent's regiment, rode into Madrid. Almost immediately, on the Prado, he met the French Generals Leval, Fonblanque and Vinot. All of them glared at him, Leval in particular showing undisguised hatred in his face. As the commanding officer in Madrid and the senior officer present, he then questioned Andrew in a laconic and sneering manner which openly implied contempt. Having first demanded and been told his name and rank, he then asked the question which was dominating his mind.

> 'Is it you who have published proclamations against the emperor, and sent them to me by express?'
> Andrew replied that it was.
> 'Very pretty productions they are!' snorted Leval with curling lip, ' I am surprised that an officer of a civilized country should have put his name to such things.'
> 'I am not aware of their being in any respect unworthy of a British officer,' said Andrew, determined not to be cowed. To which Laval, ever more infuriated at failing to see him lose face,

retorted, 'These publications, sir, will cost you dear; in the meantime you will go to prison, there to remain until your fate is decided.'

This conversation had hardly ended before the General ordered Colonel Prévost, one of his aides-de-camp, to take Andrew to his quarter. There he was to write an order by which General Hugo, the Governor of Madrid, might know what Leval meant to be done with him. They entered the Calle Alcala and, in the house of the Marques de Alcanizas, a note was dictated ordering him to the dreaded dungeons of the Retiro.

He was pushed into a low, dark room, already crowded with ten very rough-looking Spaniards who swore, spat and scratched as they pleased. The atmosphere was stifling, the weather being sultry and hot. The one tiny window, closely barred, let in only the minimum of air. Andrew became increasingly desperate, feeling he must suffocate if not released, yet here, in what he called 'this horrid receptacle' he was held for three long days.

At last, after frequent and increasingly desperate appeals, General Leval relented in his persecution by allowing him to be transferred to the Carcel de la Corte, the prison of the court. Here he was not allowed to leave his cell nor to communicate with anyone except his servant and the keeper of the prison. Nevertheless, 'it was a paradise compared to the habitation I had just left.'

He did his best to persuade the keeper to help him escape, but the man was too terrified of the consequences of being found out. He did, however, whisper that the French were leaving Madrid and that he himself must be ready to depart with a convoy the next morning.

General Leval had not done with Andrew, however, for further humiliation was inflicted on him during the march. His servant was allowed to ride one of the baggage horses, but he himself had to tramp along under the full heat of the sun, nearly suffocated by dust. Fortunately the scenes around him were bizarre enough to distract his mind.

Madrid, on this morning, presented one of those remarkable scenes incident to the war. The bustle attending a march of troops being accompanied by the confused departure of a portion of its population, whose political opinions during the struggle now rendered it unsafe to stay behind. Persons of rank,

216

forced from their hitherto comfortable homes, were intermixed with all orders of the community, and alike contemptuously treated by the French troops. Quantities of carriages, cars, wagons or laden mules, were urged on to join the cavalcade, while numerous groups of the remaining population witnessed their departure with silent but expressive contempt. One of the groups in the line of march consisted of my former companions in the Retiro, wretched in appearance and some of them incapable of undergoing any great degree of bodily fatigue. Their lamentations or declarations of inability were listened to with stoical indifference and the bayonets of the amused French soldiery goaded them forward on their way.

Near to the village of Guadarrama the convoy halted for the night. The fields became covered with the motley encampment; women and children that had previously never slept without the substantial walls of their habitations now had to derive shelter from the vehicles in which they travelled and in which, crowded and comfortless, they were destined to pass the night.

Andrew himself endured even greater privation, being forced to sleep in an open field without shelter of any kind. The next night was worse for the column halted on the summit of the Guadarrama in the teeth of a ferocious storm. 'Even the French infantry, accustomed to campaigning in all its less desirable features, expressed their unqualified horror at the night.' The ground was so wet that he could not lie down and his guards refused to allow him even to huddle against a tree to try to find some protection from the piercing wind and drenching rain.

Thankfully, next morning, the cavalcade began its descent down the mountain towards Old Castile. Near to the Fonda San Rafael they were passed by General Leval with his staff. Doubtless the General felt great satisfaction at the sight of his hated prisoner, the man who had dared to insult the Emperor, trailing along, like a common felon, between guards.

The next stop was near Segovia, where, 'the inhabitants having produced some articles of bedding, affording shelter from the rain, [the night] was passed in comparative luxury.'

Despite the adverse conditions of his visit Andrew was enchanted with Segovia, the main feature being the aqueduct, built by the

217

Roman Emperor Trajan, consisting of 160 arches, stretching across the valley.

> The castle, seated on a lofty and precipitous rock, forms an object alike conspicuous and noble. As a state prison it long possessed celebrity and its walls have at different periods become the receptacle of misfortune, or of crime. There is a gloomy magnitude about the castle of Segovia, which, added to its elevated and domineering situation, appears to have eminently adapted it for the twofold purposes of striking terror and, in most cases, ensuring security, to the persons of un-fortunates who too frequently became its inmates.

Andrew by this time, having somehow ingratiated himself with a Spanish family, was travelling in their covered car. General Hugo, the *ci-devant* Governor of Madrid, in command of the troops escort-ing the convoy, singled out the Spanish, who had collaborated with the French, for singularly brutal treatment. On one occasion, when a Spanish Marques got out of his coach, Andrew heard him say to his family that death would be preferable to the indignity and misery to which he was subjected.

Despite the fact that these people had been traitors to their country by collaborating with the French, Andrew found it impossible not to pity them in their present wretched state. Rejected by their own people, they were now equally despised by those whom they had befriended during the occupation of their country, who now, as they themselves retreated, showed them open contempt.

Andrew arrived at Cueller on 31 May where he was once more imprisoned. Now, for the first time in four days, he had a roof over his head, although the building itself was in a near dilapidated state.

> A more wretched habitation cannot be well imagined, its in-security also so manifest that a guard of infantry was ordered to accompany me, a sentinel from which remained constantly in the same apartment. From the commencement of this march, not a moment had passed during which relaxed vigilance on the part of my guards had presented the slightest chance of affording an escape . . . .
> On the 2nd of June, after marching without intermission

except for very brief periods during the preceding day and night, we arrived in the vicinity of Valladolid, but were not permitted to enter within its walls; and having crossed the Pisuerga, encamped on the right bank of that river. The main body of the Army of the South, having passed the Duero by different routes, were assembled in the neighbourhood of the city. Everything bespoke the rapid and continued retreat of the French army . . . .

When in the bivouac of the 2nd June an immense train of artillery, accompanied by its ambulances, passed to the rear. I demanded, with no slight degree of satisfaction, where these cannon were directed, perceiving at the same time a despondency of manner in the French officers, as they hesitatingly declared it to be but the result of a change of quarters.

During this day's march we passed through the populous village of Cigales, crowded with French soldiery, and then the temporary headquarters of Joseph Bonaparte. Induced by the apparent magnitude of the town promising a plentiful supply, and being destitute of provisions, I sent my servant, mounted on a pony, purchased the day preceding, with instructions to return as soon as possible. From that moment I never either saw or received information as to what became of him.

This somewhat blunt statement belies Andrew's very deep distress at the loss of this man who had bravely volunteered to stay with him when he was taken prisoner. Probably he was the groom, whom the French soldiers had pulled out with such merriment from below a mattress on the night when Andrew was captured at Polan. Closely guarded as he now was, and bereft of rights as a prisoner who had not given his parole, Andrew could only beseech those around him to make enquiries,

His fears for the man's safety increased when, on the next day's march, a soldier of the *88me Regiment* told him that he had seen his servant on the previous evening, when he had told him to tell his master that he would rejoin him on the following day. Andrew did not believe this. His servant could not speak French; therefore such a message could hardly have been sent. Furthermore, mounted on a pony, he was greatly more mobile than a straggling foot soldier, who, on his own admission, had fallen into the rear of the company.

The day passed without a sign. Never was his servant either heard of or seen again. Andrew, helpless as he was to make further investigation, had to accept the most probable explanation that, captured by French stragglers, the man had been robbed and killed.

Now bereft of his one companion, he was still at the mercy of his captors, among whom only a few showed him any form of compassion.

On the 6th [June] the convoy arrived at Burgos and for a short space of time halted in the suburb on the bank of the Arlanzon. From thence I was conveyed to the prison, and received by its keeper with cordiality and kindness. For the first time on our route the presence of French soldiers was not deemed necessary and I enjoyed the solitude to which I was consigned.

On the morning of the 10th I left the prison of Burgos taking the route for Briviesca.

The French armies were now in full retreat and it was understood that Lord Wellington was rapidly advancing. A sergeant of the 10th Hussars, taken in an affair at Morales, joined the column of prisoners, and from him I learned with satisfaction [of] the brilliant commencement of the campaign.

30

'WHAT HAS BECOME OF LORD WELLINGTON?'

From what the sergeant told him Andrew discovered that 22 May had been the day on which Wellington had begun to advance north-east from Portugal on the first stage of his avowed intent to drive the French from Spain.

From Lamego on the Douro, from Ciudad Rodrigo on the Agueda and from Coria on the Alagon, the different Corps of the allied army had begun a pincer movement to surround the French. Advancing in the early summer, the finest season of the year, through districts where fruit was already ripe and grass nearly knee high, the allies, following the retreating French, had every reason to be confident that their Commander-in-Chief would again lead them to victory, which, since the triumph of Salamanca, was something they were learning to expect.

Andrew had left his prison at Burgos and been taken to Briviesca on 10 May. Only two days later, on the 12th, Joseph Bonaparte, abandoning the town, had taken the road which Andrew had just travelled with his guards through Briviesca to Pancorbo. Before leaving Burgos Joseph had ordered the castle to be mined. The walls were meant to fall inwards but instead (due to incompetence) they had burst outwards, coming down on an unfortunate column of infantry of which no less than 300 were killed. [10]

Joseph Bonaparte, having left Burgos to head for Pancorbo with the Army of the Centre, then led the retreat of the enemy's troops towards the Ebro, Behind came the Army of the South, and lastly that of Portugal.

Andrew, while told of what was happening, had still to endure the mortification of remaining in captivity with no immediate hope of release.

At Briviesca, where the prisoners were put into a church, he slept in one of the stone niches of a chapel where, in intervals of wakefulness, he resigned himself to being marched to one of the French depots which he took to be his ultimate fate.

Next day, however, came amazing news. The gendarmes arrived to assemble the rest of the prisoners for the day's march, but Andrew, to his enormous delight, was told to stay where he was. So back he went to his recess in the chapel wall, soon to find himself entirely alone in the now empty church.

Prisoners and guards had disappeared, the loud and rapid talking of the French soldiery, intermixed with the occasional eloquence of my native country, died away, and the sound of the closing gate, as the last person left the interior, reverberated in loud echoes through the spacious building.

That I should have been selected from others proceeding to France originated in the desire of Count Gazan of restoring to liberty a captain of the French artillery taken at Badajoz. This he expected to accomplish by agreeing to an exchange, and the preceding evening had written to General Lamartinière, *Chef d'etat major* of the Army of Portugal ordering my detention at Briviesca until his arrival'.

Unfortunately for Andrew, Count Gazan was totally unaware that General Lamartinière not only detested all British officers but nursed a particular loathing for Andrew, the distributor of anti-Napoleonic propaganda.

Footsteps were again heard within the porch, and soon after a gendarme appeared directing me to follow him; whither was a matter of conjecture, from which I was speedily relieved by being conducted into a small vaulted chamber, without a single article of furniture of any description. Its floor was covered with straw, apparently not of the cleanest description, and the confined heat within was excessive. The inhabitants of the straw, rejoicing in the presence of a victim, flew up and commenced re-creating on my limbs; insects of a similar class have seldom bit more voraciously, or continued their attacks with greater perseverance. This place was worse than the Retiro, and only wanted its inmates to make it totally insupportable.

Mercifully help was at hand in the person of Baron D'Orsay, colonel of the *122me* of the line, who soon came to the dungeon. The Baron spoke to Andrew in a way that immediately put his mind at rest, 'and left no doubt of removal from the horrid place to which malignity had consigned me'. Sure enough, having agreed to free him on parole, the baron then instructed the adjutant of his regiment to help him to find a quarter in the town.

The adjutant, probably in total ignorance of Andrew's contretemps with de Lamartinière, could not have picked a worse location.

Unfortunately that selected was exactly opposite to General Lamartinière's who was perceived pacing the length of his apartment, in conversation with other officers, and apparently not in a very agreeable turn of mind. He considered the presence of a British officer very offensive; a gendarme was directed to remove me from his sight, and to continue my companion until further orders.

The look and appearance of this French general is fresh in my recollection. I have seldom seen hatred more strongly depicted than in the occasional glances of his bloated countenance, as, turning towards the window from whence I surveyed him, he seemed to regret that inflicting summary punishment was not within his jurisdiction . . . . In the street at Briviesca was the last time I ever had the misfortune of seeing him.

Baron D'Orsay, who apologized for the rudeness of his superior officer, was himself the epitome of the French aristocracy. Descended from an old and distinguished family, 'his appearance was particularly handsome, his politeness perfectly natural and unconstrained.' Andrew spent two days with him, being greatly entertained by his reminiscences of the imperial court. D'Orsay had actually been at the Tuileries when, after the retreat from Moscow, Napoleon had paid his famous tribute to the heroic Marshal Ney.

Never had the Emperor appeared in the midst of a more brilliant circle. The Prince of Moskowa [Ney] was late in arriving, but, on being perceived, Napoleon, turning to the nobles and the marshals by whom he was surrounded, exclaimed, *'Voila le brave des braves!'*

The Baron himself was no coward. His regiment, the *122me*, which formed part of General Bonnét's Division, had been particularly noticed by the Duke of Ragusa [Marmont] for its gallant conduct at the battle of Salamanca. Having admitted that the battle had been lost by the Army of Portugal, which had suffered such horrendous casualties, Baron D'Orsay then launched into a long discussion on the merits and shortcomings of various other corps. Above all he expressed his delight that his own Division had been publicly recognized by the British for 'its vigorous and determined conduct'.

Thus did Andrew, still technically a prisoner, spend two memorable days with an enemy he greatly admired. Shortly, he would find another with whom, after an initial impasse, he would establish a mutual rapport.

On the 14th the headquarters of the Army of the South arrived at Briviesca and I was soon after ordered to attend the General-in-Chief, Count Gazan. Having, from the officer accompanying me, ascertained my identity, he immediately commenced animadverting on my conduct at Toledo and proclamations which seem to have given such umbrage to the French army. His lecture appeared to be more one of necessity than inclination, . It was couched in very different terms from those of General Leval, and a kindliness of manner bespoke no personally hostile feeling on the part of Count Gazan. Combating the truth of the news from Germany, he talked slightingly of the allied powers, and concluded by assuring me, *'Si l'Empereur a perdu une armée, il a encore une autre.'*

The most agreeable part of the interview was its finale, when the Count stated that, in consequence of an application from Lord Wellington, he would propose an officer now in England as an exchange, offering, at the same time, to forward a letter from me requesting this might be agreed to, and if it was so, promising I should be immediately sent to the advance posts.

But meanwhile what had become of Wellington? No one, least of all his enemies, appeared to have any idea.

On the 16th, during the march of the Army of the South from Briviesca to Pancorbo, Colonel Arnaud, first aide-de-camp to the General-in-Chief, rode up in the line of the march, expressing his surprise at the non-appearance of the allies. What could have become of Lord Wellington? The French troops, in full retreat, were permitted to move leisurely along, without being harassed or urged forward, not a carriage of any description being lost. To him it appeared inexplicable. However, the mystery was destined to be solved without delay.

As the French army slowly retreated Wellington had rapidly advanced. He had crossed the Douro on 1 and 2 June, the Carrion on the 7th and the Pisuerga on the 8th, 9th and 10th. Then, having first reconnoitred with four divisions of infantry, and five of cavalry, at the sight of which King Joseph fled, he had occupied Burgos on the 12th. He had entered the town to find the castle still smoking from the firing of mines which had killed so many French soldiers. Wellington had then immediately ordered the destruction of the remaining fortifications which, during the siege of the previous autumn, had caused the death of Charles Somers Cocks among so many others of his men. This done, he had left the place of such unhappy memory to continue his pursuit of the enemy to the banks of the Ebro. The French could not believe what was happening!

> Their generals were convinced that the routes to the left of the road from Burgos to Vitoria were totally impracticable for the movement of an army. Reports from the local people had only confirmed what they already knew about the district, making it all the more extraordinary that the allies did not appear to be pursuing them on the line of their immediate retreat.
>
> Notwithstanding these supposed insurmountable diffi-culties, the British generals unhesitatingly marched forward, and having turned the strong pass of Pancorbo, all the obstruc-tions between it and Miranda and the right flank of the enemy's armies, the allies crossed the Ebro by the bridges of San Martin, Rocamonde and Arenas.

It was not until the evening of the 18th that General Gazan learned, to his astonishment, that the whole allied army was on the left bank of the river.

This was probably the most masterly movement made during the Peninsular War. All the confident and matured arrangements of the French army were at once overset. Hurry and confusion followed the knowledge of what had happened and an immediate night march was the consequence. Drums beat in all directions, cavalry filed past, while the town of Pancorbo, crowded with the unwieldy ambulances containing plunder accompanying the army, presented a scene of strange confusion.

Having left a garrison of 800 men in the fort, General Gazan marched his army towards Miranda, which continued to be the headquarters of the Army of the Centre. There we arrived before daybreak but were permitted a very small brief interval of rest. I was now in charge of two mounted gendarmes, but permitted to ride in any part of the column of march that I wished. By this means, opportunity was afforded of seeing, at different times, the whole French army.

As the Franco-Spanish court moved with these troops, there was a great display of uniform; the civil departments of the army, officers attached to the households of the Spanish ministers, were alike loaded with embroidery. Accompanying the Army of the South, numerous ladies, dressed *en militaire* and on horseback, having forsaken the plains of Andalusia, followed the fortunes of their Gaelic lovers.

Of the cavalry, the heavy dragoons, dressed in green with brass helmets, were superior troops to the other classes of the same army serving in Spain. The chasseur regiments under the imperial government were variously dressed; and of the hussars, not two corps were in uniform alike. The horse artillery, habited in light blue, braided with black, appeared in a high state of equipment and discipline . . . .

The *gendarmerie à cheval*, at this time numerous in Spain, and selected from the elite of the cavalry regiments, were very fine in appearance, frequently acting in a body and with the distinction to be expected from veteran soldiers: their long blue clothing, cocked hats and broad buff belts gave them a very distinct appearance from any other class of the French cavalry. The elite of the dragoon regiments, wearing furred grenadier caps, were men of great stature and martial appearance.

226

Three things in particular impressed Andrew about the French troops. Firstly their efficiency despite what appeared to be lack of discipline. Secondly the camaraderie between ranks. Thanks to conscription, the privates and non-commissioned officers were frequently better born than the officers, the odious General de Lamartinière being a case in point: 'I have witnessed a sergeant of infantry walking in familiar conversation with and his arm locked in that of his officer.' Thirdly he greatly admired the stoical attitude of the ordinary French soldier, who,

> under the most unenviable circumstances . . . instead of staring about to discover all the miseries of his bivouac, had already half-unroofed the nearest habitation for the purpose of composing his fire. When the blaze was kindled and his knees . . . in close contact with the crackling wood, a shrug of the shoulder denoted the commencement of a long tirade of complaints, which, until the fire was lighted and the soup in a state of preparation, he had neither time nor inclination to think of or to compose.
>
> In marching, the French infantry appeared indefatigable, their progress equally remarkable for the rapidity with which they passed over the ground, or the distances performed, encumbered by long and heavy great-coats which were constantly worn. The soldiers, not satisfied with the burdens they were necessitated to carry, were occasionally seen conveying articles of a superfluous description. In the line of march roulette tables were not unfrequently to be observed borne on the shoulders of the soldiery.
>
> After a long and fatiguing march of thirty-two miles, the Army of the South entered Vitoria on the evening of the 19th. A more crowded town has seldom been witnessed. The court of Joseph Bonaparte, his guards, the various convoys from the interior, the headquarters of the Army of the Centre, and some of the cavalry, already occupied the buildings or added to the confusion in the streets. The numerous staff and civil departments of Gazan's army, formed a most embarrassing addition to this already very unmanageable assemblage.
>
> The whole of the convoys, excepting that of the king, and the baggage immediately appertaining to the different armies, left Vitoria on the morning of the 20th, defiling by the route

leading to Irun. The carriages and wagons extended as far as the eye could reach, winding through the rich and beautiful valley . . . .

The situation of Vitoria is particularly picturesque and beautiful. At the period I am detailing everything about it had become eminently interesting from the situation of two powerful armies having arrived in close contact, under circumstances that rendered it nearly a matter of certainty that its neighbourhood must become the arena of a very serious conflict.

During the morning of the 20th great excitement, attended with feverish and unsteady feeling, seemed to have possession of the inhabitants and their numerous visitors. The immense convoy that had left Vitoria appeared to have produced slight effect in relieving the crowded state of the town, the street still presenting scenes of the utmost confusion, without any effort being apparent by which order was sought to be restored.

In the midst of this chaos, an aide-de-camp of Count Gazan arrived with orders that I should immediately proceed to his headquarters. On leaving Vitoria, to the left of the fine avenue of trees leading into the city, my attention was drawn to the reserve parks of the French armies. In point of number I had never seen so many pieces of artillery assembled, nor can I conceive anything more regular, beautifully arranged or in better order, than was this very imposing display of cannon. The French Colonel particularly called my attention to this sight, and, as if determined it should be my last impression of the French army, ordered my eyes to be bound up immediately after.

We soon arrived at the village of Ariñez, where I was presented to the officers of the *état major* and conducted to the house occupied by the General-in-Chief.'

In the morning Colonel Alexander Gordon, aide-de-camp to Lord Wellington, had arrived at the advance posts, with a letter from his lordship agreeing to the exchange proposed by General Gazan, who, faithful to his promise, determined at once that I should be conveyed to the nearest of the allied troops.

During the time occupied in preparing an escort the French officers conversed with great cheerfulness and apparent

228

cordiality, and Madame Gazan, considering it a possible contingency, ironically requested, in the event of her being captured by the allies, that I would exert myself to obtain for her a favourable reception.

This sally occasioned considerable mirth, which was not diminished upon my departure, an event witnessed by the whole staff. Mounted on a very diminutive horse, my eyes bound up, the appearance of a low and cocked hat then worn by the British army and the constant subject of derision by the enemy, all contrived to complete, in their opinion, a most grotesque figure. Nor were the French officers restrained in the mirth thereby drawn forth. They, however, closed the scene by protestations of kindness and good wishes. I was too happy at the prospect of rejoining my companions to be either hurt or affected by the amusement produced at my expense, and after repeated adieus, quitted the presence of those careless and apparently happy persons.[11]

Brother of Lord Aberdeen (Hadden HSE)
Died of wounds at Waterloo. 6/1815.

31

THE WATCHER AT THE BATTLE OF VITORIA

General Gazan had given Andrew a letter for Wellington, in which he said that he had agreed to his parole, but only on condition that until the officer with whom the exchange had been made left England he could not serve in any capacity against France.

In consequence of this arrangement, I was destined to be present at the battle about to take place merely as a spectator. Later in the evening, accompanied by Lord Charles Fitzroy, I rode to the quarters of Sir Rowland Hill and anxiously antici- pated the great events now with certainty to occur on the succeeding day.

It was rather a singular coincidence of circumstances that the intelligence of the Emperor Napoleon having, in Germany, concluded an armistice on the 4th of June, should have arrived at Vitoria in time to be, for the first time, communicated by a British officer to his commander the day preceding the great battle that ensued.

The morning of the 21st of June [1813] was extremely brilliant. A clearer or more beautiful atmosphere never favoured the progress of a gigantic conflict. The Corps of Sir Rowland Hill marched in the direction of the great road leading from Burgos to Vitoria, crossing near to Puebla, the same route which I had, two days previously, travelled with the French army. Sir Rowland, being intrusted with the service of turning the left flank of the enemy, commanded the extreme right.

PAMPLONA

The French armies were positioned on the extensive line of country from the Heights of Puebla, to the south-west of Vitoria, to the high ground above Gamara Mayor to the north-west of the town. This meant that virtually the whole of the French force was aligned between the south bank of the Zadorra and Vitoria, a distance of about twelve miles. The Armies of Portugal and of the South were in the first line, while that of the Centre with the cavalry, was in reserve. They were placed so that, in the event of a disaster, they had two means of escape, one by the route leading to Bayonne, the other by the road towards Pamplona.

The French had placed most of their cannon in the middle of their lines, near to the village of Gomecho, which they thought to be the most vulnerable part of their position. Andrew, however, calculated, as it proved correctly, that, in view of the fact that they were opposed by an army large enough to manoeuvre at the same time against all parts of its line, their position was extended to a dangerous extent.

The battle began when part of the Spanish Division, commanded by General Morillo, scrambled up through tree-covered slopes to attack the left flank of the French on the summit of the Heights of Puebla. General Morillo was twice wounded and Colonel Cadogan, sent by Hill to assist him, was killed.

231

It being probable, from having so recently left the French army, that there might be some points on which Lord Wellington would wish to question me, with the approbation of Sir Rowland Hill, I proceeded, soon after the firing commenced, to his Lordship, and had the honour of being with him during the whole course of that most eventful day.

The headquarters staff, when I rode up, were stationed on an eminence considerably elevated above the line of the Zadorra, on its right bank, and nearly opposite to the village of Ariñez. Lord Wellington was on foot, with his glass, surveying the whole extent of either army, and particularly the progress of the contest on the Heights of La Puebla.

Dressed in a short grey coat, closely buttoned over his embroidered Spanish sash, a feathered hat alone denoted his rank; but upon approaching, the greatest stranger could not long have remained in ignorance of his presiding over the destinies of Britain, Portugal and Spain.

Upon a remark being made that the troops of Sir Rowland Hill did not seem to be making much impression on the enemy's left, Lord Wellington declared the contrary to be the fact, and that he saw the Highlanders advancing. It was with no slight degree of exultation I heard this tribute to my countrymen, and with my glass perceived the waving tartans of the 92nd [The Gordon Highlanders] as the soldiers of that distinguished regiment marched along the ridge of the Puebla Heights in pursuit of the enemy. Distant as they were, in imagination I conceived they strode with unusual firmness, and, on the mountain summit, emulated the unconquerable qualities of their ancestors.

Meanwhile Hill's Division in Subijana de Alava, just to the east of Puebla, was being repeatedly attacked. Then, when the smoke of guns was seen to the north-east of Vitoria, it was realized that Sir Thomas Graham's artillery had entered the battle above the River Zadorra, at the east end of the French line.

There was still no sign of the centre columns of the allied army, which in fact had got lost in the hills, but at last a messenger galloped up to report to Wellington that Lord Dalhousie had arrived at Mendoza with the 3rd and 7th Divisions. The Light and 4th Divisions had already crossed the Zadorra by the bridges of

Nanclares and Tres Puentes. They were quickly followed by Sir Thomas Picton and Lord Dalhousie, so that the battle was now being fought, south of the river, for a distance of several miles.

Andrew, from his vantage point east of the river, described the unforgettable drama that was taking place.

At the moment of the allied divisions passing the river was exhibited one of the most animating scenes ever beheld. The whole country appeared filled with columns of troops, the sun shone bright, not a cloud obscured the brilliant and glowing atmosphere. From right to left, as far as the eye could reach, scarcely the most diminutive space intervened between bodies of troops, either already engaged or rapidly advancing into action, artillery and musketry were heard in one continued uninterrupted volume of sound, and although the great force of French cannon had not yet opened upon the assailants, the fire had already become exceedingly violent.

On the high ground on the west side of the Zadorra, Wellington, almost deafened by gunfire, continued to give orders to be carried by dispatch riders to the commanders of his army of 90,000 men. Below him, on the flat ground on the other side of the river, he could clearly see how the village of Ariñez was being desperately defended by the French Army of the South. It was a moment of crisis, for, as the 88th (Connaught Rangers) were driven back, the future of the battle seemed doubtful. Wellington, however, remained totally unmoved. Even in the heat of such a desperate battle, he retained that grasp of detail which epitomized the clarity of his mind.

Immediately after the repulse of the first attack on Ariñez, when musket balls were flying around him in all directions, his Lordship, wishing to dispatch an order, turned round and directed me to proceed with it, when, instantly recollecting the situation in which I was placed, he said, 'No, you cannot do it,' and another officer, who had just come up, was entrusted with the message.

Andrew, remembering this incident, humbly confessed his astonishment that 'his (Wellington's) mind continued so unshaken by events

233

as to remember the circumstances under which was placed so insignificant a person'.

Soon after this General Alava and some of the confidential members of his staff begged him to take more care of his own safety, but totally without effect. He continued issuing orders from nearly the same spot until Ariñez (finally taken by the 74th and 45th Regiments) was in possession of the British line, and the French were in full retreat towards Vitoria.

> It was after the abandonment of the first position, that the French artillery, placed in rapidly constructed field works, opened on the advancing columns of the allied army. Through this tremendous fire Lord Wellington had to pass as he galloped [on his chestnut charger Copenhagen] to the right of his army for the purpose of ascertaining the stage of the battle in that direction. His route being in a nearly parallel line, he ran the gauntlet of about eighty pieces of cannon, and fortunately escaped untouched.

The French retreat began in perfect order. It was only when the artillery was abandoned that it lost its formation. Cannons were then thrown into the ditches and narrow ravines to prevent them being used by the advancing allies, where, overturned and mixed with tumbrils and the bodies of dead or wounded soldiers, they gave clear indication of defeat.

Then, as if further proof was needed of what was taking place, a long train of carriages, wagons and animals of burden could be seen, in a state of total congestion, on the road leaving Vitoria. Wellington, seeing the direction they were taking, asked Andrew if they were heading for Irun, the road to which, he correctly assumed, was more to the left. On being told that the mass of fugitives were on the Pamplona road, he then ordered hot pursuit.

At this moment the Second Division [led by Sir Rowland Hill], extending in line up to the heights to the right, 'had a most brilliant appearance'. Having fought magnificently, driving the enemy from its immediate front, it had been halted and Hill now awaited orders to move forward in pursuit of the flying French

> The enemy's troops having entirely disappeared from in front of Vitoria, the commander of the forces proceeded towards

that town . . . . Such a scene as the town presented has seldom been witnessed. Cannon, overturned carriages, broken-down wagons, forsaken tumbrils, wounded soldiers, civilians, women, children, dead horses and mules absolutely covered the face of the country; while its inhabitants, *and others,* had commenced the work of pillage. To the accumulated plunder of Andalusia were added the collections made by the other armies; the personal baggage of the king, Fourgons having inscribed upon them in large characters *Domaine Extérieur de S.M, l'Empereur,* wagons of every description and a military chest containing a large sum recently received from France for payment of the troops, but which had not yet been distributed; jewels, pictures, embroidery, silks, everything that was costly and portable, seemed to have been assiduously transported, adding to the unmilitary state of these encumbered armies.

Removed from their frames and rolled up, some of the finest Italian pictures from the royal collections were found in Joseph Bonaparte's carriage.

While all this was happening on the part of the battlefield where Wellington headed the pursuit, Sir Thomas Graham, in command of the left flank of the allies, was still facing obstinate resistance from the Army of Portugal.

The French troops, stationed on ground that was easy to defend, outnumbered his own. They fought with great courage until about noon when, beaten back, they were forced to abandon the defence of the Bayonne road. This meant that the French lost, not only that line of retreat, but also that their whole army, now outflanked on both flanks, was facing a massive attack on its centre.

Despite what must by then have been recognized as impending disaster, the French still strongly defended the fortified villages of Abechuco and Gamara Mayor on the stretch of the river immediately to the north of Vitoria. The village of Abechuco was carried by the light battalions of the German Legion, after which the bridge nearby, one of six across the Zadorra, was open to the allied troops.

Most fiercely contested was the bridge at Gamara where nearly five hundred men of the 5th Division were killed or wounded during the battle. Captain George Hay of the Royals, who must have been a relation of Andrew's, was carried, mortally wounded, from the

235

bridge. His father, General Hay, having searched for him throughout the night, eventually found the house in Vitoria to which he had been taken, only to learn that his son had just died.

More fortunate was Andrew's friend Lord Tweedale who was saved because he lost his sword of an usual and easily recognizable design. The weapon, with its long Spanish blade, the point covered in blood, was found by one of Wellington's staff while delivering a message. It transpired that during the chaos of the pursuit Tweedale, charging some French dragoons, had been thrown off his horse and left lying unconscious under trampling hoofs. Eventually, when hauled out from beneath a pile of corpses, he was found to be wounded and badly bruised, but alive.

The French army, once driven out of Vitoria, made no attempt to rally or to check the allies now in full pursuit. Guns and equipment were abandoned in what became a mad rush to escape.

> In all parts of the field, the artillerymen were seen flying, after having left their cannon to be captured by the advancing troops.
>
> Never previously had so large a body of British artillery been engaged as at Vitoria, and there were casualties in every brigade.

When he was some way beyond Vitoria in the direction of Pamplona Wellington rode to the summit of a knoll, from where he could clearly see the line of the retreating army for over a mile. Andrew, who was with him, described the amazing scene, which, even many years later, remained imprinted on his mind.

> It is impossible ever to forget the scene opened to view upon gaining the ascent. The valley beneath represented one dense mass, not in column, but extended over the surface of a flat containing several hundred acres. On this spot, the now confused multitude were obstructed by their own irregular and precipitate efforts at escape. Little movement was discernible and inevitable destruction seemed to await a crowd of not less than twenty thousand people. Immediate orders were sent for horse artillery, and in a few minutes Captain Ross's troop, regardless of roads, had crowned the summit of the commanding height, from whence he showered down balls and

howitzers shells upon the terrified masses, now urged into efforts at accelerated flight.

Darkness brought an end to the pursuit. Wellington and his staff, Andrew among them, returned to Vitoria 'which two days ago previously I had witnessed lighted up in honour of Joseph Bonaparte, was now blazing with illumination for his total discomfiture.'[12]

32

THE FRENCH GENERAL'S WIFE

Soon after entering the town, one of the aides-de-camp, who was there already, told Andrew that Madame Gazan's carriage was among those left on the field. He being the only person in the British army whom she knew, she had, apparently, been sending numerous messages begging him to help her in the disastrous situation in which she now found herself placed.

Andrew went immediately to see what help he could give, being really sorry for her in her dreadful plight. 'A more unenviable situation can scarcely be imagined,' he wrote, but he then adds naïvely that 'with the sprightliness and unconcern of her country, she did not appear feeling it to the fullest extent'.

Obviously the General's vivacious wife was delighted to have the handsome young British officer, to whom she had taken such a liking, once more by her side.

In the confusion occasioned by the rush of carriages and the near approach of the firing, a *gendarme à cheval* rode up, proffering his assistance to the wife of his General. Her first impulse was securing the safety of her child, which the soldier undertook to be answerable for; and having placed the boy before him, rode off, soon disappearing in the crowd. General Darriceau, wounded and retiring from the field, rode up and spoke to her, but any attempt at extricating her carriage would have been fruitless and in it she remained until surrounded by the British cavalry. On being brought back to Vitoria, she proceeded to the house of two Spanish ladies, her former acquaintances, and there I found her residing.

At her request I visited the depot of prisoners, from whence her servants were restored. I then placed her remaining carriage in safety, endeavoured to quiet her fears for the safety of her child, assured her there could be no doubt of Lord Wellington admitting her immediate return to her husband; after which, having procured a guard, I placed sentinels at the entrance of her quarters to prevent intrusion and took leave for the night.

Early the next morning (the 22nd) he returned to escort Madame Gazan in her search for her carriages, which, in the chaos of the previous day, had been abandoned. She had left Andalusia with no less than three wagons, loaded with all the possessions that she and her husband had acquired from the Spaniards during the occupation of their country. Andrew, knowing looting to be a time-honoured perquisite of soldier and citizen alike, realized that it would be little short of miraculous if anything of value remained, Nevertheless, Madame Gazan, determined on finding her treasures, insisted a search must be made.

Inevitably, and it would seem stoically, she faced up to disappointment as she saw the dereliction of which she had been warned by Andrew. The field was literally strewed with manuscripts, broken trunks or shattered carriages, but naturally not a vestige remained of anything worth the trouble of transporting it back to France.

Being speedily convinced of this fact we returned to Vitoria, and soon after followed the route of the army towards Salvatierra. Considering it my duty and feeling happy of the opportunity of, in a slight degree, returning the kindness of Count Gazan, by securing the safety of his wife, I remained near to her carriage, or rode within sight of it during the course of the forenoon. Lord Wellington desired me to request Madame Gazan would dine with him on the 22nd. At the accustomed hour I accompanied her to his Lordship's.

The evening passed very agreeably. She was in every respect treated with the utmost courtesy, and the following morning rejoined her husband and child.

Thus, on the day after one of the most ferocious battles in history, when an estimated eight thousand of her countrymen had been either wounded or killed (compared to about five thousand, one hundred on the allied side)[13] the wife of the French Commander-in-Chief, displayed her charms at the dinner table of the man who had vanquished her husband. We have Andrew's word for it that the evening was a great success, partly it would seem because the Duke of Wellington, like his young intelligence officer, had an eye for a pretty lady, as has often been told.

> General Gazan had by then retreated to Pamplona, where in the strong fortress, protected by a large garrison, he was reunited with his wife and their little boy. They had departed, crossing the frontier to France, before the town was blockaded by the Second Division, commanded by Sir Rowland Hill.
>
> In the meantime Sir Thomas Graham, on the Bayonne road, pursued Foy to the walled town of Tolosa. There, having first manoeuvred to explore the possibilities of attack, he blew open the gates with artillery. The French soldiers fled as Graham's troops forced their way into the town. Disappearing into darkness, they then crossed the Bidassoa into France without attempting further resistance.

The fort of Santa Engracia at Pancorbo surrendered on 1 July to the Spanish army of the Condé del Abisbal. Then only the garrisons of Pamplona and San Sebastian remained in the hands of the French. Of the four hundred thousand men with whom Napoleon had attempted to conquer the Peninsula now only those of the two garrisons and the much-diminished army of Marshal Suchet remained on Spanish soil.

Andrew, who sketched the town showing the army bivouacs in the foreground, also left a good description:

> Pamplona, the ancient Pompeiopolis, founded by Pompey the Great, is an extensive city and one of the strongest fortified places in the whole of the Peninsula. Situated on a perfect level, it is not commanded by any domineering or neighbouring height . . . . This formidable place the commander of the forces prepared to besiege, but subsequently resolved to reduce by blockade.
>
> The probable re-advance of the French army, for the purpose of withdrawing the garrisons, rendering it important to

assemble the whole British force on the immediate frontier, Lord Dalhousie delivered over the conduct of the blockade to Don Carlos España, who, with a force of about nine thousand Spaniards, was intrusted with that important service.

Not being permitted to serve with the army, I left Sir Rowland Hill's headquarters at Orcayan, on the 2nd July, taking the route for Madrid; resolved to remain in that city until apprised by the military secretary that the cartel, restoring me to unrestricted liberty, had arrived from England.

Andrew reached Madrid to find that most of the Spanish grandees, who had fled to Cadiz to avoid the French occupation, were now returning to the capital. French collaborators, who still lurked in the city, were living behind closed doors. Elsewhere in central Europe the situation was critical. Napoleon had recently made a truce with Germany and the Russian and Prussian governments were reputedly anxious to reach a similar agreement. Therefore it was widely expected that Napoleon would once more direct his undivided energies to the Peninsular War.

Under these circumstances nothing could have been better timed than the Battle of Vitoria. The same courier that conveyed to his brother a notification of the armistice might, in returning to Napoleon, have been the bearer of intelligence announcing the total defeat of his armies, and the circumstance of his being driven from the territory that no longer, in the most trivial respect, acknowledged his supremacy. One month deferred, the armies on the Ebro would have been reinforced by sixty thousand men and thereby have become too powerful to admit of the great impression created by the energetic and well-timed advance of the allied army.

At Madrid the battles of the Pyrenees occasioned much exultation . . . . Vitoria, it was conceived, had given such a blow to the French power in Spain that Joseph Bonaparte's return to the capital was a speculation no longer entertained.

The capital gradually resumed its former appearance. The Prado again became crowded, the theatres well-attended, the opera once more graced by the presence of the Spanish aristocracy, the amphitheatre for the bullfights delighted the population of Madrid, and the recollections of war alone remained. The hotel of the Prince of Peace was in a state of preparation to receive the regency, and report announced their early return from Cadiz.

From the midst of these scenes I was recalled by the receipt of a letter enclosing my cartel of exchange and announcing that no further obstacle intervened to prevent my serving with the army.

On the 27th August I left Madrid and at twelve o'clock on the night of 1 September reached San Sebastian. From some officers of the 4th Regiment I learned that the town had been captured by assault the previous day.[14]

33

SAN SEBASTIAN

The scenery in this neighbourhood is picturesque and beautiful in the extreme. A great variety of ground is enlivened by luxuriant orchards and extensive olive plantations, while broken and precipitous rocky heights occasionally give variety to a landscape closed by the magnificent background of the Pyrenees.

The town of San Sebastian is situated on a peninsula, at the extremity of which, washed by the tempestuous sea of the Bay of Biscay, rises a remarkable conical rocky height, called Monte Orgullo, upon the point of whose summit stands the citadel or castle of La Mota. The whole extent of this singular eminence is distinctly separated from the town by an outer line

San Sebastian

of defence at its base; while batteries erected on the southern ascent, aid and protect the defences in the main body of the place. The town, previous to the siege, contained a large population; the entire space within the works being closely built upon, and numerously inhabited, the streets regular; its plaza spacious, and the houses handsome and commodious.

Thus, in 1813, did Andrew describe the town of San Sebastian, which he also depicted so accurately in a sketch.

The peninsula on which it is built, on three sides surrounded by water, is connected by only a narrow isthmus to the mainland of north-west Spain. The main road leading from the town to the castle-keep ran from the convent of Santa Teresa to the Mirador battery on a rocky point at the east end of the ridge. From there it continued to the battery of Del Principe, which was sited still higher, and nearly on a line, with the battery of De la Reyna.

The convent of Santa Teresa, the arsenal and the battery of St Elmo on the northern side, above the estuary of the River Uremea, were the town's nearest points of communication with the castle rock. Although the town itself had been taken by the allies, 1,300 men of the French garrison, who had escaped, remained defiant in the castle.[15]

On 1 September Wellington arrived in the trenches and there decided upon the quickest and most effective way of forcing the surrender of La Mota. Subsequently he ordered batteries to be built within range of the castle while mortars constantly pounded the walls.

On the morning of 2 September Andrew, who wanted to see for himself the state of affairs in the town, left Sir James Leith's quarter and walked along the isthmus and through the trenches until he reached the place where Leith had been wounded. Here too had died Colonel Richard Fletcher, chief engineer of Wellington's army, designer of the lines of Torres Vedras and one of his closest friends.

Used as he was to scenes of carnage, Andrew, nonetheless, was shocked by what he saw. The whole of the gradual ascent of the isthmus was covered in dead bodies. There had been no time to bury them since the battle of the day before. 'Stript and naked, therefore, they lay on the ground where they had individually fallen, but in such numbers that on a similar space was never witnessed a more dreadful scene of slaughter.'

Behind the isthmus columns of smoke and ashes formed such a thick fog that only occasionally could he glimpse the towering castle keep. He could, however, clearly hear the guns firing from the castle itself and from its batteries, the noise being louder and more regular then the mutter of musketry fire: 'Above all this was distinguishable the thunder of British mortar batteries, as, from the right attack, they poured shells upon the devoted rock, whose surface became furrowed and torn up by their repeated explosions.'

Andrew, having climbed up the face of the breach, walked along the curtain to find himself faced with a scene of indescribable havoc and destruction. The heat from the blazing houses was almost suffocating and from the midst of this mass of fire he could hear what he knew to be the shouts of soldiers looting the conquered town. (As had already happened at Badajoz, the troops could not be denied the immemorial privilege of pillaging the captured city.)

Never, in any war, was a town more wantonly destroyed than San Sebastian. In the high wind nothing could stop sparks flying through buildings, crammed close together in a limited space, so that fires raged unchecked. Roofs fell in and in some places stones from ruined walls crashed down to block the streets. Such was the inferno that, even at midday, the pall of smoke made a thick cloud over the town.

Andrew, groping his way down the great flight of steps leading from the curtain, found General Hay blackened with smoke and dust. Hay, who had not had a moment's rest since the battle, was trying to stop the troops from looting and to force those, still relatively sober, to try to put out the fires which were burning in every direction.

So desperate had the situation become that, in an effort to restore order, halberds (military weapons, partly axe, partly spear, mounted on long poles) had been put up in the plaza, fronting the entrance from the isthmus to the town. However, the threat of these instruments of punishment, to which men were tied when being flogged, did not have much effect in reducing the amount of pillage inflicted on the unfortunate citizens by soldiers running riot within the captured town. Still less did the ravagers care that the French garrison seemed determined to fight until their last bullet was spent.

The French held not only the castle but, extraordinary as it may seem, actually occupied the top storey of a nearby convent where British troops were lodged below, as Andrew describes:

The convent of Santa Teresa, being the building in immediate contact with the enemy, was occupied in the lower part by a party of the 9th Regiment while the upper stories were

245

inhabited by the French infantry . . . . Towards evening General Hay, Captain James Stewart and myself proceeded to the north-west angle of the place. I proceeded to visit the 9th Regiment in the convent while Captain Stewart proposed detailing to General Hay his views of dislodging the enemy from the upper part of the building. For this purpose he led the General to the bulwark and, clambering up, proceeded to point out the situation of the enemy's posts, as also what he recommended concerning them. A French sentinel, not fifty yards distant, on perceiving two officers reconnoitring, took a deliberate aim, and firing his ball it entered Captain Stewart's left temple passing directly through his head. He continued in a state of insensibility for some minutes and then expired.

The next day (3 September) early in the afternoon, Sir Thomas Graham, deciding that the French commander of the garrison, General Rey, must by then have realized further resistance to be useless, sent a flag of truce with proposals to negotiate. Several hours were given to allow the General to make up his mind and word went round that, at the end of this time, a salvo from the mortar batteries would be the signal if the attack on the castle was to continue. General Rey remained obstinate and a flight of shells, exactly at the hour indicated, was then seen sailing through the sky. By this time it was obvious that General Rey would not surrender until the batteries, ordered by Wellington to be trained on the castle, were causing serious destruction to the building.

Arrangements having been completed for a very energetic attack upon the castle defences and it being understood that the batteries would open on the morning of the 8th, at half-past nine I was in the hornwork [to the south of the town] with Colonel Dickson. The artillerymen were at their posts, everything in readiness, and at ten o'clock, by preconcerted signal, fifty-nine pieces of heavy ordnance commenced a rapid and terrific fire. Standing in the battery, close in rear of the twenty-four pounders, the noise of the other batteries was inaudible: but, in looking around, columns of smoke ascended in all directions, while dust and fragments of stone, flying from the masonry of the Mirador, indicated the perfect direction and overpowering effect of the British artillery.

The enemy, apparently astonished at the tremendous nature of the cannonade, tardily returned the fire by a few discharges from the battery De la Reyna, but, perceiving the feeble effects of this last effort, it was speedily discontinued.

About one o'clock a flag of truce appeared flying on the battery of Mirador and the firing ceased.

The Chevalier Songeon, Colonel and *Chef d'état major* of the garrison, soon after descended into the town, where, having met Colonel De Lancey, Colonel Dickson, and Colonel Bouverie, nominated by Sir Thomas Graham to negotiate on behalf of the allies, the terms were speedily arranged, by which the garrison surrendered prisoners of war, and at four o'clock in the evening the Mirador and battery Del Gobernador were occupied by British troops.

The following morning the garrison marched out with the honours of war. At its head, with sword drawn and firm step, appeared General Rey, accompanied by Colonel Songeon, and the officers of his staff. As a token of respect we saluted him as he passed. The old General dropt his sword in return to the civilities of the British officers, and leading the remains of his brave battalions to the glacis, there deposited their arms, with a well-founded confidence of having nobly done his duty, and persevered to the utmost in an energetic defence.

On the evening of the 9th September the Spanish ensign floated over the ruined walls of San Sebastian, while a constantly spreading conflagration, of ten days endurance, had not yet completed the destruction of the devoted town. [16]

34

INTO FRANCE

Andrew, with his love of exploring, was determined to see as much of the country as was possible.

On the morning of 29 September he left Sir James Leith and, having crossed over the Uremea, (the river which flows to the east of San Sebastian into the Bay of Biscay) he joined General Pack. The General, who had recovered from his wound, was travelling in the same direction to resume the command of his brigade of the 6th Division which was stationed at Maya. Having decided to follow the route via Lesaca, they stayed for the night of the 29th at Oyarzun on the great road to Bayonne, which was then the headquarters of Sir Thomas Graham.

From Oyarzun to Lesaca the road ran through a long valley to reach the base of the great mountain of Haya. Then, gradually climbing, it wound through ravines and over heights covered with magnificent trees.

In one of the loveliest spots of this wild and beautiful country Lord Aylmer's brigade was encamped. The white tents of the troops caught the eye against the dark foliage of the chestnut and ilex, while the laughter and shouts of soldiers brought life to this deserted place.

Andrew and General Pack, having stayed three days at headquarters, arrived at Maya on 4 October, where the General's quarter was situated in the valley directly under the pass leading into France. On the 6th Andrew rode to Roncesvalles, then the headquarters of Sir Rowland Hill, and saw and sketched the famous pass over the Pyrenees which, for over a thousand years, had featured in the history of Europe.

In 778 Roland, commanding the rearguard of Charlemagne's

RONCESVALLES

army, had been attacked and killed in the Pass by the Basques. Nearly six hundred years had then passed before the Black Prince rode across on his way to the Battle of Nájera, or Navarrette in 1367.[17]

It was now less than three months since 25 July when Marshal Soult had launched an attack against the 4th Division of the British army, commanded by General Sir Lowry Cole, who, greatly outnumbered, had eventually been forced to withdraw down the road towards Pamplona.[18] Three days later, however, following the Battle of Sorauren, the French, outmanoeuvred by Wellington, had been defeated and driven back into France.

Andrew found the abbey at the foot of the pass, surrounded by the habitations of the abbots, to be the nucleus of a fair-sized village. The Prior's House, built by the government to shelter travellers crossing the frontier, proved to be both large and comfortable. He sketched the village, depicting the old stone buildings against the vast panorama of mountain and sky.

In his journal he describes the sharp contrast of the country on either side of the pass.

While towards France the scenery is bold and majestic, it assumes, in the direction of Pamplona, a tamer, but not less beautiful character. The valley of Burguete, rich in cultivation and ornamented by the finest wood, is extended beneath the eye, and the sun illuminating its varied tints, rendering them more striking from being contrasted with the sombre appearance of Roncesvalles, while the dark masses of pines and forest trees clothing to its summit the grand mountain barrier, partially hid in mist and vapour, give increased magnitude to objects naturally of stupendous description.

Immediately from the abbey of Roncesvalles, the great route commences a gradual ascent terminated at the summit of the Altobiscar mountain, from whence a descent of three leagues leads to the town of St Jean Pied de Port.

From the loftiest part of the road a magnificent view is presented to the traveller. To his right appear, in great variety and majesty, the range of Pyrenees towards Jaca, including the Pic du Midi, and other conspicuous features of the chain. In advance, to the left, extends the French coast, with the city of Bayonne forming a splendid break in the otherwise unvaried line. Directly in front, and displayed to a great distance, appear the fertile plains of Gascony, while in the immediate vicinity of the route, valleys, rendered impervious by luxuriant foliage, cataracts, rocks, and the wilder accompaniments of splendid mountain scenery, are visible in constant and endless variety.

It was on 7 October 1813 that Lord Wellington invaded France. It fell to the lot of the 5th Division to be the first British troops whose colours waved over the 'sacred territory of Napoleon'. Andrew bore witness to the extraordinary scene as, with men cheering and the bands playing the national anthem, the regiments, ignoring the fierce fire of the enemy from the opposite bank, waded through the Bidassoa in perfect formation. General Robinson, up to his middle in water, shot at by musket and cannon, strode through the river on foot at the head of his brigade. Following this the French troops, from their defensive positions, made three desperate but futile attempts to stop the advance of General Hay's brigade

The Bidassoa, for some distance the frontier between France and Spain, rises in the valley of Bastan, from where, after rather a circuitous course, it runs into the sea near to Fuentarrabia. On its right bank Sir Thomas Graham, with the 1st and 5th Divisions and some Portuguese troops, had established a footing which was not attacked by the French. The result was that while the left of the allied army was fighting a brisk offensive battle in enemy territory, both the centre and the right remained largely inactive. So difficult were communications that, extraordinary as it may seem, on the same day on which Sir Thomas Graham passed the Bidassoa the officers of Sir Rowland Hill's corps, none of them having the least idea of the battle in progress near the coast, had races on the plain of Burguete.

The great wooden bridge of Irun, on the Bayonne road, had been destroyed on the orders of General Foy, retreating from the defeat of Vitoria. The allies, however, carried a pontoon train with the army, so that, immediately after their encampment on the right bank of the Bidassoa, a makeshift bridge was strung across the river.

The Duke of Dalmatia (Marshal Soult) had established his headquarters in St Jean de Luz, with his army strongly entrenched, extending from the coast to St Jean Pied de Port. The position of Lord Wellington's army was as follows:

The 1st and 5th Divisions, with the brigade of Lord Aylmer, the Portuguese of General Bradford and Wilson and the Spanish force of General Giron, encamped in France, extending to the great mountain of La Rhune. The Light and Fourth Divisions occupied the heights in front of Vera, the army of reserve of Andalusia, with the 7th British Division on their right, near to Echelar, the Third Division between Echelar and Maya, the Sixth in position at the latter, with Sir John Hamilton's Portuguese Division in reserve, at Ariscoon, one brigade of the Second Division at Alduides, the remainder of that Division, and the Spanish corps of General Morillo, were at Roncesvalles, the cavalry rear of the army were principally cantoned in the valley of the Ebro: head-quarters removed from Lesaca to Vera.

Marshal Soult, knowing only too well that the fall of Pamplona would incite a wave of Spanish patriotism, began to make an entrenched camp along the course of the Nivelle, from St Jean de Luz by Serrez and the Heights of Ainhoe, to a minor chain of the Pyrenees, north-east of the Maya Pass. Formidable redoubts on the left bank of the river strengthened the mountain of La Petite Rhune, In addition, the heights of Ascain, protected by numerous redoubts, covered the reaches of the river for some distance to the east, completing the defences in communication with those to the extreme left of the French army.

In front of the right of this very formidable position, in advance of Andaye, and with their left resting on the shores of the Bay of Biscay, were encamped the First and Fifth Divisions of the allied army. Field works strengthened the ground thus occupied and a large force of British artillery was prepared to resist any effort that might be made to force back the allies from the right bank of the Bidassoa.

On the 25th of October, having returned from Roncesvalles, Lord Charles Fitzroy and myself entered France from Irun and proceeded along the great chaussée until arrived at the position of the troops. From thence, accompanied by General Robinson, I rode to the advanced posts, in close contact with those of the enemy, and there distinctly perceived the numerous retrenchments in progress to render his position as invulnerable as possible.

On the same day General Cassan proposed terms for the surrender of Pamplona, now reduced to the last extremity by a lengthened and rigorously observed blockade, but the allies, aware of the circumstances under which the garrison must necessarily be placed, determined not to accede to the proposition, and the French governor persevered in resistance until his last day's supply of limited rations was in process of distribution of the troops. At length, on 31 October, he surrendered the place, which, with its defences in a perfect state, a garrison of 4,000 men and 200 pieces of ordnance mounted on its walls, became the most bloodless prize of the allied army.

Thus was wrested from the imperial troops their last stronghold in the northern province of Spain, and with that great event may be said to have closed the Peninsular war.[19]

35

THE FINAL TRIUMPH
– TOULOUSE

Andrew Leith-Hay's assertion that the surrender of Pamplona ended the Peninsular War is correct in that it applies to Portugal and Spain. However, just across the frontier, on the French side of the Pyrenees, five months of hazardous fighting lay ahead.

Following the surrender of Pamplona, Wellington again took the offensive against the French. On 10 November 1813 he won a spectacular victory on the south side of the River Nivelle which runs into the Bay of Biscay at St Jean de Luz. A month later, in December, he was less dramatically successful in the battle of the river Nive, just south of the city of Bayonne. The French garrison there defied him but, with the help of the Royal Navy, he succeeded in crossing the River Adour to the west of the city.

Then, on 24 February 1814, the allied armies began to march east from Bayonne to Orthez, on the Gave de Pau, where, on the 27th, Marshal Soult, having been heavily defeated, was forced to retreat. The Marshal withdrew to Toulouse where, on 10 April, Wellington won the last of the great battles of what is termed 'The Peninsular War.'

On the evening of the victory Colonel Frederick Ponsonby of the 12th Light Dragoons* galloped into the town on a horse lathered with sweat, with the news of Napoleon's reported abdication.

---

* Colonel Frederick Ponsonby, a very dashing officer, described by Andrew Leith-Hay as 'not easily checked', had already achieved fame by charging with Colonel Elley at Talavera and again for nearly capturing Marshal Marmont, the Duke of Ragusa at Salamanca.

Rumour ran wild until two days later Captain Cook arrived from Paris to confirm that the Emperor, his capital held by the allies, had indeed acknowledged defeat.

Doctor McGrigor, Wellington's Surgeon General, now coping with the great number of wounded men of both sides, described the amazing reaction of the French town's population to the news.

> I happened at this time to dine with the Duke. He had intended to go to the theatre in the evening and it so happened that I was the only one of his staff who was in the way to accompany him. I shall never forget the outburst of enthusiasm with which he was received when they discovered him in the stage box. The whole audience stood up, while the orchestra gave us our national air of *God save the King*.[20]

Thus in a theatre, in the conquered French city of Toulouse, did his enemies acclaim the British commander, the 'leopard' whom Napoleon had sworn he would throw back into the sea, who, from the moment of his landing in Portugal on 1 August 1808 had proved himself a military tactician equal, if not superior, to the French emperor who had held all Europe in his thrall.

EPILOGUE

ANDREW LEITH-HAY

Andrew's two volumes on the Peninsular War, in which, as an intelligence officer, he made many sketches, appeared in 1831. The account ends with his description of the final stages of the siege of Pamplona, apparently the last time he saw action in Spain.

Following the armistice with France he was named a knight commander of the order of Charles III of Spain and a member of the Legion of Honour.

In 1816 he married Mary Margaret, daughter of William Clark of Buckland House, Devonshire. In the same year his uncle General Leith was appointed to the governorship of Barbados and Andrew, now a Lieutenant-Colonel, went with him as military secretary, assistant quartermaster-general and adjutant-general. His new wife, assuming that she accompanied him, may have found the climate unsuitable for, from 21 November 1817 to 30 September 1819, as a Captain in the 2nd Foot, he was placed on half-pay. Shortly after this, having retired from the army, he completed the two volumes of his *Narrative of the Peninsular War,'* before starting a new career in politics, Much involved in the agitation preceding the passing of the Reform Bill, he became member for the Elgin Burghs on 29 December 1832.

Once in parliament, his fluency as a speaker and knowledge of the army attracted the attention of the Prime Minister, Lord Melbourne, who, while giving him the lucrative appointment of Clerk of the Ordnance on 19 June 1834, also made him a knight of Hanover.

Appointed Governor of Bermuda on 6 February 1838, he resigned his seat in parliament. However, the death of his father and his subsequent inheritance of the Leith Hall estate prevented him from taking up his post.

On 7 July 1841 he was again elected for the Elgin Burghs, in which capacity he continued to sit in parliament until 23 July 1847. After losing his seat at the next election, he then failed to win the city of Aberdeen.

By this time he was much embroiled in the history and in the current affairs of his native county. His book *The Castellated Architecture of Aberdeenshire,* appearing in 1849, was much acclaimed. The lithographs of the principal castles and houses, like those of his *Narrative of the Peninsular War,* are reproductions of his sketches, in addition to which the text, containing a great deal of information, is entirely his own work.

He died aged seventy-seven at Leith Hall in Aberdeenshire on 13 October 1862.[21]

COLQUHOUN GRANT

Colquhoun returned from Scotland to join his regiment, the 11th Foot, in time to fight at Toulouse, the final battle of the Peninsular War. Following the armistice, he applied for a vacancy at the Senior Department of the Royal Military College, then at Farnham in Surrey. He was there when Napoleon escaped from Elba and Britain was again at war with France.

Subsequently, from the army headquarters at the Horse Guards, every regiment was summoned to arms. Colquhoun, now officially Head of Intelligence in the British army in the field, reported to the Commander-in-Chief in Brussels on 12 May. From there he was sent to Mons to organize agents in Belgium who would report on the movements of the French.

The main reason for this was that Wellington desperately needed to know on which of the four main roads leading to Ghent and Brussels from France the enemy would approach. The shortest way from Paris to Brussels was through Mons, which was heavily defended. Between Mons and the Ardennes, however, lay what was known as the 'Charleroi Gap, ' a stretch of thirty miles on which few fortifications existed.

On 13 June one of his secret agents sent a message to Colquhoun, telling him that '*Les routes encomblées de troupes et de material, les officeirs de toutes grades parlent haut que la grande bataille sera livrée avant trois jours.'* Colquhoun, taking this to mean that the French were heading for the Charleroi Gap, sent a courier galloping to Brussels to give Wellington this vital news.

Unfortunately the messenger was stopped by a cavalry patrol. He was taken to the Brigade Commander, Major General Dörnberg, and the obtuse Hanoverian, having read Colquhoun's report, returned it to him insisting that 'so far from convincing him that the Emperor was advancing for battle, it assured him of the contrary'. Colquhoun, on the courier's return, at once took the message himself to Wellington, whom he found on the field of Quatre Bras. Had he only received it earlier, the battle, in all probability, would not have been fought on the field of Waterloo.

On 19 June Colquhoun wrote from Waterloo to his sister Mary, wife of Doctor James McGrigor, telling her that he was well, having 'lost only a horse'.

Following the war Colquhoun lived for some time in semi-retirement in his family home in Forres. In 1820 he married Margaret, second daughter of James Brodie of Brodie, laird of Brodie Castle nearby.

In the following year, 1821, Colquhoun was gazetted a lieutenant-colonel in the Dorsetshire Regiment, the 54th. He was then posted to India with his wife and Walter, their only child, who was just a year old. While there, for his services in Spain and Portugal, he was made a Companion of the Order of the Bath.

In 1824 the Regiment was sent to Burma where a strenuous campaign and bouts of tropical disease ruined Colquhoun's health. He returned to Madras, but, in October 1826 the Regiment was ordered to the Malabar Coast. Here Colquhoun's wife Margaret became so ill that it was decided that she and Walter must return to Scotland. He himself would follow as soon as possible. Sadly, however, Margaret died in St Helena on the voyage home. Walter was taken to her brother's home at Brodie Castle, near Forres, to live with her relations.

Early in 1829 Colquhoun himself came back to Britain, invalided out of the army and plainly very ill. His brother-in-law, now Sir James McGrigor, did all that he could to help him but it was decided, almost as a last resort, that he should take the waters at Aix-la-Chapelle, Here, on the night of 28 September, 1829, he died, his little boy beside him. He was only forty-eight.[22]

SOURCE NOTES

Part 1, (pp 1–43)

1 Napier, Sir W, *History of the War in the Peninsula*. abridged edition. p xxix
2 Ibid, pp 26–7.
3 Paget, Sir J, *Wellington's Peninsular War,* p 16.
4 Marshal Lefèbvre, born of a humble family in 1755, had gained rapid promotion in the army during the French Revolution. He was created Duke of Danzig by Napoleon after that city had capitulated to the besieging French forces in May 1807.
5 Lord William Bentinck, second son of the 3rd Duke of Portland, a serving soldier and Colonel of the 11th Dragoons, was at that time British envoy to the Spanish Junta in Madrid. Later, as Governor-General of India, he was renowned for his liberal views, the abolishment of suttee being only one of his reforms.
6 George Canning (1770–1827) was Foreign Minister from 1807–10.
7 See Napier, Sir W., pp 38–9.
8 Ibid, pp 45–6.
9 Paget, Sir J., p 16.
10 Napier gives Lord Henry Paget's regiment as the 10th Hussars. However, Andrew states categorically that Paget ordered the 15th Hussars to charge without waiting for the 10th Hussars, which, under Genral Slade, had marched directly for the town of Mallorga, the headquarters of the British army. See Leith-Hay, Vol.1. pp 92–3.
11 Ibid, p 75.
12 Paget, Sir J., p 82.
13 For full details of this campaign see Leith-Hay, Vol. 1, pp 1–133.

Part 2, (pp 45–111)

1 Paget, Sir J., p 21
2 For the letters of Charles Cocks at this period see Page. J, *Iintelligence Officer in the Peninsula,* pp 19–25

3   See Paget, Sir J., pp 87–8
4   Page, J., p 28
5   Ibid
6   Ibid, pp 27–31 for Charles Cocks's letters of this period
7   Paget, Sir J., p 93
8   Napier, Sir W., abridged edition, p 92
9   Paget, Sir J., p 94
10 Ibid, pp 96–7
11 For Andrew's description of Talavera see Vol 1, pp 142–170
12 Paget, Sir J., p 27
13 See Leith-Hay, Vol 1, pp 174–191
14 See Napier, Sir W., abridged edition, p 118
15 Leith-Hay, Vol. 1, pp 192–212
16 For Charles Cocks's letters and journal at this period see Page, J.,
    pp 43–57
17 Paget, Sir J., p 34
18 Ibid, p 33
19 Napier, Sir W., abridged edition, p 118
20 Ibid, pp 120–1
21 Haswell, J., *The First Respectable Spy*, p 140
22 Page, J., p 67
23 Leith-Hay, Vol 1, pp 307–8
24 Napier, Sir W., abridged edition, p xl
25 Page, J., pp 74–6
26 Wellington. *The Despatches of Field Marshal Arthur, Duke of
    Wellington*, Vol 6, to Lt-Gen.Sir S. Cotton Bt., 6 Sept, 1810
27 Napier, Sir W., abridged edition, pp 130–1
28 Ibid
29 Wellington. *The Despatches of Field Marshal Arthur, Duke of
    Wellington*. Vol 6, to Lt-Gen.Sir S. Cotton Bt., 6 Sept, 1810
30 Page, J., pp 67–80
31 Paget, Sir J., pp 103–4
32 Ibid, p 104
33 Sutlers = provision merchants following the army who sold food
    and drink to the soldiers.
34 Paget, Sir J., p 104.
35 For a more detailed description of the Battle of Busaco see Leith-
    Hay, Vol 1, pp 230–40

Part 3 (pp. 113–185)

1 Page, J., pp 82–3
2 Ibid, p 84
3 Napier, Sir W., abridged edition, pp 149–150
4 Leith-Hay, Vol 1, pp 240–7
5 Napier, Sir W., abridged Edition, pp 152–6
6 Paget, Sir J., p 114
7 Leith-Hay, Vol 1, pp 257–263
8 Ibid, pp 248–266
9 Haswell, J., pp 123–6
10 McGrigor, Sir J., p 189
11 Haswell, J., p 139
12 Napier, Sir W., pp 202–9
13 Page, J., pp 139–141
14 Ibid, pp 226–274
15 Paget, Sir J., p 144
16 Page, J., p 165
17 For further details see Haswell, J., *The First Respectable Spy*, pp 154–7
18 Napier, Sir W., p 285
19 Leith-Hay, Vol 1, p 292
20 McGrigor, Sir J., p 183
21 Ibid, pp 184–86
22 See Leith-Hay, Vol 1, pp 299–305
23 Paget, Sir J., p 42
24 McGrigor, Sir J., p 188, pp 190–5
25 Ibid, p 193
26 The two main sources for the story of Colquhoun's capture and escape are firstly Sir James McGrigor, *The Scalpel and the Sword*, pp 188–192; secondly, Haswell, J., *The First Respectable Spy*, pp 167–189
27 Leith-Hay, Vol 2, pp 8–65
28 Page, J., p 190
29 Ibid,. p 191
30 Paget, Sir J., p 165
31 Page, J., pp 197–8
32 Ibid, pp 198–9
33 Ibid, p 205
34 Ibid, p 204

Part 4 (pp 187–254)

1   Leith-Hay, Vol 2, p 83
2   Paget, Sir J., p 168
3   Leith-Hay, Vol 2, pp 107–9
4   McGrigor, Sir J., p 208
5   George Hay, Marquess of Tweedale, born in 1787, was two years younger than Andrew, being then aged twenty-five. He had succeeded his father in 1809 after both his parents had died, as prisoners of Napoleon, in the fortress of Verdun. Acting as ADC to Wellington, he had been wounded at the Battle of Busaco on 27 September 1810. Subsequently, having commanded both the 30th Regiment and the 2nd Life Guards, he became a Field Marshal and as such was Governor and Commander-in-Chief of Madras from 1842–48. He died, aged nearly ninety, in 1876.
6   For further details see Leith-Hay, Vol 2, pp 116–143
7   Haswell, J., p 201
8   McGrigor, Sir J., pp 193–5
9   For more details of the events of this chapter see Haswell J., *The First Respectable Spy*, pp 188–204
10 Napier, Sir W., abbreviated edition, pp 379–80
11 Leith-Hay, Vol 2, pp 142–188
12 Ibid, pp 191–211
13 Paget, Sir J., p 176
14 Leith-Hay, Vol 2, pp 211–223
15 Paget, Sir J., p 182
16 Ibid, p 183
17 Ibid, p 193
18 Ibid, p 192. See also Leith-Hay, Vol 2, pp 268–276
19 Leith-Hay, Vol 2, p 276
20 McGrigor, Sir J., pp 229–234
21 From *Dictionary of National Biography*, Vol XI, Smith, Elder & Co., 1909. Also *The Times*, 17 Oct. 1862, p 7; *Gentleman's Magazine* 1863, i, 112–13; *Men of the Times*, 1862, p 371
22 For these and further details of the life of Colquhoun Grant see Haswell J., *The First Respectable Spy*.

BIBLIOGRAPHY

The first-hand accounts which form the basis of this book are:

Leith-Hay, Major Sir Andrew, F.R.S.E. *Narrative of the Peninsular War* Volumes 1 & 2. Daniel, Lizars, 5 St David Street, and Whittaker, Treacher and Arnot, London 1831

Page, Julia, *Intelligence Officer in the Peninsula*. Letters & Diaries of Major the Hon. Edward Charles Cocks, 1786–1812 Hippocrene Books Inc. New York.

Haswell, Jock, *The First Respectable Spy*, The Life and Times of Colquhoun Grant, Wellington's Head of Intelligence, Hamish Hamilton, London, 1969

Napier, General Sir William, *History of the War in the Peninsula* Abridged and with an introduction by Charles Stuart, University of Chicago Press, 1979

McGrigor, Sir James, *The Autobiography and Services of Sir James McGrigor Bt. Late Director of the Army Medical Department*, Longmans Green, 1861. Republished under the title *The Scalpel and the Sword*, edited and with additions by Mary McGrigor. Scottish Cultural Press, 2000

Additional information:

Paget, Sir Julian, *Wellington's Peninsular War*, Leo Cooper, London, 1990

Longford, E. *The Years of the Sword*, (Panther edition, 1972)

Wilkin, Captain W.H., *The Life of Sir David Baird*, George Allen, London. 1912

Warre, Lieut-Gen Sir William, edited by the Rev Edward Warre, *Letters from Peninsula 1808–1812*

Rifleman Harris, Recollections of. Ed. Christopher Hibbert, Leo Cooper, 1970

Blanco, Richard. L., *Wellington's Surgeon General: Sir James McGrigor*. Duke University Press, Durham, N.C., 1974

Verner, Colonel Willoughby. *History and Campaigns of the Rifle Brigade*, part 11, 1809–1813. John Bale, Sons & Danielson, London, 1919

INDEX